Praise for *Sa*

"The small town of Independence, where authors Joan DeDecker Busby and Carol DeDecker Wiens were growing up between 1935 and 1951, lies about midway along the narrow Owens Valley of Eastern California. From high above, on the Sierra Nevada's sheer eastern flank, the town appears, as it did to a young Joan DeDecker in the late 1930s, as a 'postage stamp' of green in the vast sagebrush expanse of the valley below.

Such observations fill the pages of this thoughtfully crafted and engaging memoir of the authors' 'uncommon' childhood. Individual vignettes, based on their own recollections and the diaries of their remarkable mother, Mary DeDecker, are arranged as alternating voices to reflect each sister's emerging sense of place in the Owens Valley. Gradually widening circles of discovery and self-reliance take the girls, guided by uncommonly wise parents, beyond home to community, across the sagebrush valley, and into the Sierra wilderness they grow to love.

These are stories to savor. With clarity and immediacy they bring to life the ordinary and the unusual of the sisters' small-town upbringing—their mother's laundry day, the Depression-era hobo at the back door, playing the tuba at graduation, guard towers at nearby Manzanar War Relocation Center, encounters with mountaineer Norman Clyde in the Sierra backcountry.

The book's finely-etched details will be familiar to those who know the Owens Valley or have lived there—these were the teenage 'DeDecker Girls' of my own Independence childhood. But more broadly, as the authors convey their maturing connection to the natural world, they remind us of the countless and unexpected ways this time of discovery we call childhood can shape the values and passions that define us as adults."

—Jane Wehrey, historian and author of *Voices From This Long Brown Land: Oral Recollections of Owens Valley Lives and Manzanar Pasts; Manzanar;* and *The Owens Valley*

"*Sage & Sierra* is more than a charming memoir—it is a spot-on picture of small town life in rural California set in the 1940s and 1950s, as seen through the eyes of two young sisters. Interesting, funny, insightful and nostalgic, it is filled with colorful characters and engaging stories of family, friends, and community, as well as paying tribute to and honoring the natural environment. While reading, I was reminded of my own cherished memories of growing up in a small town during the 1950s . . . Sunday drives with my family, walking to school with neighborhood friends, baseball in our vacant lot, summer vacations into the High Sierra.

As a Museum Curator and Public Historian, the narratives are priceless gems, weaving together the history, politics, and socio-cultural climate of the times, preserving the rich heritage of the Owens Valley and Eastern Sierra for generations to come. It is a pleasure to read!"

—Roberta Harlan, Curator of Collections & Exhibits,
Eastern California Museum

Sage & Sierra

June, 2018
Joan De Decker Bexley

Sage & Sierra

A MEMOIR

Growing Up in Owens Valley

Carol DeDecker Wiens & Joan DeDecker Busby

PIGGY ROCK PRESS

Mt. Williamson and Symmes Creek, from a few miles southwest of Independence, 2013.

Let's have done with stranger faces, let's be quit
of staring eyes,
Let's go back across Mohave where the hills of
Inyo rise.
There's a word we've lost between us we shall
never hear again
In the mindless clang of engines where they bray
the hearts of men.
Let's go seek it east of Kearsarge where the
seven-mile shadows run,
From the great gray bulk of Williamson heaved
up against the sun.

Mary Austin

SAGE AND SIERRA: GROWING UP IN OWENS VALLEY—A MEMOIR

PIGGY ROCK PRESS
967 E. Parkcenter Blvd, P.O. Box 132
Boise, Idaho 83706

For information about this title or to order other books and/or electronic media, contact Carol DeDecker Wiens at dncwiens@gmail.com or Joan DeDecker Busby at busbymill@sbcglobal.net

Library of Congress Control Number: 2017954455

ISBN: 978-0-9992863-0-2 (print)
978-0-9992863-1-9 (eBook)

Printed in the United States of America

Cover and interior design by 1106 Design

Photographs, unless otherwise credited, are from the DeDecker Family Collection

Maps by Carol DeDecker Wiens

PIGGY ROCK PRESS

To Paul and Mary DeDecker,
our parents, our companions, and our inspiration
And to the people of Independence,
past and present

Contents

MAP 1

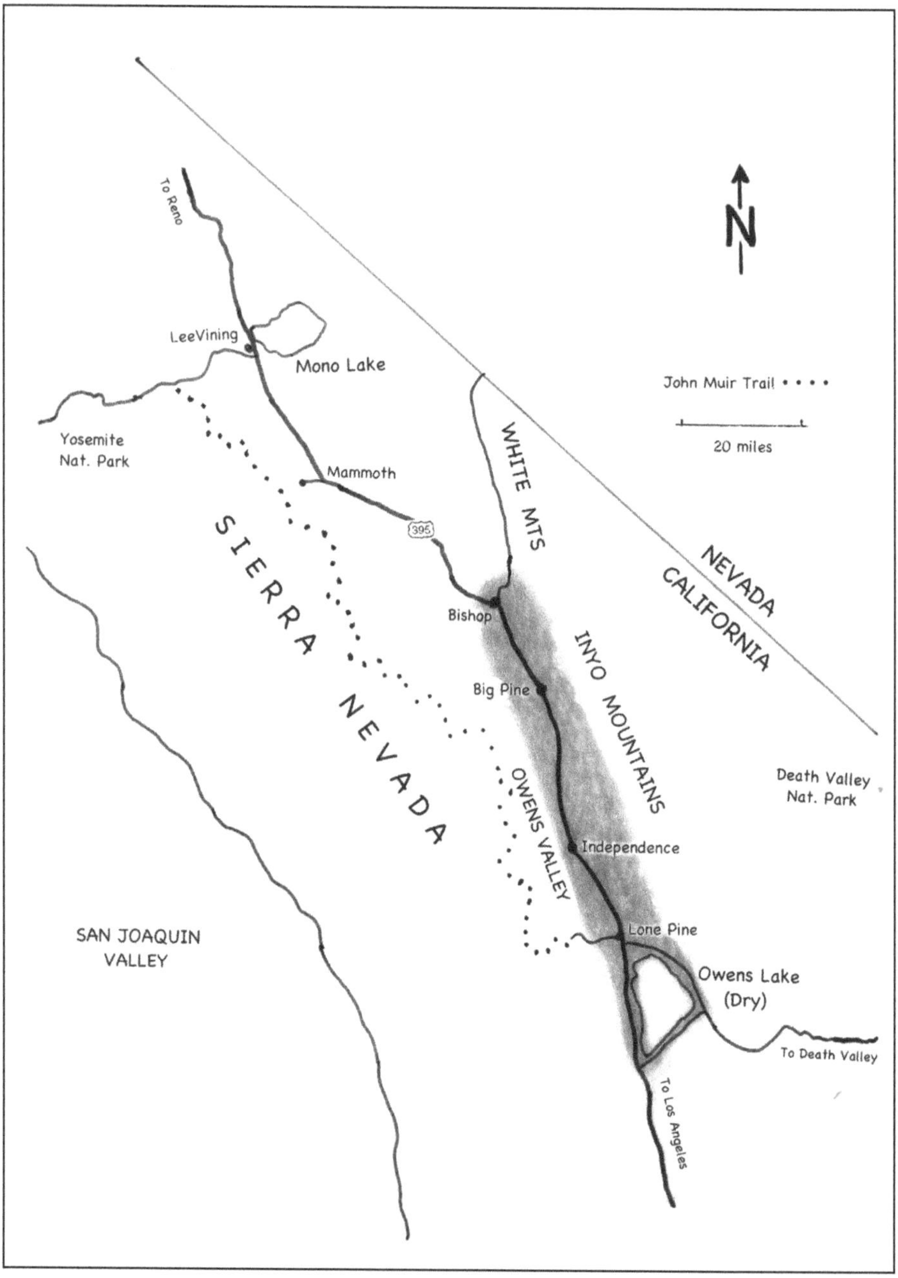
To Reno
LeeVining
Mono Lake
Yosemite
Nat. Park
Mammoth
395
SIERRA NEVADA
WHITE MTS
Bishop
Big Pine
INYO MOUNTAINS
NEVADA
CALIFORNIA
John Muir Trail
20 miles
Death Valley
Nat. Park
OWENS VALLEY
Independence
Lone Pine
Owens Lake
(Dry)
To Death Valley
To Los Angeles
SAN JOAQUIN
VALLEY
N

MAP 2

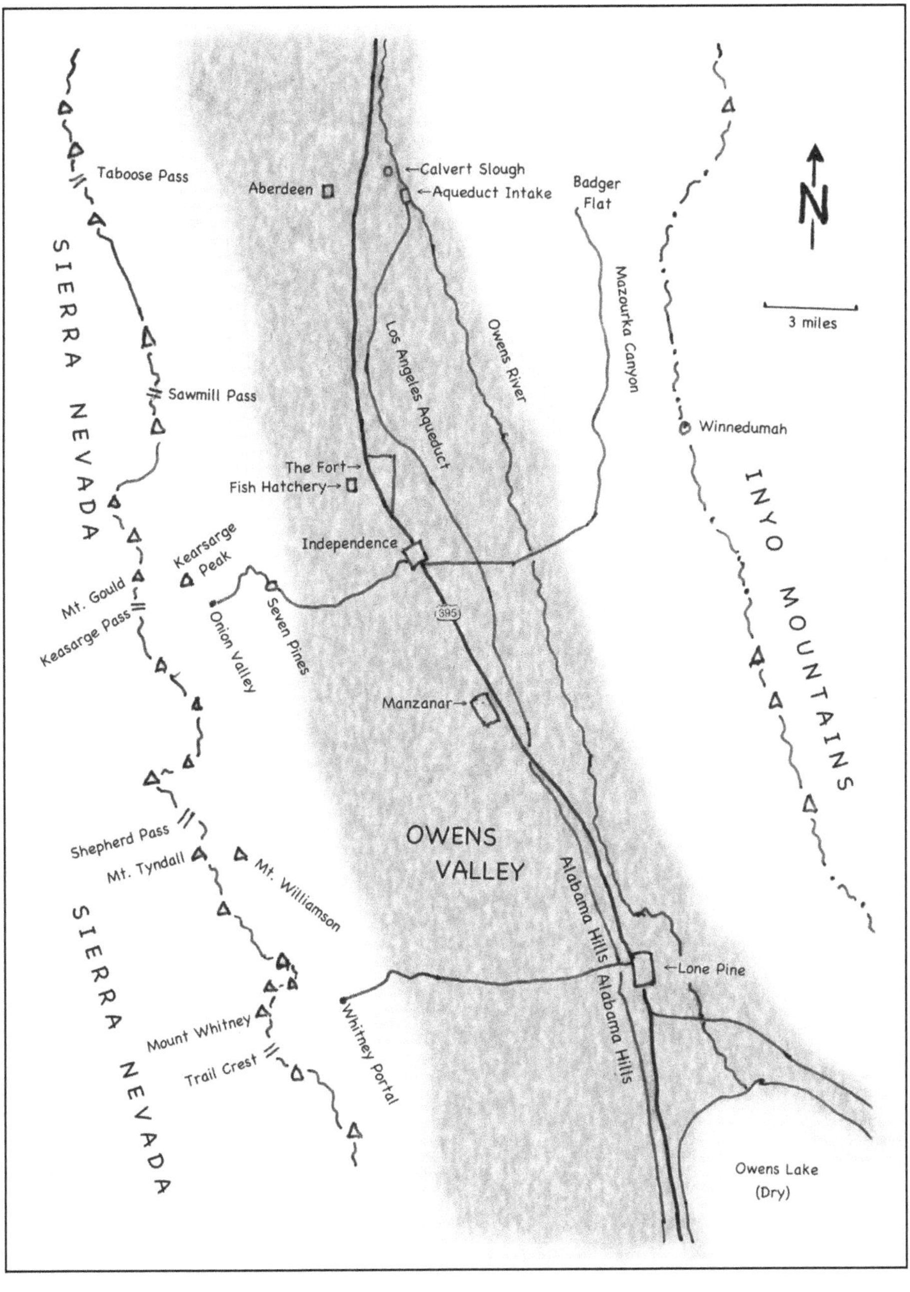

Taboose Pass
Aberdeen
Calvert Slough
Aqueduct Intake
Badger Flat
SIERRA NEVADA
Mazourka Canyon
Owens River
Los Angeles Aqueduct
3 miles
Sawmill Pass
Winnedumah
The Fort
Fish Hatchery
INYO MOUNTAINS
Independence
Kearsarge Peak
Mt. Gould
Keasarge Pass
Onion Valley
Seven Pines
395
Manzanar
Shepherd Pass
Mt. Tyndall
Mt. Williamson
OWENS VALLEY
Alabama Hills
SIERRA NEVADA
Lone Pine
Alabama Hills
Mount Whitney
Whitney Portal
Trail Crest
Owens Lake (Dry)

MAP 3

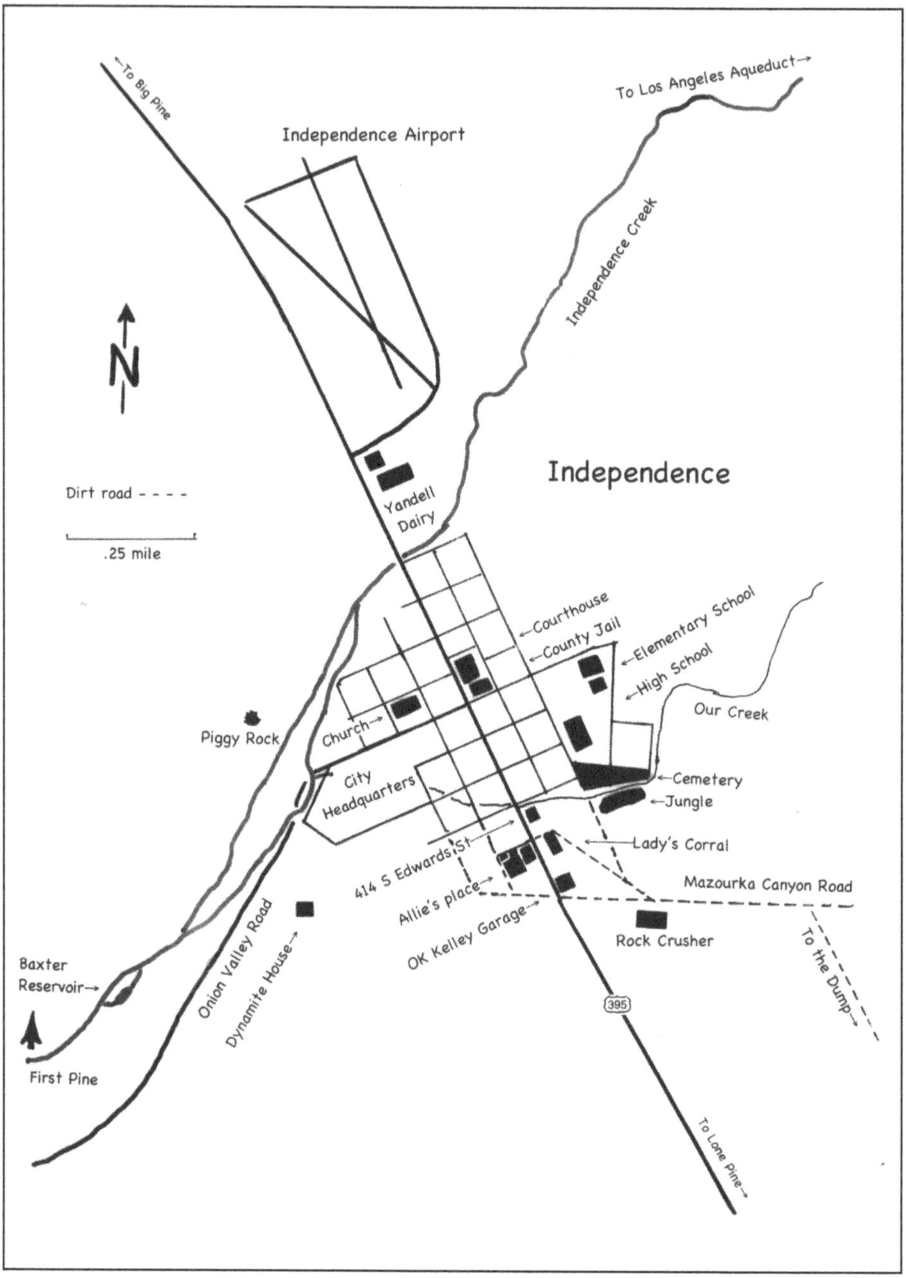
To Big Pine
Independence Airport
To Los Angeles Aqueduct
Independence Creek
N
Independence
Dirt road
.25 mile
Yandell Dairy
Courthouse
County Jail
Elementary School
High School
Our Creek
Piggy Rock
Church
City Headquarters
Cemetery
Jungle
Lady's Corral
414 S Edwards St
Allie's place
OK Kelley Garage
Mazourka Canyon Road
Rock Crusher
To the Dump
395
Baxter Reservoir
First Pine
Onion Valley Road
Dynamite House
To Lone Pine

Preface

On an August evening in 2008, residents of Owens Valley, California, gathered on the Eastern Sierra Museum lawn in Independence. My sister and I had been invited to share stories of our childhood. We would attempt to explain that the life we loved in the town and valley included much more than the house on Edwards Street.

"Home" extended from the valley floor to the snow-capped peaks of the Sierra and to the crest of the Inyo Mountains. "Home" was the morning sun on Mt. Williamson, the smell of rain on sagebrush, and the murmur of Independence Creek as it flowed through our backyard.

Our enthusiastic audience appreciated how our stories and photographs provided a view into a bygone era—an era that deserves to be remembered. We described a simple but satisfying childhood with both the joys and limitations of living in a small town.

Our talk that evening caused Joan and me to reflect on what it was that made those years in Independence so special. While growing up, we couldn't fully know that ours was an uncommon childhood. Now we realize that three things made it possible—the time, the place, and the wisdom of parents who gave us the freedom to roam.

Life in the 1930s and 1940s was far different from today. We were too young to comprehend the hard times of the Great Depression when there weren't enough jobs and many families were impoverished. Before our move to Independence, our father had struggled to stay employed. Our mother recycled everything she could. She kept a ball of used string and another ball of used rubber bands. She made a soapy slush with remnants of soap bars for our laundry. The frugality we learned from our parents remains with our generation and with us. The Depression taught us how to get along with less.

World War II brought jobs for everyone, but austerity stayed with us. Wartime rationing was necessary and shortages were common. With limited gasoline and a national speed limit of 35 mph, people stayed close to home. The war focused our country on a common goal and fostered cooperation. After experiencing the Great Depression and World War II, our father often said, "Hard times never hurt anyone."

The landscape of our childhood was equally important. Living in the same valley, the same town and the same house our entire childhood grounded us with an intense sense of place. We belonged to this place, and it belonged to us.

The townsfolk had a strong commitment to the community, especially to the schools. While not affluent, Independence was economically stable and had permanent employment opportunities. It was both the seat of Inyo County and the Owens Valley headquarters of the City of Los Angeles Department of Water and Power, which transports Sierra water to Los Angeles.

The town had few shops and no movie theater, and our house had no telephone or television. But we had much more—a valley with miles of open sagebrush country bounded by a mountain range on each side.

When we were young, Joan and I were content to play inside our big fenced yard, but before long, we were out the back gate. Eventually, we were wandering beyond the edges of town. Later, on bikes or horseback, we explored the creeks and foothills. With a sack lunch and a mention to Mama of the direction we were headed, we had only to be home by suppertime. The world around us was safe because it was impossible to get lost in the sagebrush, and safe from "strangers" because there were none.

Most important, our parents fostered an appreciation of our world—the town, the valley, and the mountains. Few other local families shared our fascination with the land, and many newcomers couldn't wait to return to the Los Angeles area. On family vacations and weekend hikes, we became acquainted with the dirt roads, the creeks, and the mountain passes. As children, we felt so comfortable in the outdoors that it became our real home.

Mountain memories stay with us. We can close our eyes and recall how our house felt when we returned from our first long Sierra trip. After living with granite boulders and broad vistas for two weeks, the bedroom linoleum was too smooth, and the living room rug too soft. The walls and ceilings echoed.

Looking back on those years, we realize that our connection with the natural world gave us a lasting awareness. Nature teaches children many things—it promotes self-confidence, enhances curiosity, demands responsibility, and delivers consequences for poor decisions. Not least, it cultivates an unbreakable appreciation of natural beauty. We didn't know that our family's move to Independence on a cold November day in 1935 would change our lives forever.

Since the decades of our childhood, our country's population has almost tripled. The pace of life has accelerated. Choices and expectations have expanded. Digital distractions have changed the way children spend their time. But the natural world is still there, waiting to teach our grandchildren, and their children, life's essential lessons!

—Carol DeDecker Wiens

Part One

414 SOUTH EDWARDS STREET
1935–1938

414 South Edwards Street

Joan

I was three-and-a-half, but Carol was only two when we moved to the far away place that our relatives called "Up North." I have no memories of the drive there and few of the house where we first lived. But I knew we had come from "Down Below" where our grandmas and grandpas lived and that they were sad when we said "goodbye." Eventually, I learned we had come from North Hollywood, California, and that our new home was in Independence.

A few weeks later, we moved to a larger house. On that frosty morning, I hugged my box of green doll dishes against my chest as I walked across the lawn to the front porch where Daddy and a friend were squeezing a mattress through the door. "Go around to the back door, Joan," Daddy said sharply. "This mattress is heavy." His words hurt my feelings. Moving was exciting and I wanted to help.

Carol ran around inside yelling to hear the echoes of the empty house. We wandered from room to room, opening doors and looking into empty cupboards. A screened porch spread across the front of the house from which an entry door led to a living room with a wide opening into the dining room. I knew Mama would like the two cupboards in the dining room. They had glass doors and were separated by three deep drawers. She called it a "built-in buffet." The kitchen was like a hall leading to a screened back porch, so we would have to eat in the dining room.

Behind the living room were two bedrooms, one closet and a bathroom. Just above the bathroom sink was a row of four toothbrush hooks, three brass ones and one green one.

"I get the green one," I announced to Carol.

"No, I want the green one," she protested.

"But I get it because I'm older," I told her.

Carol ran off to complain to Mama, who was looking out the windows and saying happily, "This house is like a birdcage!" When I asked her why, she explained it was because there were so many windows. Through the front windows I could see sagebrush and the snowy mountains she called the "Sierra Nevada." I couldn't see out of the high kitchen windows in the other direction, so she lifted me to see more sagebrush and mountains.

Joan and Carol at 414 South Edwards Street, 1936.

I said, "Those mountains look different."

"Yes, they are different and they're called the Inyos," she replied.

Carol kept saying, "Me too," and Mama lifted her up to see.

"Your hands feel like ice," Mama said. "Let's see if Daddy is ready to put up the stove."

When he finished bringing in all of our furniture and boxes, we watched as he poked our stovepipe up through the hole in the dining room ceiling and connected it to our wood stove. Soon we were all holding our hands near the warm metal while Mama cautioned us not to touch it.

Then Daddy moved Carol's crib and my cot into our bedroom. Mama made up our beds while I carefully arranged my doll dishes on our dresser.

With Mama in our front yard, 1937.

Mama's Diary

Carol

Years later, we learned from Mama's diary that the move to Independence was for a job. During the Great Depression, Daddy couldn't turn down any opportunity for steady employment even though it meant moving to a little town 230 miles away from their friends and families.

On her first evening, Mama wrote, "November 15, 1935. Moved our family and all our belongings to Independence, California. Said goodbye to everyone. We are regular villains to take the kids so far away . . . Left folks at 4 a.m., Paul driving the truck and I the car. Nice trip! Kids good! Beautiful country up here. Got unpacked and the wood stove up this evening. Washed cupboards. Waffles for supper, Kids tired."

Daddy's job was driving a truck for the City of Los Angeles, Department of Water and Power. He hauled construction materials from the City headquarters in Independence to a water project near LeeVining, one hundred miles to the north. Sometimes he drove a gasoline truck or a bus filled with construction workers.

Although Daddy and Mama worried about the size of the town, and whether there would be good schools and opportunities for us girls, they were quickly captivated by the wild beauty of the landscape. The morning after our arrival Mama wrote, "Got a big jolt when I saw how close the high mountains are!"

We moved into a tiny house on Jackson Street. Mama complained, "The house is filthy dirty and a terrible job to clean. Hard to find a place for everything. We are cooking on our wood stove and a hot plate loaned to us." The next day, "Washed kitchen woodwork and got the last things unpacked and we are pretty well settled tonight. We are nice and cozy, but crowded. The kids are full of pep, but good."

We had no kitchen stove, no water heater, and no bathtub. Our water came from almost-frozen Independence Creek. She wrote,

Paul and Mary DeDecker, 1929.

"Bathed the girls in a bucket of water I heated on the wood stove. Washed by heating water in pans, pails, etc. Not bad after I got started. Rinse water so cold it numbed my hands."

Mama enjoyed getting to know Independence. "Went to the store and got some groceries. Funny old fashioned place . . . looked around a bit and saw Winnedumah Rock." It was a local landmark on the crest of the Inyo Mountains across the valley from the Sierra.

The wind blew and the house was cold and drafty. We borrowed a gasoline range for cooking. Mama wrote, "Kids are ornery because they can't play outside, the gas stove works terrible and I'm getting tired of the hours Paul keeps. He's driving a bus for a while. Only home 4 hours a day, noon to 4 pm. Still, I like Independence!"

Daddy worked long and irregular hours driving the bus and big trucks on icy mountain roads. He was hours or even days late getting home after a storm, working many overtime hours, and often not getting enough sleep.

City truck in Mono County, 1936.

He also had chores to do at home. Wood stoves heated most of the houses in Independence—so chopping and stacking firewood was an endless job in the winter. "Paul and Buster went after a load of wood and were gone most of the day. Buster opened the store and let us have some groceries." Buster was the store butcher.

Although Mama grumbled about the little house and Daddy's long hours, she was enjoying making new friends, "Went to see Mrs. Warner's new baby today" . . . "Charlie Pitts and his wife were over to play bridge in the evening" . . . "Mrs. Jewett came to ask me to a luncheon for Mrs. Edwards."

She was enthralled by the beauty of the Sierra and wrote about it often. "Got a glimpse of the mountains with snow on them. Beautiful by moonlight! I am anxious for spring to come so we can get out more."

Just after Christmas Mama wrote, "We have rented a larger house down on the highway. Am anxious to have a bath in a real bathtub with plenty of hot water!"

Not long after we moved to 414 South Edwards Street, Daddy had a new job in the City office in town. Mama was happy that he wasn't driving on icy roads. Joan and I liked it because he walked home for lunch. Daddy liked it because he could work in the yard every afternoon.

Uptown with Mama

Joan

Carol and I liked to go uptown with Mama to help with her errands. She pulled us in our red wagon across the highway to the sidewalk that ran for one block. The next block had a dirt path under a row of old locust trees. The third and fourth blocks were the "Uptown," with sidewalks on both sides of the street.

Shops included the grocery, drug, and hardware stores, a small dress shop, and two cafes. The largest buildings were the Independence Hotel, the Winnedumah Hotel, the Inyo County Courthouse, and the American Legion Hall. Because it had a stage and the biggest room in town, the Legion Hall was used for school programs, dances, basketball games, and an occasional movie.

Our first stop was the post office. Nettie Fausel was in charge, and she put letters in the boxes. Mama turned the dial on Box 78 back and forth until the door magically opened. She always hoped for letters from her family and usually there were several. We didn't have a telephone so they wrote almost every day. Nettie and her husband, Max, lived in the back part of the post office building. Max ran the barbershop next door and Daddy was one of his customers.

Next, we crossed the highway to the grocery store. In the back of the store, Buster Scroggins, wearing a white hat and apron, cut and wrapped our pork chops and stew meat. He was Daddy's friend and always happy to see us. The clerk weighed our parsnips, carrots, and celery and wrapped them in newspaper. At the checkout stand we watched the cash register keys go up and down, up and down, and then the money drawer slid out! Mama put the groceries in the wagon and we all walked home.

We rarely went to the drugstore, but Carol and I soon learned that ice cream cones came from the soda fountain along one wall. We carefully examined the display of penny candy: peppermint, root beer, lemon drops, and butterscotch. Candy and ice cream were rare treats, and begging never worked.

The courthouse was the most important building in town. Tall cedar and sequoia trees grew in the back lawn. A wide sidewalk and rose garden led to steps spreading across the front of the building and up to a landing where four giant columns stood, holding up what Mama said was a "portico," a kind of pointy roof. The courthouse had three floors, counting the basement, where the library was located.

Uptown Independence looking northwest, c. 1937.
County of Inyo, Eastern California Museum

We visited the library once a week to return our old books and check out new ones. The librarian, Miss Margrave, and her assistant, Mrs. Best, were friendly and helpful. Carol and I were always eager to search out new books on the low table with the little chairs. *And To Think That I Saw It On Mulberry Street* by Dr. Seuss and *The Story of Ferdinand* by Munro Leaf were my favorites. I checked them out over and over again.

The museum was down a long hall from the library. It interested Mama but not us girls. She had to ask for the key to unlock the glass door. Even with the lights on, it was a dark, gloomy place. Everything there seemed old and brownish, all crowded together in glass cases. We wrinkled up our noses and whispered to Mama, "Let's go." But she was attracted to the dried flower display rack, and she looked at each plant for a long time.

Uptown Independence looking south, c. 1937.
County of Inyo, Eastern California Museum

Up two flights of stairs was the courtroom with its oak benches and chairs. Carol and I were impressed with the shiny brass spittoons. They were placed in corners of the courtroom, near the door, and down the hall. It was hard to imagine so much spit!

The jail and a small park with shady trees and benches were next to the courthouse. The park was an oasis of peace and quiet, and, on hot summer days, old men often sat on the benches and talked or dozed.

Sometimes, Mama took us to visit her new friend, Bessie Poole. We liked to play with her son Tommy, who was Carol's age. He had a set of cardboard sewing cards. Mrs. Poole threaded a blunt needle with colorful yarn for each of us, and we followed the holes to make a picture.

Mrs. Poole's white hair was a puzzle to me. "How can she have white hair when she isn't even old yet?" I whispered to Mama. On the way home she explained the concept of prematurely gray.

It took time for Carol and me to really know the town and its wide streets lined with leafy trees that kept down the summer heat. We learned where our friends lived and that Edwards Street was named after the man who had laid out the town. Also called "The Highway," it ran north and south through the center of town, parallel to the mountain ranges on each side of the valley. East was where the sun came up over the Inyo Mountains and west was where it went down over the Sierra Nevada. Getting lost was never going to be a problem.

Although we loved to be out and about in town to meet new people and listen to Mama talk with them, in those early years most of our time was spent in our own big yard.

A Perfect World

Carol

Our front yard looked like a park with its thick lawn, trees, and flowers. I knew from photographs that it hadn't always looked like that. Daddy had revived the mostly dead grass with goat manure and water and made flowerbeds between the fence and lawn for hollyhocks, sweet peas, and petunias. Now that he didn't drive a truck anymore, he had time after work to plant flowers. We had violets and snapdragons growing along the house and trellises of red roses near the front door. Two spreading locusts, a small spruce tree, and a weeping willow kept the front yard shady in the summer. Graceful willow branches hung over the fishpond.

The backyard was dirt, not the dusty sort, but clean, coarse gravel washed down from the Sierra. In the spring, it was hard to walk barefoot until our feet toughened. A creek ran through the northeast corner of the backyard and out under the fence. It was lined on both sides with locust trees. Our dirt driveway entered from the side street and crossed the creek on a plank bridge. A wire fence, with front and back gates, enclosed the entire yard. For me, the creek, bridge, and the many trees gave our yard a feeling of enchantment. In summer, it was an oasis of green in the surrounding sagebrush.

Daddy kept the backyard as tidy as the front yard. Leaves were raked and the fruit trees pruned. Wood for the stove was stacked neatly next to the nectarine tree. Daddy's lumber pile was organized with the portion set aside for us to use separated from the bigger boards that he needed. In addition to the trees along the creek, we had the cool sanctuary of a grape arbor, two tall poplars, and four fruit trees.

In early summer, Joan and I had a hard time waiting for the fruit to ripen.

"Those nectarines will taste a whole lot better when they get ripe," Mama would scold when she found us behind the woodpile sampling the green fruit.

"But we like them like this," I smiled. She looked dubious as I crunched on a sour mouthful.

Although the lawn was comfortable for bare feet, we found more things to do in the backyard. We excavated lakes and rivers by the water faucet for our stick boats. On the hard-packed gravel driveway, we drew lines for hopscotch and played jump rope.

Joan and I liked to walk on the smooth rocks along the edge of the creek. Holding onto tree trunks kept us from slipping into the water. She led the way. In spots that were a stretch for my short legs, she called back to me cheerfully, "I'm not sure you can do this one, Honey."

And I hollered, "Wait for me! I'm coming!"

Daddy enjoyed building projects, and we soon had swings, a pull-up bar, a teeter-totter, and a playhouse. The latticed playhouse had a built-in table on one end, a built-in bench on the other end, and two windows. Mama made yellow curtains for the windows.

One day, when Joan and I were in the playhouse garnishing our lovely mud pies with green grapes, Joan called out, "Daddy, come in! We made some mud pies just for you!"

He leaned his rake against the mulberry tree and came in saying, "Yum, those sure look good," and he enthusiastically popped one into his mouth.

When we heard him crunching Joan cried, "Oh no, Daddy!" She ran to the house with me right on her heels. "Mama, Mama, Daddy didn't know it was pretend food," Joan burst out.

Mama whispered to us, "Don't worry, he was playing a trick on you. He probably tossed the mud pie out the window when you weren't looking and was eating a gingersnap that he pulled from his pocket."

When we were older, we learned to dam the creek with boards from our section of Daddy's lumber pile. The water was cold because it came down from the Sierra snow, but we splashed with our friends until we were goose-pimpled and shivering. Then we all ran to the fishpond where the sun kept the water warm, and the slime on the bottom was soft and comfortable. We slithered around on our stomachs until we were warm enough to get out to lie on the lawn in the sun.

Daddy kept a stack of wooden blocks behind the garage to use when he jacked up the car to work on the engine. We used them to

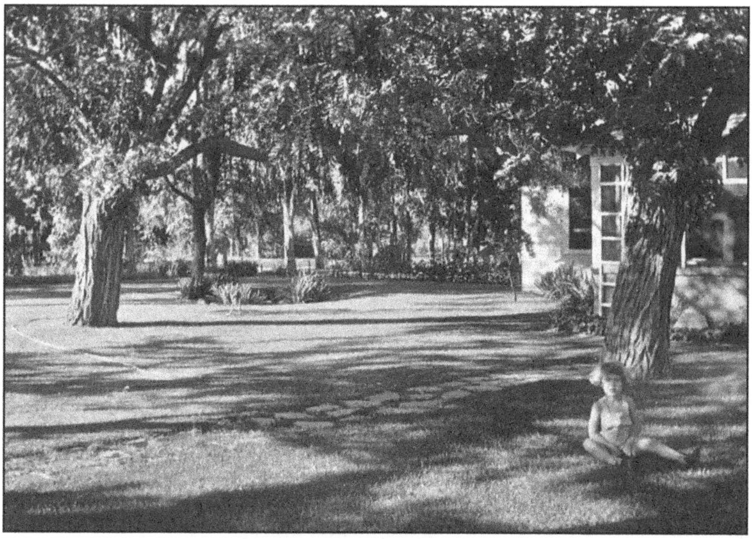

Carol in our front yard, 1938.

make "structures." When we finished a project, Daddy always returned the blocks to their spot behind the garage.

They were heavy for Joan and me to move around the yard so we pulled them in our wagon. Once, we built a two-block high clubhouse with three neighbor girls. The building project was a success, but we disagreed who should be president.

Roberta said, "I should be president because I am the oldest."

Janice objected, "It was my idea to have a club."

Joan argued, "But the clubhouse is in my yard."

Janice's little sister asked, "What is a club?"

And I said, "It's hot. Let's go play in the creek."

One night, when we were drying the dishes I said, "I think we have the nicest yard in Independence. No one else has a creek with a bridge and so many trees."

Joan agreed, "I'm glad that Daddy likes to build things, like the swings and the playhouse."

In our backyard with our cousins, 1938.
(See Appendix for names)

Mama smiled, "I like the way it looks—trim and tidy with so many colorful flowers. But most of all, I'm glad that Daddy enjoys working in it.

We were never at a loss for something to do in our special and spacious yard. It was a perfect world!

Our Sunday Drives

Joan

There were many unpaved roads in Owens Valley, and Mama and Daddy seemed eager to explore them all. On a spring Sunday, soon after our move to town, we packed a picnic lunch and drove up a steep dirt road through the sagebrush to Grays Meadow at the base of the Sierra. It was not much of a meadow, but more of a damp area along Independence Creek six miles above town. The black oaks, willows, and birch trees had leafed-out along the noisy stream, and wildflowers were blooming. We spread a blanket on the grassy bank and enjoyed the warmth of the spring sun.

After lunch, Daddy fished while the rest of us followed the trail along the creek to Seven Pines, where summer cabins were scattered under the tall Jeffrey pines. In later years, Carol and I would envy our friends with cabins there in the cool shade, above the heat of the valley. Just above Seven Pines, Independence Creek tumbled out of its narrow canyon and flowed down through the sagebrush to Independence.

On another Sunday, we drove right past Grays Meadow and Seven Pines and on up to Onion Valley, another eight miles. The narrow mountain road was frightening with hairpin turns, steep hillsides, and views down into the canyon far below. Mama pointed out the foundations of buildings swept away by an avalanche many years ago. I was relieved when we reached Onion Valley, a fairly flat area surrounded by peaks with patches of snow. We parked where the road ended and the hiking trails began. Daddy told us people came here to camp or fish at the nearby lakes, or to hire a packer to take them over Kearsarge Pass to Bullfrog Lake.

It was chilly at 9,000 feet, and Carol and I put on our sweaters before running into the meadow to admire the flowers. I met an impressive plant called the corn lily. It came up to my chin and looked like a giant corn stalk with fat leaves and topped by a cluster of tiny white flowers. Some of the stalks were taller than I was.

We walked over to see the cabins and corrals of the pack station and to visit the horses and mules. The animals were friendly when we poked handfuls of grass through the fence. Then we wandered through the campground. No campers were there because it was still spring. We ate our lunch at a picnic table to the sound of waterfalls and streams all around us.

On the return drive, Daddy parked the car in a wide spot so we could look at the view below. "Pay attention now and don't get too close to the edge," he reminded us as we scrambled out of the car. One look down took our breath away. Far below us the narrow road zigzagged down several thousand feet to Seven Pines, around rocky ridges and boulder-strewn slopes. Mama pointed out our town on the valley floor, a dark green postage stamp in a vast sea of sagebrush.

"What are those other green places?" I asked, and she told us they were alfalfa fields where ranchers grew feed for their cattle. She pointed out Independence Creek, a line of green winding from Seven Pines across the sagebrush to the town. The highway sparkled when sunlight reflected from car and truck windows.

We continued down the steep gravel road, the tires making a crunching sound and our ears popping as we dropped in elevation.

On later trips to Onion Valley, Carol would ask me, "Are you going to drive up this road when you are a grownup?"

"No," I always said. "It's way too scary."

When relatives visited, we often took them on picnics to some of our favorite places. We loved the Fish Hatchery on Oak Creek. The eggs and hatchlings were housed in a handsome building made of cobblestones with a tower and tile roof. The superintendent and his family lived in the tower. The building was surrounded with lawn, trees, and flowerbeds and with ponds for the growing trout. The smallest pond held the largest trout, and when we came near, they roiled the water expecting to be fed. In the huge hatchery room, we kids liked to stand on the end of the troughs and watch the fingerlings swimming against the current.

Our Grandpa Foster often camped with friends farther up Oak Creek. They put up their tents in the cool shade of the willows, cooked over a campfire, and enjoyed the fishing.

Our younger cousins, Sydney Ann and Clinton, always wanted to go to the Alabama Hills, above Lone Pine. It was a goblin world of sculptured boulders, perfect for hide-and-seek and exploring. On the drive home, we could usually persuade Daddy to take what we called the "Whoopee Road," a narrow road with deep ups and downs. He drove fast and we gasped as our stomachs dropped in the dips. At the top of the hills we all yelled, "Whoopee!"

This was just the beginning of all there was to see. For our family, it was as important to return to favorite a place, as it was to explore new ones.

Fort Independence

Joan

"I know it's just north of town, but I don't know exactly where." Mama was always curious. She'd been hearing about "The Fort" ever since we had arrived in Independence, and she wanted to know what it was.

She inquired at the library and the museum and learned that the fort had been built in 1862 by the United States Army to control the conflicts between Owens Valley settlers and the Paiute Indians. The Paiutes had lived in the area for centuries, and they naturally resented the newcomers. They lived in family groups and weren't farmers, so they depended on hunting deer and other animals and gathered pine nuts and seeds. During difficult winters, they killed the settlers' cattle, and skirmishes led to the deaths of both Indians and settlers until the fort was built. After the conflicts were over, the fort was abandoned in 1877.

Mama also learned that all the buildings were gone, and there was nothing left of the fort itself. It had included a parade ground surrounded by wooden buildings for housing the officers, adobe barracks for the soldiers, a hospital, and a school. Because the American flag was first raised over the new fort on July 4, 1862, it was named "Camp Independence." Several years later, the settlement three miles away was named "Independence."

After reading all the available information and studying the old photographs, maps, and drawings, Mama wanted to see the site. She came home from the museum waving a sketch map she'd made and said, "Paul, let's drive out there this weekend to look around."

On Saturday morning, we drove north from town for three miles where Daddy made a right turn off the highway onto a dirt road.

Mama read aloud from her directions. "This has to be it."

We eagerly jumped out and explored the grassy field, hoping to find at least some old boards or adobe bricks. There was nothing, only bushes and clumps of dry grass.

Daddy commented, "People have probably used all of the wood and adobe for other buildings, lumber has always been in short supply here."

As we climbed back into the car Mama remarked, "That was disappointing, as we should have expected. But now that we're here, let's look around a little. I read that the soldiers lived in caves while they waited for their barracks to be built. She looked at her map and said, "I think we should turn left here."

We drove down a short lane and parked at the edge of a steep gully. A path led us into a dry wash where wide openings had been carved into the hard gravel bank to create rooms. I was not impressed and commented, "Why would anyone want to sleep in such a dry, dusty place."

"I don't think those soldiers had a choice in where they would sleep," Mama laughed. "A gravel roof is better than no roof."

Nearby, we stopped to look at a tiny school building. "It was built years later, for the Fort Independence Indian Reservation kids," Daddy said. "Some of this area was given to the Paiutes about twenty-five years ago. They have water rights in Oak Creek and own many acres of land. Some Paiute families live in Independence, and some of them live here. I don't know how many." He pointed out the irrigation ditches around each field, all lined with locust trees and yellow sunflowers. He drove slowly, and we could see turn-offs to their homes.

Finally Daddy said, "Well, I think that's about it. Have you seen enough, Mary? We've learned all we can, and it's time for lunch."

I was disappointed in our visit to Fort Independence and complained on the way home, "I've looked at the scary pictures in Daddy's National Geographic magazines of forts and soldiers and Indians attacking the stockades, and it all looked exciting. Even though Mama told us there had never been a stockade here, I thought there would be something more to see."

The Hobo

Joan

Sometimes the bigger world came right to our door. One day, a stranger knocked at the back screen porch and Mama answered. She didn't open the door but talked to him through the screen. I watched and listened. The man wore an old jacket and shabby pants and had brown hair and a stubbly beard. He asked Mama if he could do some work around the yard in exchange for a meal.

I quickly scanned our backyard. There was not a weed to be seen, an irrigation ditch encircled each fruit tree, and there were no weeds or trash piles. Our playhouse, swings, and the grape arbor were all neat and tidy. I couldn't see any work for the man to do and I glanced at Mama with dismay.

She told him her husband had finished all of the chores. There was a long silence. Finally, she realized he was hungry.

"Would you like something to eat?" she asked.

"Yes, ma'am," was the quick reply. She fixed him a big plate of beef stew, sliced tomatoes and buttered bread. He sat on the back steps and ate hungrily, saying, "Thank you ma'am," as he handed her back the empty plate.

Mama talked to him for a while. She gave him a rose-colored wool blanket and suggestions about where he might earn a meal. With a "Thanks again, ma'am" he walked across the bridge and was gone.

Mama told me he might have come on the freight train to Kearsarge Station and walked the four miles into town. She went on to say that during the Depression a lot of people couldn't find jobs or enough to eat. She looked very sad.

Joan Learns to Read

Joan

Feeling very grown up, I walked by myself the several blocks to the Methodist Church. I was going to school! Although the district lacked a kindergarten program, a group of parents worked together to provide a morning kindergarten at the church social hall. Ours was the first and last class for many years. The mothers helped out on different days. As a snack, we had graham crackers and tomato juice or milk. I liked drawing pictures and playing games, but most of all I loved being with the other children. There were fourteen students. Three of us would spend thirteen school years together.

I felt even more grown up when Mama walked with me the four blocks to the elementary school the following September. There were two classrooms in the main building for the first four grades. The fifth and sixth grades were together in the Annex, a large room in an adjacent building.

In front of the school, a low hedge protected a rose garden and patch of lawn. The rest of the yard was gravel, with swings, a slide, a teeter-totter, and shady elms. A group of tall cedars grew in a back corner. The little kids played under the trees and the big kids climbed high in their long horizontal branches. When Carol started school, she thought it was more fun to play in the trees than on the playground.

Ah, Miss Lyete! My first-grade teacher was young, pretty, and nice, and had dark wavy hair. On the first day, she wore a yellow dress with a tiered skirt and black edging. It was her first teaching assignment. She taught nine first-graders and eleven second-graders. Right away, she started us first-graders on phonics and writing the alphabet letters. While she was giving lessons to the first-graders, two rowdy second-grade boys caused her no end of grief, and both spent time either with tape across their mouths or sitting in the cloakroom. This treatment didn't seem to change or even bother them. At the time, I simply considered them naughty boys. Looking back, I think they were two bright but bored little boys, not interested in being "good."

Joan's kindergarten class—Joan with doll, 1937.
(See Appendix for names)

I was thrilled to be reading. At home, I practiced aloud to Mama while she sewed. She was equally thrilled because she and Daddy had just splurged on an electric sewing machine, a great improvement from her old treadle model. We both were happy as I read to her while she sewed.

The Swan Family Visits

Carol

The Swan family arrived in an old black pickup truck. The covered back end was filled with kids, camping equipment, and fishing poles. Mr. and Mrs. Swan and the grandma rode in the cab. I watched them all pile out, wildly enthusiastic about camping on Independence Creek and hiking in the mountains. I was too young to remember them as our neighbors when we had lived in North Hollywood.

Our parents were delighted to join them on a hike up to the lakes above Onion Valley. Daddy was eager to try his luck at fishing, and Mama was always ready to hike up a new trail. Joan, almost six years old, was invited to go along, but I was to spend the day in Onion Valley with the grandma.

The grandma wanted to sit in our car. All day! I wanted to play outside. I looked out the window for a while, wiggling and squirming, before I announced decidedly, "I'm going to get out to look at the creek."

"Oh no!" the she replied sternly. "You might fall in."

I squirmed some more and said, "It's too hot in here." She rolled down her window, just a bit.

Finally I tried, "Well, I need to go to the outhouse."

She took me by the hand and delivered me to the outhouse and back to the stuffy car. So I sat in the driver's seat and played with the pedals and pushed and pulled all the buttons and knobs on the dashboard while the grandma scolded. She had never learned to drive and worried I might start the engine, or worse, I might release the brake and we would roll down the hill and into the creek.

She probably was a nice grandma, but she hadn't brought any books to read to me. I learned later that she was from Sweden and didn't read English.

I didn't feel any happier when the hikers returned, talking about the fish they'd caught, their snowball fights, and other trip delights. They had visited Gilbert, Flower, and Matlock lakes and had a picnic. It had been an exciting day and I had missed it all!

I think Mama felt as sorry for me as I did for myself when I said, "The grandma made me stay in the car all day!"

Mama explained, "I had expected that she would let you play in the meadow and take you to pet the horses. I'm sorry that I didn't suggest that to her. I think she feels uncomfortable in our mountains, and she wanted to keep you safe."

That night when the Swan family got out their Fourth of July fireworks, I forgot my disappointment. They had rockets and amazing firecrackers that sizzled and flared. Best of all were the worms that twisted and wiggled on the flat rocks of the walk between our house and the front gate. And the sparklers! While the kids ran around on the lawn twirling sparklers, the dads set off the rockets out on the side street.

The Swan family returned to Owens Valley many times to camp, hike, and fish with our family. By their next visit, I was old enough to go along.

Women's Work

Joan

Carol and I stood in the screened back porch and watched with wonder as the clothes, all bubbly and squishy in the washing machine, went through the electric wringer and came out flattened like boards.

"Don't touch the wringer," Mama warned. She showed us once again how to push the release lever while repeating one of her disaster stories about someone catching a hand or an arm in the rubber rollers. Of course that stimulated our interest, but it was many years before she allowed us to use the wringer.

On washday, right after our usual breakfast of fruit, toast, bacon and eggs, she set up the back porch. She put our big galvanized washtub on a bench next to the electric washer. Then she filled both the washing machine and washtub with buckets of hot water from the kitchen tap.

In went the sheets, and after some time in the machine, they were put through the wringer and into the rinse tub, swished by hand to remove the soap, wrung again, and placed in our bathtub for a final rinse. In that last rinse of sheets and other white items, she would add a little of Mrs. Stewart's Bluing, a concentrated solution that somehow helped the whites look whiter. Then everything went through the wringer one final time.

A few selected items, like our dresses and our parents' best clothes, were dipped in a starch mixture at the kitchen sink. When ironed, they would be stiff and hold their shape.

Carol and I did our job at the kitchen sink. We turned every sock inside out, swished it around in the water to get out any sand, and then turned it right side out again. We didn't think it was necessary and grumbled to Mama, "Why do we need to rinse the inside of socks?" Mama had high standards.

She carried the washed clothes outside to the clothesline Daddy had built on the side lawn. In summer, the desert heat dried them almost as fast as Mama hung them up. The sheets felt crisp and smelled good. If the wind blew, clothes weren't left on the line for long or they'd get whipped, worn, and sandy. And the wind blew hard and often.

Our washday lunch was cornmeal mush with a spoonful of butter on top. It was a brief rest for Mama. By the end of the day, a week's worth of laundry would be done. She emptied the tubs of water, scrubbed the floors, remade the beds, and cooked dinner. She looked so tired.

Then there was the ironing, always the ironing. Most of our clothes were made of cotton, so they came off the line stiff and wrinkled. Mama stacked them on the oilcloth-covered dining room table, filled a bowl with water, and got out her u-shaped brush. She sprinkled a shirt on one side, turned it over and sprinkled the other side, then rolled it tightly and placed it in the small washtub. She carefully tucked towels over the sprinkled clothes. In a few hours the moisture would spread uniformly and make them easy to iron, but if she waited too many days the dreaded mildew would begin to set in. As ironing was not Mama's favorite chore, she checked frequently for that telltale odor.

A few years later, when it was time to teach Carol and me how to iron, we practiced on Daddy's boxer shorts, handkerchiefs and pillowcases. It wasn't as easy as it looked and although Mama was patient, she expected a good job.

As homemakers, Mama and the other women in town spent hours on laundry chores. Over the years, as we cycled through ever-improving washing machines, Mama's workload decreased. New fabrics required less ironing. She was happy to have more time to study the desert plants and pursue other expanding interests.

My Big Sister

Carol

Joan was a year and a half older than I was. I followed her around and tried to imitate her. When she was loud and unruly, so was I, until Daddy looked up from his newspaper and said, "No rough-housing in here. You girls go outside."

I tried to keep up with her, but she could talk faster, run farther, and climb higher in the peach tree. Luckily, I didn't follow her lead when she tasted the paste Daddy was using to lay new linoleum on the kitchen floor. It looked like chocolate sauce. Or when she drank the pickle juice. Even if she was bossy at times, I respected her immense knowledge. We had plenty of conflicts, but it was her nature to be kind. She was patient when she taught me to jump rope in the driveway and to play jacks on the dining room floor.

I was heartbroken when Joan started kindergarten. "Are you going to school AGAIN?" I asked her every morning of the first week of the school year.

"Yes, because I am five and we have music and stories and paint-brushes," she said proudly.

Unfortunately, there was no kindergarten the following year when I was five. Joan's was the first and only kindergarten class in years—a special program organized by parents. So I was home alone for a second year. During those years, Carol Walters was my neighborhood playmate. She lived across the highway with her mother, an older sister named Janice, and a housekeeper named Helen. Because she was a year younger than I, Mama called her "Little Carol." I enjoyed being the wise and bossy one for a change.

Little Carol and I usually played in our backyard, probably because it had swings and a playhouse. Or, perhaps, it was because Helen liked to listen undisturbed to her afternoon radio soap operas. When her programs were over, Helen came to take Little Carol home. But if I got too bossy and Little Carol was ready to go home earlier, she called, "H-E-L-E-N" from our side of the highway. She was not allowed to cross without an adult.

During those two years, I waited impatiently for Joan to get home from school. She was my favorite playmate, but as we grew older our interests began to differ. While she and her friends read books on a blanket under the locust trees, my friends and I climbed the trees or played in the fishpond.

Eventually, we realized our temperaments were not the same. Being outgoing and sociable, Joan was attracted to conversation and interaction. She was a listener and a talker and enjoyed stories about other people. She understood their feelings. When Mama's friends came to visit, Joan paid attention to the conversation. I preferred action in the back yard, knowing that Joan would give me any exciting information I had missed.

We were also different in another way. When Joan was sad or upset she would talk to Mama about the problem, but when I felt that way I went into the closet and sat in the rag box. It was a dark and comfortable place to think things over. I asked myself, "Why did you shoot green nectarines at Geraldine McLaurin with your new slingshot when she rode by on her bike?" After a lot of thought, I still didn't know the why, but in the case of the nectarines I didn't need to confess because Mrs. McLaurin had already come over to talk to Daddy.

He sat me down and said, "Carol, it's not a good idea to shoot anything at anyone. You need to march over right now and apologize to Geraldine and her mother." He took away my slingshot, and I felt both guilty and sad. That was a special slingshot I had made from a red manzanita branch.

Not all of my thoughts in the rag box were unpleasant. The day after the nectarine incident, Mrs. McLaurin knocked on the front door again and said, "Carol, we're going to Pinyon Creek for a picnic this evening, and we hope you can come with us." I never understood why I did some of the things that got me into trouble, but the rag box was the place to be while I tried to figure out how to fix them. I learned that apologizing helped.

When I grew too big to fit in the rag box, I would slide under our lower bunk bed where it was quiet, and the linoleum was smooth and consoling. That's where I went the one and only time that Daddy come home drunk from his office Christmas party. And when we got the news that my grandpa DeDecker had died. I was in the fifth grade when Grandpa was killed by a hit-and-run-driver. It was the worst day in all of our lives, and I had a lot to think about. It helped me to have a quiet thinking place.

Joan had a strong sense of justice and fairness. When she felt something was unfair, she would state her case and stubbornly stick to her opinion. She did more arguing with Daddy than I would have dared. They frequently disagreed about cutting down trees in the yard, and she lobbied for years, unsuccessfully, to get a dog. I admired her willingness to stand up for her ideas, but I was reluctant to confront authority. When I wanted to do something I knew would not be readily approved, I did it first and worried about the consequences later.

This tactic worked well for me because I believed I had good judgment about the outcome. I found I wasn't always right. There was the time my third grade friend and I walked from her house at the Fish Hatchery to my house in Independence, three miles through the sagebrush, forgetting to tell her mother where we were going. And there was the event on the rickety raft at Flower Lake when the wind blew Marilyn and me into the middle of the lake and I didn't know how to swim. But all in all, I generally made good decisions.

Mama expected her daughters to be well mannered and ladylike. I recall our departure to Barbara's fifth birthday party when Mama reminded us to thank both Barbara and Mrs. Yandell for inviting us to the party.

We were usually polite—that was the easy part—but Joan was much better than I at being ladylike.

She asked me, "Why don't you like dresses and long curls?"

I said, "Well, it's hard to climb a tree in a dress, and curls take too much time." In the photos Mama framed for Daddy's office desk, Joan was sitting on a chair with long curls and wearing a pretty dress. In my photo, I was sitting out on the long limb of the big locust tree in the front yard wearing jeans and a sweatshirt, with my usual short hair.

At Phyllis Shaffer's eighth birthday party, I tore the pocket of the dress Mama had just finished sewing.

When I got home with my pocket dangling she scolded, "Carol, I work hard to make you nice dresses and you don't take care of them."

It was one of the few times I felt she was being unreasonable. "Mama," I said, "Someone had to climb over the fence to retrieve the ball, and I didn't know there was a loose wire on the top."

"But the Shaffer's yard does have a front gate," she said rather sharply.

It was harder than she thought to be ladylike.

Part One

Even though we were different in many ways, Joan and I agreed on the important things in life, the foremost being an appreciation for the outside world. We shared a curiosity and an enthusiasm for investigating the wild things around us, first in our own backyard and later in the desert beyond the fence.

I was glad I had a sister. With a few exceptions, Joan was a good-natured and lively companion.

Our Particular Parents

Carol

Daddy was particular about everything. His garage workbench and his sock drawer were always tidy. When he said, "Don't forget to put my hammer away when you're through with it," we wouldn't dream of not doing so. He was particular about how the front yard looked, and he didn't like weeds in the backyard either. In the summer, when he walked home for lunch, he moved the sprinklers that watered the lawn and the hoses that irrigated the fruit trees in the backyard. Most days, after work, he pulled weeds in the flowerbeds or pruned the roses.

For breakfast, he always had the same thing—fruit, two eggs, bacon, cereal, toast, and coffee.

For supper, he liked everything. When it was time for dessert, Mama would ask, "Do you want canned peaches or pie?"

After some thought he would say, "I think I'll have pie tonight."

It was a joke, because we all knew he would always choose pie, just as he always had tea with milk in it with dinner. The only thing he wouldn't eat were olives.

After supper he liked to read the newspaper and hear the news on the radio.

On weekends, he often went fishing in the creeks that flowed down from the mountains. Sometimes Mama, Joan, and I went along. We all liked to explore while he fished.

Our father was predictable. Joan and I usually knew what he would say or do or think. That made life easy. Knowing what to expect avoided arguments. He was generous about helping us, and we didn't make unreasonable demands.

In spite of his particularity, he had a good sense of humor and loved practical jokes. When he was dating Mama, his mother had said, "Paul, I'd like to meet the young woman you seem to be very serious about."

He nodded, "I'll bring her home for supper on Sunday." But he also took Mama's two sisters along and would not tell his mother which of the three was his girl.

During the 1930s, it was common for young women to have a "Hope Chest." It was generally a cedar chest, which she would fill with her embroidered pillowcases and crocheted doilies. Mama was not interested in doilies or Hope Chests, but her younger sister, Hazel, filled hers with such things.

At Christmas, Daddy said, "I think Hazel needs a broom for her chest." He sawed the handle of a new broom in two so it would fit into the chest and connected the two pieces with a hinge. He sent her the broom along with instructions on how to use it. Joan and I were too young to catch the humor, but we recall a photo of Aunt Hazel pretending to sweep the floor with a crooked broom.

* * * * *

Mama cooked and washed the clothes. She cleaned the house often because she was particular too. She often reminded us, "Pick up your toys and make your beds before you go out to play."

Once a week she did the laundry with an exacting routine that took all day. She hung it on the clothesline in a certain way—the socks on one line and the shirts on another. It was difficult for us to help her because she was so particular.

We always wondered why she never wanted us to help with the cooking. We knew it was dangerous for us to use our gasoline stove, because it was tricky even for Mama to pump and light it safely. However, after she got her first electric range, she still didn't let us cook. I suspect that she just didn't want a messy kitchen.

Our kitchen was so tiny that it had to be tidy. The stove, refrigerator, and water heater filled one wall. The sink and drain board filled the opposite wall. Doorways filled the two end walls. We washed the dishes immediately after each meal so the space wouldn't be cluttered.

Even washing the dishes wasn't simple at our house. Our friends asked, "Why does your mother pour a tea kettle of boiling water on the dishes before she dries them?"

We hadn't noticed that most people didn't rinse that way. Later, we understood that some of her peculiarities went back to the tuberculosis hospital where she had worked after graduating from high school. Before the days of antibiotics, tuberculosis was difficult to cure and sanitation procedures, such as scalding dishes, were imperative.

Mama was especially particular about our behavior. We needed to eat whatever was served, to be home on time, and to say "please" and "thank you."

Although Mama was particular about how the house looked, her overriding interest was going to see new places and learning new things. She liked to walk through the sagebrush and drive down dirt roads. She wanted to learn the names of the birds that migrated through the valley and read books about the mining days.

But more than anything else, she liked to look at the mountains and hike up the creeks while Daddy fished. We were all happy when he would say on a Saturday morning, "It looks like a good day for fishing. Let's go up Oak Creek."

Joan and I got along well with our particular parents.

Hazel and the Hula

Joan

Oh, Hawaii! The land of warm water and sandy beaches, exotic flowers, perfumed leis, and graceful dancers in grass skirts. All of this, and more, were the topics of Aunt Hazel's letters from that far-away paradise. She was Mama's youngest sister and had sailed there on the *SS Malola* in 1936 to marry Clarence Smith, a marine. They had been engaged for some time.

Their wedding was small and no family members were present, but we could tell by the photographs she sent that it had been elegant. Aunt Hazel always looked stylish, even when she stood in our front yard to have her photo taken with various nieces and nephews. For her wedding, she wore a long, slim, white satin dress and carried an armful of long-stemmed white roses. Beside her stood handsome, dark-haired Uncle Clarence, wearing a white jacket and black pants. They looked solemn, but happy.

The Hawaiian wonder that most impressed Carol and me was the pineapple drinking fountain featured on Aunt Hazel's plantation tour. Here one could drink all of that delicious juice one wanted. It was hard to imagine.

After two years in Hawaii, she sailed for home on the *SS Lurline*, with Uncle Clarence to follow on a military vessel. Mama drove with us girls all the way from Independence to Los Angeles to meet Hazel's

Our new car, 1937.

ship. It would dock the next morning and Uncle Bud, one of Mama's brothers, drove us to the pier. We were late and he drove so fast I was frightened. But finally we walked up the gangplank and there was Aunt Hazel.

She wore a finger-length cloak over a blue dress, and had several leis around her neck. As elegant as ever. But I also remember that she was upset because we were late and had not been present for the ship's arrival. I knew Mama felt unappreciated when she murmured, "She doesn't realize how much effort it took for us to get here." Aunt Hazel often seemed upset about something.

She had not only learned to dance the hula, but also brought us grass skirts, tissue paper leis, ankle decorations, and phonograph records of the songs. She let us shake her feathered gourd to the rhythm of the music. When Aunt Hazel danced and shook the gourd, it seemed to take on a dazzling life of its own. She gave us a Hawaiian doll dressed in a grass skirt and leis. And she taught us some of the dances. The ones I remember best were *A Little Brown Gal in a Little Grass Skirt* and *Malihini Mele.* I loved learning the hula, even to Aunt Hazel's exacting standards, and swayed my hips, remembered always to smile, and danced at variety shows and events around town. When I was

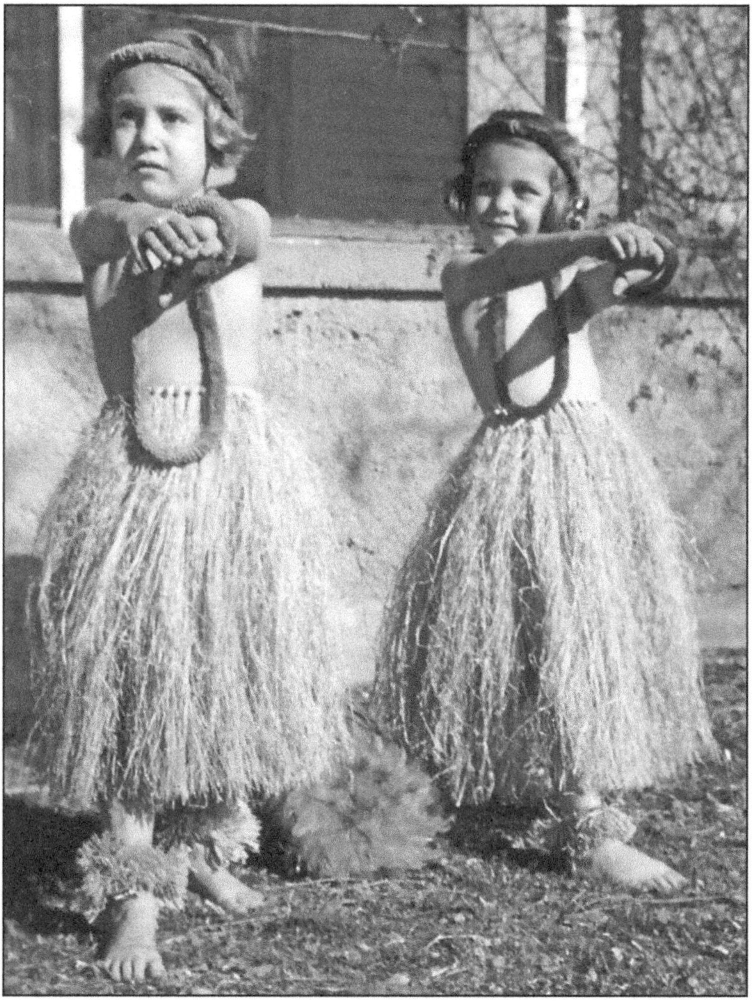

Hula girls, 1938.

seven, the local newspaper reported, "Joan DeDecker captivated her audience with her Hawaiian dance, which she did as the PTA number."

Carol was not so enamored with the hula and soon dropped out of our joint appearances. When Mama had us pose in front of the house in our grass skirts for a snapshot, Carol complained that Daddy had just fertilized the lawn with goat manure. She didn't care much for the hula, and the smelly lumps under her bare feet didn't help.

Cycle of the Seasons

Joan

As the months and years went by, we began to recognize the cycle of the seasons and to anticipate and appreciate the changing colors outside and our changing activities.

In spring, the fruit trees bloomed—nectarine, apricot, peach, and mulberry, each with different colored blossoms. The purple lilacs by the back porch smelled spicy. Daffodils and tulips brightened the flowerbeds. The orioles returned to the locust trees along the creek, hummingbirds found Mama's columbine, and robins patrolled the lawn for worms. Locust branches drooped with fragrant flowers. We tasted the sweetest part of the blossoms and compared their flavor with that of the yellow honeysuckle flowers that grew on Anton's fence across the street. Daddy's violets bloomed and bloomed, and we smelled their perfume as we ran past. Frequent windstorms brought dust and whipped the buds and blossoms. Spring was a season of longer days and sweet-smelling surprises and the fun of playing outside again.

In summer, we tumbled on the lawn, built blanket tents, and ran through the sprinklers with our friends. Cedar waxwings passed through town, gorging on ripe mulberries. Thunderstorms with booming claps and lightning flashes brought brief downpours and gave the desert the delicious smell of damp sagebrush. We picnicked with friends and visiting relatives up the creeks in the shade of birch and willows. Carol and I slept on cots on the front porch and played jacks on the cool concrete floor. We ate ripe peaches and Daddy churned peach ice cream. After supper, we walked to the outdoor skating rink in the schoolyard with our clamp-on roller skates and skated around and around to the music that Mr. Tatum played on the phonograph.

Labor Day marked the beginning of fall. School began with the excitement of seeing our friends and moving to the next grade, wearing the new dresses that Mama had sewn and our new shoes. Deer hunters planned their hunts and at supper Daddy reported on who had "got their buck." The robins and orioles flew south. The Virginia creeper turned shades of red and Mama warned us again not to eat the purple berries. The town trees turned orange and yellow, and their leaves piled against the curbs. Locust leaves drifted down and collected in corners of our yard. Carol and I helped rake and burn them in the alley. Rabbitbrush bloomed bright yellow among the sagebrush, and Mama sneezed and sniffled as she studied new plants. Daddy wrapped the outdoor faucets with gunnysacks and drained the fishpond.

In winter, the cold wind blew. Friends came for Thanksgiving turkey and apple pies. We looked through pages of dolls and games and pretty dresses in the Sears Roebuck Catalog, and our parents ordered gifts. We hung school classrooms with green and red paper chains and practiced our parts for the school program in the Legion Hall. Mama sent Christmas cards and made toffee and fruitcake for friends and relatives. Christmas vacation was the time for jigsaw puzzles, board games, and phonograph records. Our family invited neighbors for Tom and Jerrys, and we children got them sprinkled with nutmeg but without the brandy. In the morning, after a snowfall, we looked out the windows and caught our breath with the beauty of a soft white blanket extending across the sagebrush to the top of the Sierra peaks. But mostly we sat close to the stove and read.

Part Two

EXPLORING OUR WORLD
1938–1941

Beyond the Fence

Carol

Mama loved our big beautiful yard. During our early years, she was concerned about Highway 395 just beyond our front gate. Whenever we went out to play, she said, "Girls, you must never open the front gate. The highway traffic is dangerous!"

With no stop signs or traffic lights, the trucks didn't slow down much as they went rumbling through town. We were so used to hearing the trucks go by that we scarcely noticed them. We understood Mama's concern, but we had no reason to go out the front gate. It was the back gate that opened to a wonderful world!

There was a tree-lined creek and miles and miles of sagebrush. The alley behind our yard dead-ended at the creek. Mama didn't worry, because there was never any traffic there.

We often waded down the creek from our back fence to the cemetery. It was only two blocks away, but to Joan and me, splashing through that tree-lined corridor seemed like a grand expedition.

"Can we take our lunch?" Joan asked Mama on an early spring day.

"Yes, how about cheese sandwiches? We helped her make them and put them in old cloth sugar bags that we tied to our belt loops.

Barefooted, we spent hours poking along looking for just the right spot to eat our picnic lunch. Actually, our creek was just a diversion ditch that took water from Independence Creek to a ranch on the east side of town. It had been carefully constructed with flat granite boulders lining the bottom and sides. At the time, I didn't consider it to be a ditch, and I still call it the South Fork of Independence Creek.

Joan said, "My feet like to feel these smooth rocks."

"Yes, but it's a little chilly today," I shivered, looking down at my red toes.

The water was cold enough all year for rainbow trout to thrive.

"Let's eat at the grove," I suggested. That was an area with more trees than the single row of locusts that lined each side of the creek.

"No, I think we should eat right now because I'm freezing," and she pointed to a sunny spot between the trees.

We couldn't wade up the creek from our house because it went through culverts under the highway and town streets. It flowed freely only through a few backyards, and we felt lucky that one of those yards was ours. When we were a few years older, we walked through the sagebrush to meet the main part of Independence Creek just above town. From there, it was a hike rather than a wade because it was a natural stream with a swift current and an uncomfortable rocky bottom. You didn't try to wade, even with shoes on.

Sometimes Joan and I sat together in our wagon for a ride downhill for two blocks to the cemetery. The side street, Pavilion Street, paralleled the creek and sloped gently eastward toward the Inyo Mountains.

As we coasted I said, "I wish we could go faster."

Joan disagreed, "We're going fast enough, but let's go back up and do it again."

Our house was near the south end of town. Only three homes, three vacant lots, and Kelley's gas station were between us and the sign on the highway that read: Welcome to INDEPENDENCE—POPULATION 720, ELEVATION 3927 FEET.

To the east, behind our back fence and gravel alley, were miles of sagebrush all the way to the Inyo Mountains. To the west, across the highway and behind a single row of houses, were more miles of sagebrush all the way to the base of the Sierra. The bushes were a mix of sagebrush, rabbitbrush, and shadscale, but Joan and I called it all "sagebrush." We loved the familiar and friendly smell of sage and the golden blooms of rabbitbrush. The shadscale fruits provided food for the stick horses we galloped through the bushes.

"Stop here, Joan!" I called out. "My horse wants to eat." And I pulled off a handful of shadscale fruits for him to eat out of my hand.

As we explored farther from home, Mama told us to stay away from the "Jungle." It was across the creek from the cemetery where some old men lived in shacks. Also, she reminded us that we must never climb on the rock crusher. It was an enticing landmark about a half mile southeast of our house. From a distance, it looked like a ship in the desert. Up close, it was a dilapidated structure several stories high, a tangle of metal and beams held together with giant nuts and bolts. Daddy told us it probably had been used to crush granite boulders when they paved the highway, but it hadn't run for many years. For some reason, we found it fascinating, and it was a frequent destination for our hiking and picnic expeditions.

As we inspected the rusty metal bits lying around, Joan excitedly pointed, "Look at this huge bolt! I'm going to take it home to put in Daddy's can of nuts and bolts."

"But look at this, Joan!" I was more interested in the layer of clay in the depressions where water had been stored during the crushing process. As the muddy water dried, it cracked into thick polygonal clay plates. "Perfect for building a fort," I exclaimed.

One day, Little Carol and I stacked these wondrous building blocks to make a structure. We named it "The Bucket of Blood Bar" for a reason I don't recall. I must have been reading about pirates. Since it so rarely rains in Owens Valley, our "bar" lasted for years.

On the next visit I said, "Joan, let's take some of this clay home."

She was enthusiastic, "Yes, we can make dishes and have an art show."

We ran to get Mama's washtub and lugged home as many clay plates as we could carry. With water added, it became smooth reddish clay, ready to mold into dishes and other artistic creations. But Daddy grew tired of our messy red clay before we got around to our art show, and we all helped to clean it up.

I was never tempted to climb up the rock crusher's shaky ladders, but Joan confessed much later that she and Janice had once scrambled to the top.

"Really? I can't believe you did that! Mama told us not to climb on those ladders. Why did you do it?"

She thought a moment and then said, "Because we wanted to see what was on top."

I was impressed that she had the bravery to climb up there and also the courage to do something that Mama had repeatedly told us not to do. I didn't have the nerve to do either one. To this day, I've kept her secret.

Another favorite place to visit was the dynamite house, located across the highway and beyond the row of houses. By itself out in the sagebrush, it was a small room dug into the ground with thick walls, no windows, a dirt floor, and a heavy door that was permanently swung open. It wasn't much to look at, but the name intrigued us. What could be more exciting than going into a dynamite house! According to Daddy, the City had stored explosives there when they were building the Los Angeles Aqueduct. He sometimes walked out there with us, perhaps he found it captivating too.

We never saw a rattlesnake on our wanderings, but there were plenty of lizards and an occasional horned toad. Startled jackrabbits skittered ahead of us through the bushes.

Part Two

From our bunk beds at night we could often hear the coyotes calling.

I said, "Joan, let's go look for them tomorrow."

She sleepily agreed, "But where do you think they are?"

"Well, if I were a coyote I'd live at the dump. Let's go see."

There was always something to do down-the-creek or out-in-the-sagebrush.

The World of Granite

Carol

Mama and Daddy were telling us about their vacation plans. Joan said, "I wish we could go with you to the mountains. It would be fun to ride a horse over a mountain."

"I know you would like to go with us, but Aunt Hazel wants you to visit her and Uncle Clarence in LeeVining that week. I think you will have a good time there."

"What will we do at their house?" I asked.

"I think they will take you on hikes and picnics, and you can take lots of books to read." Mama knew we would like that part of our visit because Joan and I had just finished first and second grade.

After five years of admiring the Sierra Nevada from our front windows, Mama and Daddy decided it was time to see what was beyond the high peaks and jagged crest. Daddy learned about some of the mountain passes from the packers and old timers in town, and a friend who worked at the fish hatchery told him stories about planting trout fingerlings in the timberline lakes.

They rented two horses and a mule from Allie Robinson for a week. He was the local packer who lived across the highway. Allie met them at the corral near the Symmes Creek trailhead with the horses and the mule. He showed them how to saddle the animals, load the pack boxes with their food and camping equipment, and hang the boxes from the packsaddle forks. He emphasized the importance of balancing the load so it wouldn't slide off.

He concluded with, "Hobble the horses at night and they won't wander far. The mule will stay with them. And feed them all some oats in the morning."

He didn't seem concerned that they'd never been in the Sierra before or that Daddy didn't know anything about horses and mules.

After their trip, I was enthralled with their tales of the horses, Frankie and Briby, and the mule, Sadie. They described the rocky trail over Shepherd Pass, the lakes and meadows, and the views from their camp in a grove of foxtail pine at 11,000 feet in the Tyndall Creek basin.

Much later, I realized what an undertaking that trip had been for them. Mama had ridden horses as a child on their family farm in Oklahoma, but Daddy had grown up in Chicago and Los Angeles and was a city boy.

Also, I didn't understand then how profound their introduction to the high Sierra wilderness had been for them. They were touched by the beauty and solitude of that wild world of granite. Few people went into the mountains then—during the week they had seen just two other parties. Daddy said with a smile, "The fishing could not have been better! I caught golden trout in Labrador Lake and Lake South America." While he fished, Mama found interesting plants and wrote notes about those she hoped to identify. That's where she first met the alpine shooting star, a common but exquisite flower of the high meadows.

The next summer, they took one horse and two mules and stayed for two weeks. Their enthusiasm made me wish Joan and I could go with them, but we had been invited to visit our aunts in southern California. Joan stayed with Aunt Hazel and Uncle Clarence who had recently moved to Inglewood. I spent the two weeks in San Fernando with Aunt Lois, Mama's other sister, and her family.

This time our parents' tales were even more exciting. Daddy told us, "It was an unusually heavy winter in the Sierra, and snow was still deep on the passes. We made a big loop over Kearsarge Pass and Glen Pass to Rae Lakes, then down Woods Creek to the South Fork of the Kings River and out over Sawmill Pass."

I can still recall their route from studying the topo map. Hearing their stories and looking at their photographs made their trip come alive. It was on the north side of Glen Pass that one of the mules slipped on the ice just below the summit. Daddy told us the story.

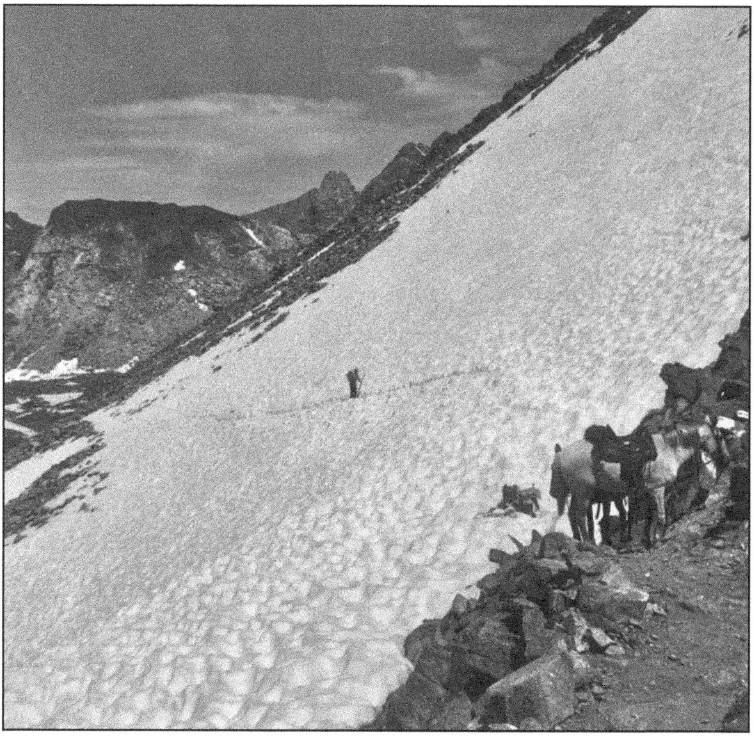

Trouble on Glen Pass, 1941.

"We watched Pinky slide down the steep snowfield. He bounced over some rocks and kept on going. We rushed down to him where he had landed among the boulders. He got up slowly, but seemed all right. I was surprised that he didn't have any broken legs."

Mama added, "It was such a relief that we didn't complain about spending many hours on that snowy slope collecting all of the things that had flown out of Pinky's load."

"What would you have done if Pinky had broken a leg?" I asked Daddy.

"I don't know what we could have done for him. I think we should talk to Allie about that."

Sometimes Mama was so taken with the beauty of a favorite camp that she described it in detail—the view down to the lake, the clump of trees where they cooked and slept, a kitchen rock that made a perfect table, and sunset on the nearby peaks. The glow on her face and the emotion in her voice made it easy to tell how much she loved those times.

Soon they were planning their trip for next summer. They were going again with one horse and two mules for two weeks. And, again, Joan and I were not invited. This time we would be staying with our neighbors across the highway. Now that we were eight and nine years old, we needed to stay in town to water the lawn and feed the rabbits. We were raising rabbits for food, and caring for them was one of our regular chores.

This time, Mama and Daddy went over Sawmill Pass and camped at beautiful Woods Lake. Then over Pinchot Pass, down to the South Fork of the Kings River, and over Cartridge Pass to Marion Lake before returning over Sawmill Pass. That route was used less than those on their previous trips, and they saw even fewer people.

Daddy said, "Cartridge Pass was close to impassable because that trail gets little use and no maintenance. But we were able to coax the animals across the bad spots. At least the snow wasn't as deep as last year."

Often on their trips they made friends with the people they met and exchanged letters for years. This summer they met a mountain climber named Art Reyman. He was camped at the old trapper's cabin on the Kings River. Around their campfire, he told them tales of his Sierra climbs, many of them first ascents.

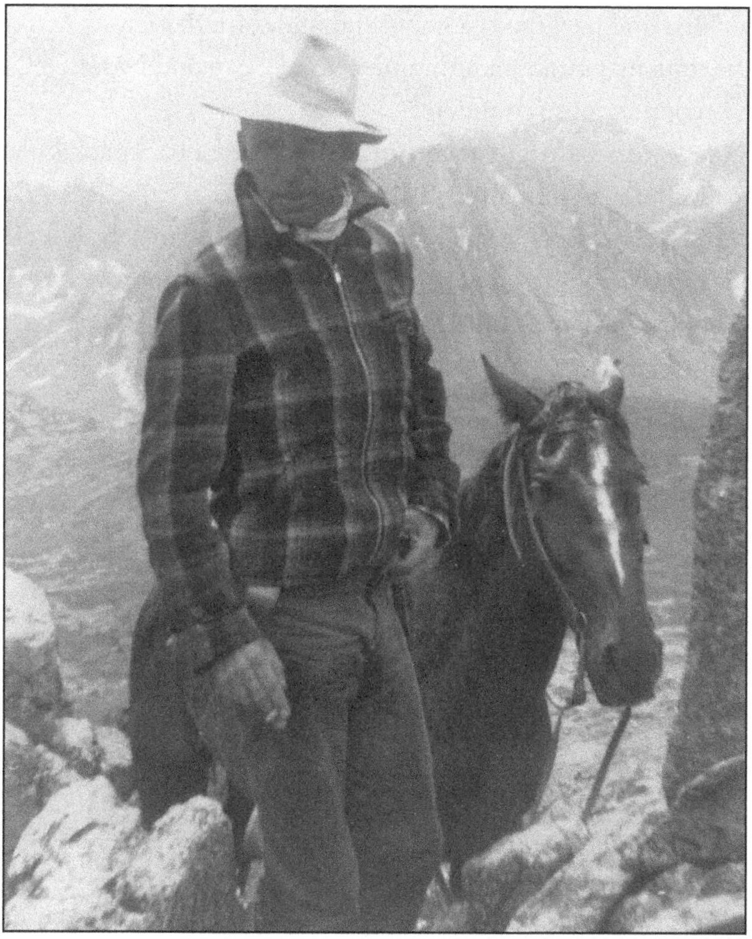

Daddy on Pinchot Pass, 1942.

As they parted, Art said, "If you have any extra coffee, I could use a little. I won't be going out for another week or two."

When we heard stories of this trip, we were again sad that we hadn't been a part of their adventure. But for our attention to the lawn and rabbits we received a yellow tent, a gift that we cherished for years. We would spend many nights with our friends in that tent set up on the lawn or out by the creek.

With each trip, Mama and Daddy were learning more. The job of catching and packing the horse and mules was easier, as was reading the topo maps and planning their food. Joan and I could tell they were becoming more confident.

A few weeks after their return, a man with a backpack knocked at our back door. Mama laughed when he said, "I came by to return the coffee I borrowed on the Kings River." Art became a close family friend. He visited often and joined us on trips for many years.

Looking back over their long marriage, my guess is that if Mama and Daddy had been asked about the highlights of their life together, near the top of the list would have been the early trips exploring the Sierra. It was the honeymoon they had never had.

Small Town Teachers

Carol

For a small town, the Independence grade school had many good teachers, but my first, second, and third grade teachers were special—Mrs. Burns, Mrs. Kearney, Mr. Rogers, and Mrs. Phillips.

Mrs. Burns was my first grade teacher. She had eight first graders and ten second graders in her classroom. I felt a bit intimidated by it all, and was glad that both Joan and Tommy Poole were there. The Pooles were the first family we met when we moved to Independence. I would see a lot of Tommy over the years because he was in my grade, and also our parents were best friends. Our families had dinners, picnics, and hikes together and Tommy sometimes seemed like a brother. We were the only members of that first grade class at our high school graduation.

Mrs. Burns taught us about farmers and cows and silos. She also taught us to read.

When the school year ended, Tommy and I were in the middle of a new reader, and Mrs. Burns invited us to have reading at her house every day until we finished the book. We read while her new baby named Susie slept. Afterwards she served us cherries and cookies.

On the last day she asked, "Would you two like to stay to watch me bathe the baby?

"Oh Yes!" I said because I'd never seen such a tiny baby.

Tommy was less enthusiastic, but polite as we watched Mrs. Burns bathe little Susie in the kitchen sink.

* * * * *

On the first day of second grade, Miss Reader said, "We have three Carols in our classroom and I think it will be confusing when I call on one Carol and a different Carol answers." So that day

"Carol Arlene" became "Arlene." Little Carol remained "Carol," and I became "Carol Lynne."

During that year, Miss Reader's name also changed. She became Mrs. Kearney, but her husband didn't live in Independence.

Mrs. Kearney talked to us often about behavior and the importance of being respectful and courteous. We wrote and illustrated stories about Sweet and Pete the Courtesy Twins. I liked the way she spoke to a girl in our class who struggled with reading. Mrs. Kearney was always patient and helpful.

On the Saturday before Christmas, I wrapped a gift for Mrs. Kearney. Joan and I had grown gourds during the summer and had painted them to give as presents to our aunts and teachers.

"Mrs. Kearney likes bright colors so I'm going to give her this red and yellow one."

Mama said, "I'm sure she'll like it."

Then she reminded me again, "You must not go to her house too early in the morning."

I waited as long as I could before running up the street. She lived just one block away. I knocked on the door many times before Mrs. Kearney answered. She appeared to have just gotten out of bed. It was Christmas vacation and her new husband was visiting. They sat with me on the couch in their bathrobes while she unwrapped her gift, and they both admired her lovely gourd stocking darner.

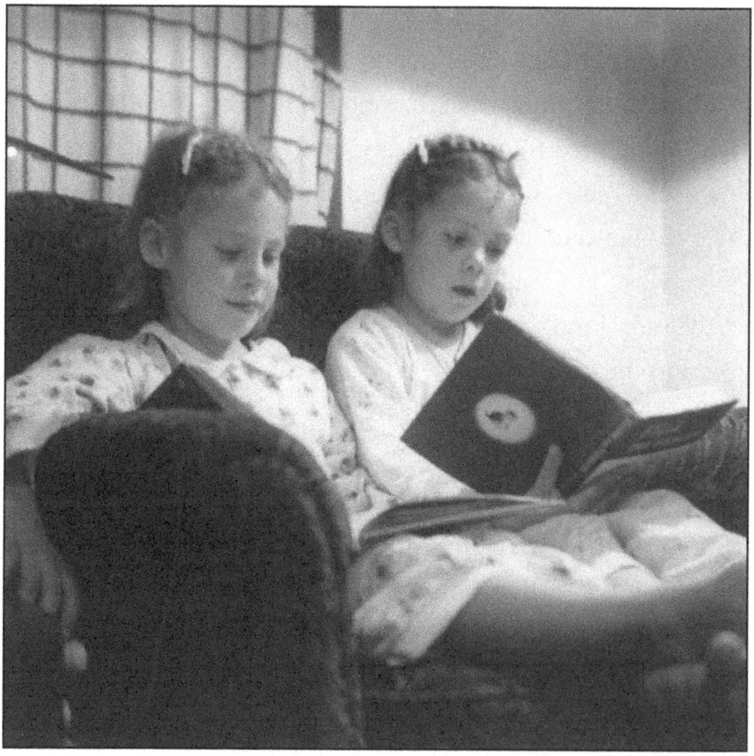

Bedtime reading, 1940.

Mrs. Kearney left Independence at the end that school year to join her husband in San Francisco. I wrote to her for years and she sent me pictures of her children.

* * * * *

Mr. Rogers was the high school band teacher, and he also came to each elementary classroom for an hour every day. He came to our room right after lunch.

"Good afternoon, boys and girls," he would say with a smile. He was young and handsome and notably short. Mr. Rogers seemed to enjoy our music hour as much as we did. Our room had a piano. He could play many songs and liked to teach us new ones.

"What kind of music shall we have today?" Hands shot up and Mr. Rogers pointed to one, "Teddy, what shall we sing first?"

As usual Teddy said, "Home on the Range!"

We all had our favorites. Stella's was, "You are my Sunshine," and mine was, "A Candy Lion." I still remember the words:

"A Candy Lion's very good,
Because he cannot bite,
Nor wander roaring for his food,
Nor eat up folks at night."

Some days, Mr. Rogers played slow and soft "relaxing music" on the phonograph. It was built into a tall brown cabinet. With its short brown legs, it was taller than we were. We watched as he flipped the lid open and put a record on the turntable. Then he stuck a handle into a hole in the side of the box and cranked. Next, he put the needle on the record, and the music played.

Mr. Rogers said, "Now we will all relax."

When our heads and outstretched arms were on our desk and our eyes were closed, Mr. Rogers moved quietly around the room, lifting one of our arms to see if we were relaxed. Usually my arm was not relaxed because I was thinking about what came next!

When we were relaxed enough, Mr. Rogers gave us each a metal-tipped stick to tap on our desks in time with the music.

When we could follow the rhythm to his satisfaction, he pointed to a cardboard box on Mrs. Kearney's desk, "Now you can each choose an instrument."

Billy usually chose the loudest—the drums. Tommy chose the cymbals. I preferred the triangles. Then we all tried to play in time with lively phonograph music. Often it was a polka, the fast music that makes you want to dance.

Many things changed after our country entered World War II, even in Owens Valley. Some of our teachers left to join the military right away, and some waited to be drafted. We were surprised when Mr. Rogers joined the army. He didn't look tall enough to be a soldier.

When he left our school he said, "I won't be shooting a gun because the army needs bandleaders. Music is important during a war because it makes people feel good." We understood. Music hour with Mr. Rogers had been a happy time for us. We hoped he would be safe.

When the war was over, Mr. Rogers came back to our school. My class was in the seventh grade, and Mr. Rogers was the high school band teacher again. Billy was playing the drums, Mr. Rogers was giving Tommy clarinet lessons, and I was playing the flute. We were happy that he had returned safely from the war.

* * * * *

My third grade year was unusual because it was taught at the Methodist Church social hall rather than at the elementary school. That was because the number of third grade students unexpectedly increased. The school could hire another teacher, but it couldn't build another classroom. Mrs. Phillips taught thirteen third graders in the social hall.

We all loved Mrs. Phillips. Like Mrs. Kearney, she taught us to be kind and considerate. We had music every day because Mrs. Phillips could play the piano. Now that we could read well, we each had a music book, and I was delighted to find "A Candy Lion" in it.

For recess, we had no swings or slides, but we played dodge ball and Red Rover on the church lawn and ran races in the alley.

Mrs. Phillips had us bring a snack every day to eat after morning recess. Then she had us lie on our rugs to rest and relax. She said, "You might think you are too old for this, but it's good for everyone to have a rest." No one complained.

We all enjoyed the one-room school experience with Mrs. Phillips.

Shirley Temple

Joan

Shirley Temple was the child movie star of the 1930s and it seemed as though every mother was grooming her daughter to follow in Shirley's footsteps. Our cousin Sydney Ann was a natural. She even lived in Hollywood. She took piano lessons and Aunt Jean said she had "talent." Her limber body made her good at acrobatics. And she was cute, smart, and good-natured—a great cousin even if she was a year younger than Carol. Aunt Jean was Daddy's sister and when her family came to visit, Carol and I watched Sydney Ann do back-flips and handstands on our lawn. She made it look so easy. During our visits to North Hollywood, we would listen to Sydney Ann's latest piano pieces while Aunt Jean chattered on and on to Mama about her daughter's latest achievements and what her teacher said, etc. etc. Mama tried to act interested even though she had heard it all before.

As a young woman, Aunt Jean had a brief career as an adagio dancer. Mama explained it as slow motion and graceful acrobatics. In one of her dresser drawers, Mama had a framed photo of Jean standing in a gauzy outfit holding one leg straight up with one arm loosely circling it. As I admired the scene, I asked Mama, "Why don't you put this picture on the wall?" She murmured something about a lack of wall space, but I knew that if it had been a photo of a mountain or a flower she would have found a place to hang it. It would be many years before I understood the cause of Mama's disinterest in Jean's dancing. She was aware of Daddy's childhood resentment of the attention Jean had received as a child dancer. Lessons and tours had caused financial stress in the family, and while he never talked about it, Mama understood Daddy's feeling of abandonment when his mother and sister were so often away.

Shirley Temple could tap dance, and it had become one of the latest rages. Barbara Yandell, Carol's classmate, had tap shoes and took lessons from our teacher, Mrs. Burns. We were invited to join the class. Carol was not interested, but I went to several sessions and loved the sound of Barbara's tap shoes on the wooden floor. Mama was reluctant to buy those expensive shoes, and we both realized that I would need a bigger size each year. Still, I've always admired those dancers who move around the stage so effortlessly tapping those wonderful rhythms.

Beyond the Town

Carol

Joan got a bicycle for Christmas when she was six years old. I was disappointed I didn't get one too, but she was expected to share and she did. With that little blue bike, our world expanded. It wasn't long until we were taking turns visiting nearby friends and riding to the post office to get the mail for Mama. She didn't worry about us because we rode down the alley to avoid traffic.

Little Carol, who also shared a bike with her older sister, was always ready to go for a ride. The town dump was a frequent destination, about a mile past the rock crusher on a dirt road. We ate our sandwiches among the mounds of tin cans, old tires, and lawn clippings. Then we searched for empty pop bottles. They were easy to find, mostly Coke and Pepsi cola bottles. When our handlebar baskets were full, we pedaled back to town and went straight to the drugstore.

Mr. Baker smiled and asked, "How are things at the dump today?" He knew where we got our bottles.

He gave us two cents for each bottle, and we climbed onto the tall swivel stools at the soda fountain to count our money.

Little Carol said, "We have forty-eight cents!"

"Let's see, you want a cherry phosphate," Mr. Baker said to her.

He turned to me, "And you want a root beer float?"

"You have a good memory!" I said.

If we had money left, we bought licorice sticks.

Occasionally, we went up the Seven Pines road a ways, never far because it was steep and we had to get off and push our bikes. The trip down was so exhilarating that one day we talked Mama into driving us all the way to Seven Pines with our bikes. She helped us unload them and went home to finish the ironing.

As soon as we started down, Little Carol and I realized the road was way too steep for our coaster brakes.

We picked up speed and Little Carol yelled, "Oh help, I can't slow down!"

"Neither can I!" I shouted.

Then my bike chain came off. I steered out into the gravel and sagebrush in an attempt to slow down. Luckily I crashed into a tall sage rather than a granite boulder. Little Carol helped me get the chain back on the sprocket.

She said, "My chain came off once and my dad showed me how to put it back on. It's not too hard."

None of us had realized how fast we would coast down the steep asphalt road. "*What had Mama been thinking*?" I wondered as we walked our bikes down the steep sections. We never made that trip again.

Joan was allowed to take longer rides with her friends, even along the highway out to the Fort.

"Because she is older," Mama said.

"Can I ride out to the Fort when I turn eight?" I asked.

She said, "Maybe," and then continued on about the importance of good judgment.

Sometimes Little Carol and I left our bicycles home and walked through the sagebrush to Piggy Rock, north of the creek and just above town. It was one of the many granite boulders sprinkled throughout the desert, and it seemed gigantic at the time. We had discovered it one day when we were out wandering in the sagebrush and had named it Piggy Rock because it looked like a pig's head. We often sat under its overhanging north side to eat lunch in the shade.

On a cold spring visit I said, "I think we should make a fire and cook our lunch the next time we come."

Little Carol nodded, "Some hot soup would be good."

The following Saturday, we took matches and some rice to cook in my blue metal lunchbox. Little Carol ran down to the creek to get water while I started a fire with sagebrush twigs. When the water boiled, we threw in the rice and stirred it with a stick.

Soon there was lots of smoke, and I yelped, "Oh no! The bottom of my lunchbox is getting black!"

This was something I hadn't considered. We put out the fire and went down to the creek to scrub off the soot. We weren't entirely successful so as soon as I got home, I put the lunchbox away in its usual place in the cupboard on the back porch. I didn't want to explain its black bottom to Mama. Although she never asked, she probably knew about our effort to cook lunch and figured we had learned something. On our next visit, we took peanut butter sandwiches.

Many times we passed Piggy Rock and hiked on up the creek. There were grassy spots among the willows and birch trees and quiet pools for wading. We never went farther than the Baxter Water Company reservoir, about a mile from town. Following Mama's stern instructions, we admired the deep water from outside the fence.

Joan and I shared her little blue bike for many years. It wasn't until well after we had outgrown it that we got a standard-size bicycle. Our Grandma DeDecker gave us hers when she was no longer able to ride. It was old, but Daddy replaced a few parts and cleaned and polished until it seemed brand new to us. Again, we shared.

Long Ago

Joan

Carol and I were playing in the backyard near the water faucet where we were making a river for our wood-bark boats. As we lengthened the channel, a piece of obsidian appeared in the gravel. It was a spearhead almost three inches long. We often found arrowhead pieces out in the sagebrush, especially after a rain when water rivulets had washed away a covering of sand, but the unbroken spearhead was a rare find.

Mama admired it and commented, "Countless artifacts must lie on the valley floor and up the canyons. The Paiute people lived here for a long, long time."

She told us that settlers came to the valley in more recent times looking for farm and cattle land. Prospectors in search of silver and gold had roamed the canyons of the mountain ranges east and west of Owens Valley, and even farther east to Death Valley and the Nevada ranges.

On family outings in the Inyos, we occasionally found a tiny cabin tucked away above a dry wash or partially dug into an embankment. We speculated about who had lived there, and when. Sometimes there were hints—rusty tin cans, pieces of crockery, or remains of mining equipment. We looked in the cabins for dates in the old newspapers stacked under a cot frame or nailed on the walls for insulation. We peered into mine shafts, examined ore piles and tailings, and wondered what the prospectors had hoped to find.

One day, when Grandpa Foster was visiting, we drove a few miles east of town to look for the deserted mining town site of Bend City. We found it between the Owens River and the base of the Inyos. Almost nothing was left of this once-thriving community except a few piles of crumbling adobe. It was hard to believe that one hundred years ago, Bend City had been considered for the Inyo County seat. While wandering about the old foundations, Mama found a gold coin and a piece of a slate pencil.

"I just can't believe that kids actually went to school out here," I marveled.

Through those glimpses of the past, we became aware that our time spent in this desert country was a tiny part of a much older story.

Our Hike to Symmes Creek

Carol

Mama loved to explore. I suspect that the mountains were often on her mind. Even though for the first few years in Owens Valley she was content to get to know the streams coming out of the canyons and to go for walks through the sagebrush, she looked up at the mountains many times a day.

One morning, when I was seven years old, Mama packed a lunch and we set off with Joan, Janice, and Little Carol for a long walk through the sagebrush towards the base of Mt. Williamson. She said we would eat lunch when we reached Symmes Creek.

The streams coming down from the Sierra had birch and willows along their banks and, from a distance, looked like a winding green line. I was doubtful about finding Symmes Creek out there in the sagebrush because I could see that the green line didn't extend much beyond the base of the mountains.

"Mama, are you sure there is a creek out here?" I asked more than once.

For what seemed like hours we crunched across the desert gravel and around each bush with me asking, "Are we almost there?" The other girls were too polite to complain.

Mama distracted us by telling us the names of the Sierra peaks that overlooked the town, from Mt. Williamson just in front of us to Mt. Baxter, eight peaks to the north. We practiced naming them—"Williamson, Keith, Bradley, University, Keasarge. Mary Austin, Black, and Baxter,"—"Williamson, Keith, Bradley, University, Keasarge. Mary Austin, Black, and Baxter," until we were out of breathe.

"I didn't know that mountains had names," Janice said.

Finally, there it was. Symmes Creek flowed clear and inviting with willows and wild roses along its banks. We lay on our stomachs in the grass and dipped our tin cups for a long drink while Mama dug in her pack for our lunch. With our feet dangling in the cold water, we munched on tuna sandwiches and apples.

Mama said, "The creek runs only a short way farther before it sinks into the gravel."

"But how did you know it was here?" I asked.

"Mr. McDougall told me. He often goes for walks through the sagebrush."

Mama and I had met him one day while walking home from the post office. She had fallen into step with him, and they started talking. Mr. McDougall was old and had a long white beard. He looked like a stranger to me, and I desperately wanted Mama to stop talking to him and hurry home. They were talking about Woods Lake, one of Daddy's favorite Sierra lakes.

Mr. McDougall spent weeks camping there every summer, causing the local folks to call him "The Mayor of Woods Lake." He lived across the highway in a tiny cabin behind Allie's corrals and became our good friend. Mama often invited him for Thanksgiving dinner, and Daddy once put a new roof on his little home. He enjoyed teaching Joan and me to play new versions of Solitaire. When he got too old to go to the mountains, he gave us his special Woods Lake coffee pot, which we cherished and used for many years.

As we tromped home from Symmes Creek, Mama told us the names of the wildflowers—yellow dandelions, apricot mallow, and blue gilias grew among the shrubs.

"What's that tiny white one?" Joan asked.

On her hands and knees with her hand lens, Mama showed us the tiny white buckwheat flowers. She was learning about the native plants from Mark Kerr, a strange man who lived in a strange house he had built of cobblestones.

As we talked about Mark Kerr, Janice said, "Did you know that he keeps rattlesnakes in his yard and collects baby snakes from their nests on Rattlesnake Hill? My dad says that hill is swarming with rattlesnakes."

Joan shuddered and asked Mama, "How many snakes are in a nest?"

"Too many!" Mama said, and she also shuddered.

Mark Kerr worked in the Independence museum and knew more about the native plants and animals than anyone else around. He enthusiastically helped Mama locate books for identifying plants. He was also interested in the history of the local Paiute and Shoshoni people. Mama considered him a valuable source of information on many subjects, but she never went to check out the snakes at Rattlesnake Hill.

I didn't complain once on the way home. I was content to know for sure that Symmes Creek was out there in the sagebrush. Visiting it was worth the long hike. When we got home, Daddy looked at his topo map and told us we had walked five miles.

That night, while Mama and I were doing the dishes, we talked about the hike and all that we had seen.

She said, as she often did, "It makes me feel so good to be outside all day."

As always, I would wonder why. It wasn't until years later that I understood the depth of her appreciation for and love of the natural world.

Our Relatives

Joan

Mama's two sisters and their families came to visit the summer that Carol and I were seven and eight—Aunt Hazel and Uncle Clarence, and Aunt Lois and Uncle Sherman with three-year-old Sharon and baby Doug. We spread picnic blankets on the grass under the big locust tree by the fishpond, and Mama and my aunts brought out plates of sandwiches and pitchers of lemonade and ice tea.

The men sat together on one of the blankets where they told jokes and talked about fishing. "Either of you want to go up Oak Creek this afternoon?" Daddy asked.

The conversation on the other blanket interested me more. Mama and her sisters were talking about what was going on with relatives and friends in North Hollywood. While we waited for the cookies to appear, I continued to listen and Carol climbed out on the long branch of the locust tree.

That night, I awoke to the sound of sobs coming from the living room where some of our visitors were sleeping. I rolled off my summer cot on the front porch and went in to listen. It was dark, but I could hear Aunt Lois crying and talking about Grandma and Uncle Harold and Uncle Bud.

"Mom just can't say anything nice about Sherman," Aunt Lois said.

Hazel added, "I wish Harold would find another place to live now that he's out of high school."

Mama gave me a hug and sent me back to bed. I was curious about the details and also upset and confused. How could this be happening after our happy time on the lawn? I lay there thinking about Grandma and why Mama and my aunts were upset with her. I had not seen Grandma Foster for a long time and knew that the mention of her name was a painful topic for Mama.

After our aunts and uncles returned home, Mama had a talk with Carol and me. She told us that Grandma Foster had always tried to control her children and had not liked Daddy or the other young men and women her children brought home. None seemed good enough to her. She told us how difficult it had been to end her visits with her mother, but she did it because she worried about how Grandma's behavior would affect us. She didn't want to go into more detail and the subject was so distressing to her that we didn't ask many questions. When we were older, she told us more about her family.

Her father, Charles Foster, was born in Illinois and had a successful farm in the Oklahoma panhandle. Her mother, Phoebe Thompson, was born in Kansas, the daughter of the first woman doctor in that state. Mama was the oldest of five children. She loved the farm and for several years rode a horse to a rural school. She was eight years old when her mother left her husband and took the children to California on the train. Mama told us how sad she had felt waving goodbye to her beloved Papa as the train pulled away.

Eventually, her father sold the farm and followed his wife. The family settled in the San Fernando Valley, near Los Angeles. Her parents separated when she was in high school and later divorced. Her brothers were often truant from school and tended to get into trouble. As the oldest child, Mama did her best to keep them on a steady path and encouraged them to complete high school. She excelled

The Frank DeDecker family, 1941.
(See Appendix for names)

as a student, and her teachers encouraged her to attend college. But after one semester, she dropped out for financial reasons and took a job as a nanny.

Daddy's father, Frank DeDecker, had French immigrant parents. His mother, Ada Gooch, was born in England and still had family there. She had sailed to New York by herself at age sixteen. Frank and Ada met and married in Chicago. After Daddy was born, they came to stay with relatives in North Hollywood. Grandpa was a house painter, always eager for work, and this took the family back to Chicago for a time, then back again to North Hollywood. Even with tight finances,

Grandma DeDecker managed to sail home to England, first in 1909 to show off her two-year-old son and again in 1937 for the coronation of King George VI.

Daddy's sister, Jean, was five years younger. She and Uncle Clint had two children, Sydney Ann and Clinton. The lives of Daddy's family members seemed calm and uncomplicated in contrast to those of Mama's relatives.

When Daddy graduated from high school, he was on his own and like his father, he hustled for work wherever he could find it. When he met Mama, he had a job at the Mulholland Ranch in San Fernando Valley. Mama was working at Olive View Sanatorium, a

Picnic in the Alabama Hills with our cousins, 1944.
(See Appendix for names)

Daddy and Uncle Clarence on our back steps, 1940.

tuberculosis hospital. Both had many friends, and they all had good times together.

Mama's albums show scenes of picnics in the nearby mountains and parties at the beach. Daddy had a new Model A and was generous about transporting her friends. But a man named George also wanted to marry Mama. The ins and outs of courtship days with these two very different men were recorded in her diary. First it was George she yearned for, then Paul. The romantic saga and her busy social life continued unabated until she chose our father.

They married a month before the stock market crash in 1929, and lived for six years in the North Hollywood area. Daddy struggled, but always managed to find work. During that time they had two babies and moved six times. While Mama and Daddy remained close to their families and we visited often, they were happy to be living a good distance away.

Household Expectations

Carol

In our home, there was little room for ambiguity. The rules were clear and consistent. We were expected to respond the first time we were asked to do something, not the second or third time. Joan and I did a fairly good job of complying without complaint, so the rules must have seemed fair. Both parents were strict and always seemed to be in agreement, so there was no point in running to one to complain about the other. We were generally good kids and respected our parents because Mama always gave us the reasons for her and Daddy's decisions.

For example, when I was seven years old I learned to be home on time for supper. There was a new girl in my second grade class named Shirley Anderson who had recently moved down the street. She had an irresistible swing that hung on long ropes from a cottonwood tree in her front yard. One afternoon while we were swinging, I knew it was getting late and that I should be getting home for supper. Shirley had not yet been called in, so we kept on swinging.

Finally, realizing it was very late, I headed for home and guiltily entered our yard through the back gate. I was afraid to peek in the window, but I felt that supper was in progress. I sat in our swing for some time trying to think of a reason for being late. I knew there was no excuse, so I sauntered in, trying to look surprised to find them eating. There was no scolding. But I knew they were annoyed because no one asked me if I'd had a good time playing with Shirley. How I envied Joan, who was angelically cutting up her pork chop without saying one word.

Later that evening, Mama reminded me, "Carol, it is rude to be late for meals." When she added, "You know better than that," I was glad that I hadn't thought of a ridiculous excuse.

I said, "I won't be late again, but it's a very nice swing."

To help prevent further problems, Mama hung a cowbell on the back porch. It had a pleasant tone and when I heard it clanging from way down the creek, I ran right home.

Joan and I also knew that our household had little tolerance for picky eaters. Mama always suggested we try everything she served, but she never insisted. We heard stories about children who had to sit at the dinner table until they ate every bite, even if it took hours. That didn't happen at our house. We were never asked what we wanted for a meal or if we liked this or that, because we were expected to like everything. We were a bit embarrassed to be known as "the kids who will eat everything," and to be held up by our friends' mothers as examples of "good eaters." But, the fact was, we truly did like just about everything Mama cooked. Joan was not fond of asparagus and I didn't much like cooked turnips, but we didn't have to eat them.

When our cousin, Sydney Ann, came to visit it was painful to watch the food battles. Mama couldn't understand why Sydney Ann wouldn't eat green vegetables or tomato soup, and neither could we. But Sydney Ann wouldn't taste either of them.

She said, "I don't like the way tomato soup looks, and I don't like the way it tastes. My mother doesn't ever make tomato soup."

Mama said, "If you have never tried it, how do you know you don't like it?"

Sydney insisted, "Tomato soup is something I don't eat!"

It was a standoff. Our cousin was as stubborn as her Aunt Mary.

Joan looked at me and whispered, "I wish she would at least try it."

In our home, there was little tolerance for disorder. There were probably several reasons for this. Daddy had grown up in a disorganized household. From my early observations, he and Grandpa liked consistency and tidiness while Grandma and Aunt Jean were more relaxed about housework.

We drove to North Hollywood several times a year to visit. Aunt Jean and her family lived next door to our DeDecker grandparents. After each visit, the conversation in the front seat on the way home began with the opinion that Aunt Jean's kitchen stove was greasy, the bathroom needed a good scrub, and our cousins should be taught to make their beds and keep their toys picked up.

I had mixed feelings. I loved Aunt Jean's spark. On each visit, we would find the entire family engaged in a new passion. Once it was badminton, and they had a court in the backyard. Grandma was having as much fun playing as the rest. Another time, it was cracking bullwhips. When canasta was the rage, it was their game. They were the first people we knew to get a television set.

I especially liked the time we arrived to find a swimming pool in their backyard. It was larger than any pool in Owens Valley, with swim lanes painted on the bottom, a diving board and dressing rooms along one side. Uncle Clint was a builder, and such projects were easy for him. Though I was always happy to get back to our orderly home, I also was a bit envious of their carefree and spontaneous lifestyle.

Another reason for order in our house was because there simply was not room for things to be lying around. We had a place for everything, as long as things were kept in their place. Actually, the only reason we could live in a small, one-closet house was because we didn't have a lot of things. During the Depression, families bought only what they could pay for in cash, and that wasn't much. Of course,

Carol washing dishes, 1941.

living in Owens Valley limited what was available, yet I don't recall that Joan and I ever felt deprived of clothes or toys.

There is no doubt that Daddy's excessive need for neatness and order caused tree pruning and removal conflicts with Joan. He didn't like trees that grew too fast, had messy fruit, or had too many leaves to rake. He was always concerned when tree roots disturbed his beautiful lawn. First, he took out a few trees in the front yard and then a few in the backyard. Next, he cut off the entire top of our shady grape arbor, leaving it at shoulder height. Then one day, Mama told us he planned to cut down the weeping willow, our favorite tree, whose branches hung over the fishpond.

"No!" Joan protested. "He can't cut down the willow tree!"

Mama told us the reasons why he wanted to remove it. "It drops leaves in the fishpond, and the roots are getting into the lawn."

When she said, "It's getting tall and he is afraid it will fall in the wind and hit the roof," Joan stormed out the front door, stood back a distance to assess the height of the tree and declared, "It's not too tall now and won't be for a long time! He just wants to cut down all of our trees."

Joan talked and talked to Daddy, but it did no good. In the spring, down it came. She almost cried when she saw the branches lying on the lawn.

We knew Daddy would like to remove even more trees, but we also knew he would check with Mama first, and that she would put her foot down if necessary. We three liked lush and shady gardens. Daddy liked them neat and trim.

Hiking with Silver

Joan

Daddy led the way up the trail and carried a canteen on a strap across his shoulder. Carol and I followed, and Mama came behind us leading Silver, an old and friendly white mule. That afternoon, we had driven about ten miles north of town to Division Creek and turned up the dirt road leading to the Sawmill Pass trailhead. Silver was in the corral waiting for us—Allie had brought him up earlier in the day. Carol and I, ages seven and almost nine, were overjoyed to be taking our first overnight trip into the mountains. We were on our way to Sawmill Lake for the long Fourth of July weekend.

The lower part of Sawmill Canyon is narrow with sheer cliffs, so the trail climbed up a sandy ridge on the north side of the canyon before dropping down to the creek. It zigzagged through sagebrush, yellow buckwheat, and red paintbrush. We climbed up and up, loose gravel giving way under each step. Sometimes it was no more than twenty steps before we switched directions, and sometimes the trail went on forever before making a turn. We stopped often for drinks from Daddy's canteen and to look down on the valley below.

"See that hill down there?" I asked. "Why is it so red?" Daddy told us it was a cinder cone formed by a small volcanic eruption. He told us about volcanoes and pointed out the black lava flows below us.

As we climbed, we passed mountain mahogany trees, some of them tall enough to provide us with welcome shade. Looking down on the trail below, we could see how far we had come. The long switchbacks made it seem as though we were barely progressing up the hill, but the short ones showed how quickly we were gaining altitude.

I was getting tired of the uphill when Mama said, "Take your time. It's better to keep going slowly than to hurry and need long rests." She gave us some Lifesavers for encouragement and said, "We've come about two miles and have one more to go," and she pointed to a rocky outcrop on the hillside above us. "Once we get up there, it will be downhill to Sawmill Creek and we'll eat supper."

The shadows had lengthened by the time we reached the top of the ridge and dropped down to the creek into a garden of willows and ferns. We were tired and ready for our sandwiches and fried rabbit and long drinks from the stream.

It was dusk when we finished supper so Daddy got out his flashlight, and we followed the trail along the creek past manzanita bushes and Jeffrey pines. To Carol and me, the darkness felt spooky, but our parents were in such high spirits we soon forgot our anxiety.

I was beginning to wonder if I could walk any farther when Daddy said, "It's leveling out. I think we're getting close." Finally we passed one last clump of manzanita and there was the meadow. It seemed to be waiting for us, silent and ghostlike in the cool darkness. Next to the trail, a quiet stream flowed between grassy banks. Soon we reached the far end of the meadow where a huge boulder stood, twice our height and just as wide, and right next to it was a flat area that had been leveled and softened with dry pine needles. "This is Camp Rock," Daddy said. He unloaded Silver, spread out our sleeping bags on the canvas tarp, and we were soon fast asleep.

The next morning, Carol and I explored a grove of aspen trees with smooth white bark and round leaves that twinkled in the breeze.

People had carved initials, names, and dates in the trunks. We played in the tall grass along the meandering stream, and watched the little trout dart to safety under the mossy banks. In all of our later Sierra travels, I've never seen a prettier scene than Sawmill Meadow on that summer morning.

At camp, Mama was cooking bacon and eggs. She opened a can of figs. We'd never had them at home, but figs were to become a family tradition at Camp Rock in Sawmill Meadow. While Mama arranged our pots and aluminum dishes and food in the pack boxes, Daddy saddled Silver.

Sawmill Lake was two steep miles up switchbacks through the Labrador tea bushes and prickly chinquapin. Red fir and foxtail pine shaded the hillsides. Mama told us the names of these new mountain plants along the way. Now that we were used to Silver, Carol and I took turns leading him. He liked to sniff Carol's straw hat, the one that Aunt Hazel had helped her make the previous summer, and we wondered if he was going to taste it.

We camped above the lake in a grassy spot next to a stream. Daddy made a sunshade with the canvas tarp and Mama stacked the pack boxes in the cooking area. We fed Silver some oats and tied him nearby.

From camp, we could look down and watch Daddy fish. He never stayed in one spot for long. He would cast out a fly several times before hopping to another rock, always on the go. Even then, I recognized the grace in his smooth and unhurried casting. One side of the lake had a steep cliff with tumbled boulders near shore, so he did not invite us to tag along while he fished. We hoped we would have trout for dinner. And we did.

Carol and Mama and I lazed around camp and read. For special occasions we could buy comic books and had chosen *Lil' Abner*, *Dagwood and Blondie*, and *Batman and Robin*. Mama caught up on back issues of *Readers' Digest*. Carol spent time climbing on the granite boulders and riding Silver's packsaddle, which Daddy had cinched down over a log.

The next day we hiked to Sawmill Pass, leaving Daddy behind to continue his fishing. The pass was two steep miles above our camp. When we saw the summit just ahead I whooped, "We're there!" But we were not. We trudged up to the next rise but that wasn't the top either. Mama explained that there often seem to be several summits to a peak or pass.

Finally, we reached the top, where a sign read "Sawmill Pass 11,350 feet." As we rested and ate lunch, Mama pointed out various peaks and basins. "Around that ridge is Woods Lake, where Mr. McDougall camps every summer, and behind that mountain is Pinchot Pass." She told us far more than I could remember, but the sweeping view helped us comprehend the vastness of the Sierra.

When we headed for home the next day, I learned how much easier it is to hike down than up. We ate lunch where we'd had dinner on the hike in, then climbed the ridge and down, down, down the sandy hillside to the trailhead. We were sweaty and tired, but it was a satisfying kind of tiredness. We put Silver in the corral and kissed his nose as we told him "goodbye." He watched us, ears forward, as we drove away. Allie would drive up to get him later in the afternoon.

Pine Nuts at Badger Flat

Carol

Joan and I wiggled in anticipation as we drove eastward from town toward the Inyo Mountains. We were on our way to Badger Flat with the Goffs to collect pine nuts. Soon we crossed the aqueduct. It was a wide, straight, and deep canal full of water on its way to Los Angeles. A little farther on, we crossed the Owens River. Only a few ponds and marshy patches fringed with cattails and willows remained along the riverbed because most of the water in Sierra streams had been diverted into the aqueduct.

About four miles from town, we crossed the narrow-gauge railroad tracks and passed the Kearsarge Station buildings. I asked Daddy about the tracks because from town we never saw or heard a train.

He explained, "The narrow-gauge was built a long time ago to carry freight and passengers from Nevada to Owens Valley. That was back when there was more mining activity than we have now. The train still runs, it's called the Slim Princess." In later years, Joan and I had classmates who lived at Kearsarge Station, but I don't recall ever seeing the train.

At the base of the Inyo Mountains, the road turned north and entered Mazourka Canyon. Mama commented on the colorful layers of rock, so different from the white granite of the Sierra across the valley.

"These mountains have fossils because they were once under the sea."

"But where did the sea go?" I asked.

She tried to explain, "The world is much older than we can imagine and many things have happened that are hard to understand."

The road got rougher and steeper. Our 1937 Plymouth wasn't meant for such travel, but Daddy was skillful at coaxing it up the bumpy spots. Sometimes he had to stop to remove rocks from the road. We began to see juniper trees on the steep hillsides, and by the time we reached Badger Flat we were in a pinyon forest.

The Paiute Indians have lived in Owens valley for centuries and have long known how to collect pine nuts. I had seen their baskets and poles in the museum in Independence. We followed their method, but instead of using deer hides, Daddy and Mr. Goff spread a canvas under a tree and shook the branches with a rake until nuts fell out of the cones. Joan and I helped Mama and Mrs. Goff pick up the nuts and soon we had pitch on our hands and clothes.

"My hands are all sticky, Joan complained. "I need to wash them."

Daddy laughed, "Water won't work, Joan. Just rub your hands in the dirt."

"But they'll get even dirtier," she objected, until she realized that he knew something we didn't about pitch.

The Goffs were new in town and also were newlyweds. Mr. Goff taught the seventh and eighth grades and Mrs. Goff was learning how to cook. The past winter, when Mama had been away for a week helping Aunt Lois with her new baby, the Goffs came to our house every night for a dinner that Mrs. Goff cooked. We all liked having them come even if she served some unusual dishes. Daddy was still teasing her about her sticky spaghetti and soupy fruit cocktail pie.

We shook many trees, and with all of us working, it didn't take long to collect several buckets of pine nuts. At home, Mama would spread the nuts on trays, sprinkle them with salt water, and roast them in the oven. I thought it would be more fun to toast them over a campfire like the Paiutes would have done. Pine nuts were a good snack, and Mama sent small packages of them to friends and family.

We sat on blankets for our picnic lunch and finally, after the cucumber sandwiches and fried rabbit, out came my luscious chocolate birthday cake. It was my eighth birthday! I had helped Mama make the cake batter by adding the ingredients as I hung over the electric mixer—watching the patterns appear and vanish as the mixing bowl turned. And I had spread the thick white frosting and decorated it with many chocolate chips.

On the drive back down the canyon, we stopped and hiked to an overlook above Santa Rita Flat for a view of Owens Valley. Long and soft brown, it spread below us as far as we could see in both directions. We could recognize Independence as the green spot in the middle of the valley and the alfalfa fields and trees of the Fort as a wide green stripe. The jagged Sierra crest rose up across the valley. On that late September day, only a few sheltered patches of snow remained on the peaks.

We all loved this valley, and this place, and collecting pine nuts with our friends, just as the Paiutes had done for hundreds of years.

Part Three

THE WAR YEARS
1941–1945

Pearl Harbor

Joan

Even though I didn't understand what they were saying, I could hear the anxiety in the grownups' voices as they talked out on the porch. They used unfamiliar words like "Hitler" and "Germany" and "Poland." Carol and I had been put to bed toe-to-toe on a cot, but I could overhear the conversation outside. It was the summer of 1940 and our family was visiting Aunt Hazel and Uncle Clarence in LeeVining.

When I asked about it the next morning, Mama assured me that our country was safe and any war was a long time in the future and far away.

Reports of Hitler's invasion of Poland were continually on the radio, and all of the news seemed to be bad. Mama and Daddy would shake their heads; it was easy to tell they were worried. Daddy never missed the Richfield Reporter news at ten o'clock, just before he went to bed. Although the *Los Angeles Times* arrived on the Greyhound bus a day late, it covered the news in greater depth than the radio.

I don't remember Pearl Harbor Day, but Mama and Daddy heard about it on the radio, and we all listened to President Roosevelt tell the American people that our country was at war!

Daddy was thirty-four years old and I worried he might have to join the army. He was not drafted because his job, providing water for Los Angeles, was classified as essential to the war effort. He considered joining the Seabees, a part of the Navy that did construction work. I was relieved when he decided against it.

All of our uncles worked in war jobs—in the shipyard at Sausalito, the security department of the Douglas Aircraft factory in Los Angeles, assembling airplanes at Lockheed Aircraft in San Fernando, and building the Alcan Highway in Alaska. Young men in Independence were drafted or joined the Service. Mr. Goff quit teaching seventh and eighth grades and joined the marines and our music teacher, Mr. Rogers, joined the army.

Wartime programs brought new people to Owens Valley. In the spring of 1942, an internment camp was built six miles south of town to house Japanese people living on the west coast. Its official name was "Manzanar War Relocation Center," but local people called it simply "Manzanar." Those who resented having 10,000 Japanese people living nearby called it the "Jap Camp."

For one year, the Compton Junior College Civilian Pilot Training Program from southern California was held in Independence. This project used the Independence airport for flight training and several high school classrooms for teaching courses in geology and meteorology. The Elliott family from Los Angeles moved to Independence to be away from possible enemy attacks while Mr. Elliott served as a military officer. Adelle Bovenkirk's family lived in town while her dad, a minister, worked at Manzanar. We school kids liked having new friends and classmates.

I remember the times that Mama and Daddy sat at our oilcloth-covered table counting out ration stamps for various items: gasoline, tires, shoes, canned goods, sugar, oil, meat, and butter. We bought white oleo, the margarine that came in a one pound sealed wrapper containing a small dye capsule. Carol and I took turns crushing the dye capsule and kneading the oleo until it turned yellow. We speculated about whether it then tasted more like butter.

The shoes we bought at Lloyd's store in Lone Pine were short-lived because they were made of less and less leather and more and more cardboard. And the soles made black streaks on the linoleum, which distressed all mothers. Carol's shoes always seemed to be worn out.

The speed limit was lowered to 35 mph, and it took many gasoline stamps for a trip to North Hollywood. During one visit, we drove to the Douglas Aircraft plant in El Segundo to pick up Uncle Clarence, who was now Chief of Security. He wore a uniform with a pistol on his belt and looked stern and official. The entire entry area was overhung with camouflage nets that gave it an eerie feeling. We heard stories about blackouts and air-raid sirens and at night saw searchlights sweeping back and forth across the sky.

Independence was united behind the war effort. The United Services Organizations (USO) held dances for service men at the Legion Hall, and Mama joined the other local women with the decorations and refreshments. We school kids pasted cartoons from the Saturday Evening Post into scrapbooks that the USO sent to soldiers.

Like many families, we had a victory garden with tomatoes, cucumbers, and squash. School children were encouraged to participate, and a team of parents and teachers visited all the gardens. Carol and I were proud of the blue ribbons we received for our vigorous Swiss chard.

Some families also raised chickens or rabbits. Daddy chose rabbits, and Carol and I shared the job of feeding and watering them twice a day. We played with the bunnies on the lawn and tried not to think about what Daddy was doing in the garage when the doors were closed. Even though our pets, Jack and Jill, were spared from the frying pan, it was hard to be enthusiastic about our frequent rabbit dinners. With meat rationing, it became a wartime practice to observe Meatless Tuesdays. Carol and I always looked forward to Mama's egg and cheese casseroles.

At school, the teachers sold savings bond stamps, which we took home and pasted into booklets. When one was filled, Daddy took it to the bank in Lone Pine and received a savings bond. There were twenty and fifty-dollar bonds and higher. Daddy also had money deducted from his paycheck for savings bonds. He told us our government needed to borrow money from the American people to build airplanes and make ammunition.

The town held metal and paper drives, and the school sponsored a silk and rayon drive contest. Silk was hard to find because women's stockings were increasingly scarce, but Mrs. Phillips, my fifth grade teacher, encouraged us to collect what we could and bring it to school

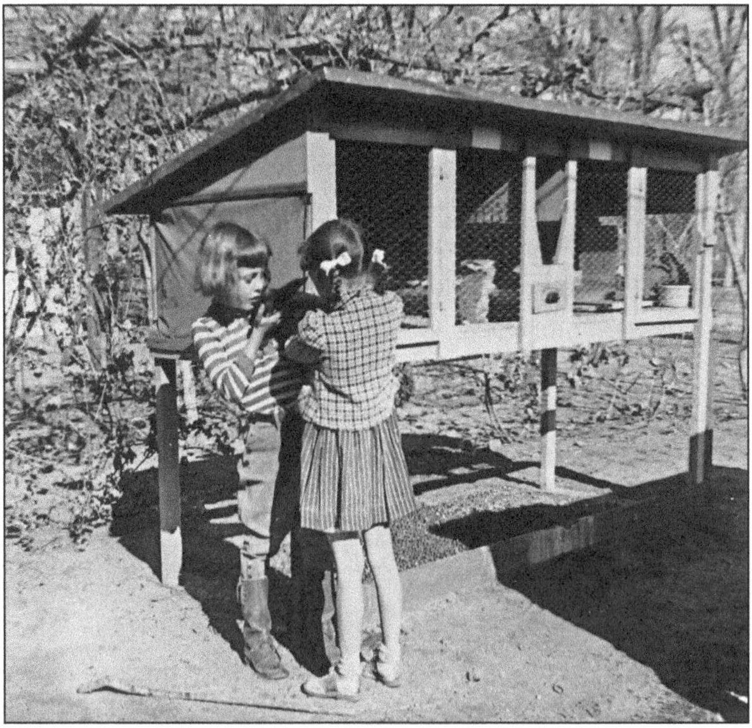

Carol and Little Carol playing with the bunnies, 1941.

to be weighed. The winner would receive a prize. One of my classmates had a group of friends help her, and they ran around town pulling a wagon. On weighing day, a member of her group nudged the scale with the toe of his shoe, and when I saw it he whispered, "If you tell you'll be really sorry." I went home crying, and it was the only time Mama went to school on my behalf. The next day, Mrs. Phillips gave the entire class a stern scolding with comments about honesty and trustworthiness. The room was silent, and I admired the way she handled the situation.

During school recesses, we kids practiced marching. A sixth grade boy always commanded the troops: "Forward march. Left turn. Right turn. About face."

Our new music teacher, Mrs. Stephens, taught us military fight songs. We sang with gusto:

"Over hill, over dale
As we hit the dusty trail,
And those caissons go rolling along.
In and out, hear them shout,
Countermarch and left about,
And those caissons go rolling along."

Mrs. Stephens was young, tall, pretty, and loved us all—and we loved her. She was married to a marine lieutenant. When she read parts of his letters to us, the War came right into our classroom. One day, she came to school aglow with exciting news. She and her husband had a private code. If he wrote in a letter that he needed a new wallet, it meant he was coming home on furlough. She explained how our government censored all letters soldiers sent home to ensure the enemy wouldn't learn about troop movements.

When the big day arrived, one of the older high school boys drove Mrs. Stephens north to Big Pine, where she could meet her husband's bus with more privacy than would have been possible at the Independence bus stop. She took several days off, and we kids were thrilled with the romance of it all.

In the summer of 1942, Carol and I stayed with neighbors while Daddy and Mama were in the mountains. Once, I climbed the cottonwood tree in their front yard. The radio was turned up and through the static I listened to the news, trying to figure out who was winning and who was losing. It appeared to be even. The War seemed to go on forever.

Manzanar

Joan

Mama, Carol, and I were going to Lone Pine on a breezy spring day in 1942 when Carol was eight and I was nine. We had shopping to do at J. C. Penney, as Mama had said she'd make us each a spring dress.

As we approached Manzanar, we spotted a row of tents. There was a new fence, higher than the old one, with barbed wire strands strung taut and close together. We knew that Manzanar had once been a town with a school, grocery store, and apple and pear orchards. The community was abandoned when the City began diverting the water from Bairs and Shepherd creeks into the aqueduct in 1913. Daddy had cut firewood from the dead trees there before he installed our coal-oil stove.

Just inside the new fence, men were building a tall skinny wooden structure that reminded me of pictures I'd seen of windmills.

"What's that?" I asked Mama.

"It's a guard tower," she said, "for watching people, if you can believe it."

Bulldozers were charging up and down like wild steers, creating huge swirls of dust, pushing the sagebrush into giant piles, scraping the desert bare.

On our next trip to Lone Pine, I looked for the fence. There it was, with even more guard towers. Now there were buildings, rows and rows of long black sheds, all exactly alike. "Barracks," Mama called them. Workers scurried everywhere, shoveling sand and gravel, pouring concrete, nailing frameworks of two-by-fours, and rolling out tarpaper to cover the sides and roofs. The scene was hazy with dust that the spring winds were sweeping from the cleared ground. Mama told us the men were building the barracks for Japanese people.

"They look like ugly places to live, all in a row," I said. "Why are they coming here?"

"Because they have to," Mama replied. "Ever since Pearl Harbor, some people have been afraid that Japan might attack the west coast, probably Los Angeles or San Francisco or even cities further north in Washington. They are worried that Japanese people who live along the coast might try to signal submarines or act as spies."

After mulling this over I asked, "Are those people Japanese or American?"

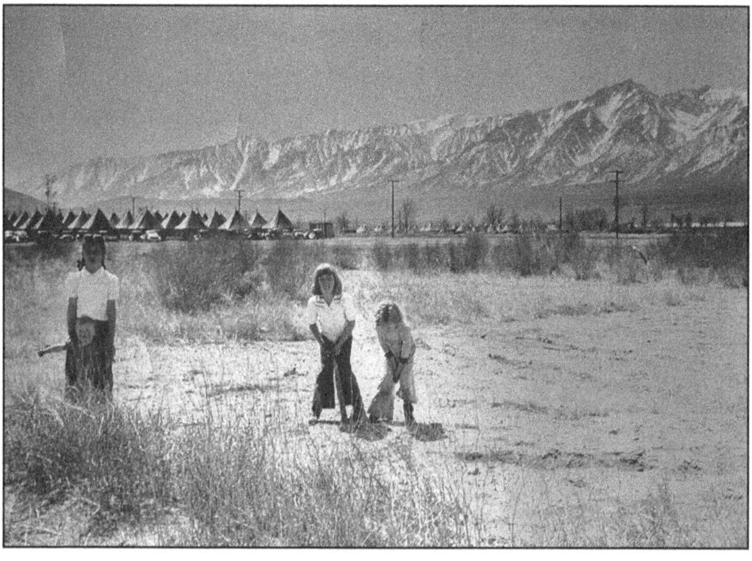

With our cousins during construction of Manzanar War Relocation Center, 1942. *(See Appendix for names)*

"Most of them are citizens or want to become citizens. But some people think that if they have to choose, they will be loyal to their homeland."

I thought about it some more as we crossed the aqueduct and skirted the edge of the Alabama Hills. From our long-anticipated visits, I knew Los Angeles as a city where there were billboards and traffic lights and spicy-smelling pepper trees, a place of aunts and uncles and cousins. But San Francisco and beyond seemed as exotic and impossibly far away as another country. It didn't make sense that people, Japanese people, from such distant places would come to our quiet valley.

The next time we passed the barbed wire fence, the barracks were occupied, no doubt about it. From the highway, we could see little figures walking from building to building, irrigating the old apple orchards, and working in communal vegetable gardens. The guard towers were manned with soldiers, sentries stood at attention at the stone entry gate with the pagoda roof, army jeeps and trucks came and went. It was hard to believe that thousands of people were now living there.

On one of those rare and wonderful nights when we talked Daddy into taking us to a movie in Lone Pine, we saw the search lights sweeping back and forth, back and forth, evil and scary in the night sky.

"Who would try to escape?" I asked, thinking about the desert to the north and south, the Inyo Mountains rising to the east, the Sierra peaks silhouetted to the west.

"That's one reason it was built here," Daddy said. "Nowhere to go and tall mountains on two sides."

"I'd go up one of the creeks and hide in a canyon," Carol said.

"But you couldn't stay there in the winter," I reminded her.

The local people had mixed feelings about whether it was right or wrong. One neighbor said he slept with a gun under his pillow,

"In case any of them Japs get out." Other people felt that U.S. citizens should not be imprisoned. Regardless of local opinions, it was a "done deal" by President Roosevelt through Executive Order 9066. This was wartime and all kinds of bad things were happening. There was a strong fear factor because the Japanese had attacked our ships in Pearl Harbor.

Not all of the barracks were used to house people. Some were used as mess halls, bathrooms, a hospital, and schoolrooms. Even though internees worked as schoolteachers, more were needed. These jobs were filled by Caucasians whose housing was just outside the fence in buildings with kitchens and bathrooms. Their children attended school in Independence, and it was exciting to have new classmates.

Although I never went inside the camp, my parents did. They were included in a group of Independence townspeople invited to a Christmas program at the new Manzanar auditorium. When they came home, I could tell by the tone of Mama's voice, and by her comments, that she had been touched and impressed by the experience. She told us about the school children dressed in dark pants or skirts and white shirts. They waited so quietly on the bleachers along one wall and sang so beautifully.

Towards the end of the War, security relaxed at Manzanar. The guard towers had long been abandoned and not many people were around.

"What's happened to everyone?" I asked Mama.

"Many of them have found jobs in other states, which means they can leave Manzanar," she told us.

"Can't they go back to their old towns and houses?" I asked.

"No, they can't live anywhere along the Pacific coast, so they have to start all over again in a different place."

"That doesn't seem fair to me," I commented.

At supper one evening, Daddy told us that Japanese fishermen sometimes crawled under the fence to hike to the high lakes behind Mt. Williamson.

"But how do they get under the fence with all of those guards around" I asked, and Daddy told us the meaning of "relaxed security."

"The guards know what's going on, but they also know how much the Japanese men like to fish."

A few weeks later, Mama and Daddy hiked up to those Williamson Creek Lakes with Art Reyman to climb Mt. Williamson from the west side. They had turned back from the summit climb because it was stormy and too dangerous to continue and were eating lunch when Mama spotted a slender stick in the rocks. It seemed out of place in that land of granite boulders far above timberline. They scrambled closer to investigate and found that the stick was a willow fishing pole. Next to it was the body of a Japanese man.

Daddy reported the discovery to the sheriff, who already knew about the missing person. Several search parties had made unsuccessful attempts to find the fisherman. Because the area was impossible to reach with pack animals, the authorities decided the body would remain where it lay, wrapped in a handmade quilt and covered by a mound of rocks. A stone cairn marks the site and a Buddhist funeral ceremony was held at Manzanar. The widow sent a letter of appreciation to Mama and Daddy.

This event made me wonder why people would break the rules to visit the Sierra. Was it the fishing they wanted, the beauty of the mountains, or the feeling of freedom? We heard various comments from townspeople who worked at Manzanar. They all agreed that the children were friendly and polite and "some of our wild town kids could learn plenty from them." The families were close-knit and through their gardening efforts, the people had made the desert bloom.

We knew that Japanese men had fought for the Allied cause. By now, I was almost a teenager, becoming aware that what I considered "fair" was called "justice." In the case of Japanese internment at Manzanar, I felt that justice and the Bill of Rights had not worked as advertised.

In early 1945, our local paper informed us that Executive Order 9066 had been rescinded and the Japanese people were free to leave Manzanar. By November, the Camp was empty. I hadn't seen anyone actually arrive nor did I see anyone leave.

Princess for a Week

Carol

Mama, Joan, and I were coming out of Joseph's Grocery in Lone Pine when we met Dr. Anthony coming down the sidewalk with her dog named "Churchill." She was one of the few doctors in Lone Pine and probably the only woman doctor in Owens Valley. Joan and I didn't like to see her because she was constantly talking to Mama about our tonsils. She was not our doctor, but evidently she considered herself a tonsil expert and seemed to believe that all tonsils should be taken out. I had great admiration for her, however, because she was the only person I had ever seen dive off the high dive at Keough's Hot Springs.

The conversation began as usual. "Mary, have you made a decision about the girls' tonsils?"

"No I haven't, not yet."

They discussed tonsils while Joan and I talked to Churchill. He was one of those bulldog types with extremely loose skin. He was friendly but strange looking in his baggy coat and pushed-in face.

Joan said, "If we could have a dog I'd want a different kind," and I agreed.

On the drive home, we talked about dogs, not tonsils. For some reason, removing children's tonsils was a growing practice, and Mama was not one to join a fad. But she loved dogs and said, "Churchill is an English bulldog, and he is named after the Prime Minister of England."

"I wish Daddy would let us get a dog, not like Churchill but a smaller one," Joan lamented.

Mama said, as she always did, "I would like one too, but you know your father doesn't want a dog digging in his flowerbeds. He works hard to keep them nice."

About a month later, just a few days after school was out for the summer, Mama announced that my tonsils would come out next week.

My first question was, "What are tonsils anyway?" My next question was, "Is Joan having hers out too?"

Joan was not, and I felt that something must be wrong with me. I didn't think Mama knew much about tonsils either, but she assured me that lots of people have them removed and not to worry. I suspect she had discussed the matter with Dr. Simon, her naturopathic doctor in North Hollywood, before making her decision. He must have agreed it was the right thing to do.

Mama consulted him often. He may have been the reason we took naps every day for years, laid under a special sun lamp aimed at our chests whenever we had a cold, and took a spoonful of that awful Stuart Formula right after dinner. She believed in gargling with salt water and pinning a damp washcloth around your throat at night for a sore throat. Perhaps not all of this was due to Dr. Simon. Mama may have learned some of it when she worked at the tuberculosis sanatorium where fresh air, daily naps, and good nutrition were the only treatments for tuberculosis.

So my tonsils came out. I don't recall being scared when they put me on a table and wheeled me into the operating room. My plan was to stay awake to see what happens when they take out tonsils.

I awoke in a bed in the Lone Pine Hospital corridor with a sore throat and feeling disappointed that I had fallen asleep and missed it all. Mama and Daddy were there, holding my hands. Mama was outraged to find my bed in the hall. It was an over-crowded five-bed hospital. We went home later that afternoon.

I spent several days lounging like a princess in my parents' bed in the back bedroom. For once in my life, I could eat whatever I wanted. I enjoyed the attention and the unusual opportunity to command, "Joan, bring me some more books, and another dish of ice cream."

The New Girl

Carol

I enjoyed being one of the best spellers in the fourth grade. I was not the smartest kid in the class, but I worked hard and was competitive. After we passed our spelling papers to the student sitting behind us for correction, Miss Deffeyus had us go to the blackboard to write misspelled words ten times. I rarely missed a word, but because it was fun to go to the blackboard, I would occasionally make an error on purpose. That changed when the new girl arrived.

Her name was Phyllis Oakeshott, and she was better than I was in spelling. She was also better in math. In fact, she was better in every subject. On top of that, she was artistic. When Miss Deffeyus asked her to draw a Christmas scene with colored chalk on the front blackboard, the whole class watched in amazement. She effortlessly created a Santa with his sleigh and reindeer that covered the entire front blackboard. We had never known even a teacher who could draw so well.

Phyllis's desk was directly across the aisle from mine and while she was outgoing and friendly, I was envious of her talents and tried to ignore her. I also began to work harder.

One day during Christmas vacation, I was sitting on our back porch steps and looked up to see Phyllis walking across our bridge and down our driveway.

With a smile she said, "I came to see if you want to play. Patsy and Marcia got a bicycle for Christmas and I'm tired of waiting for my turn to ride it around the block."

I was happy to see her and said, "I was just wishing for someone to play with. Do you want to walk down the creek?"

Phyllis and I became best friends. At school, we whispered jokes back and forth across the aisle until Miss Deffeyus said, "If you girls don't stop your giggling I'll have to move you farther apart."

After school, we played down-the-creek and up-the-creek and out-in-the-sagebrush. We read books and played cards. Joan was reading Nancy Drew books at the time, and we all searched the neighborhood for clues to a mystery to solve.

Joan practicing, 1942.

Joan and Carol on our driveway bridge, 1942.

When we walked down the creek, I said, "See these footprints? They are different, and I think we should follow them."

Phyllis got out her notebook and said, "I'll draw a picture so we won't forget how they look."

But no matter how hard we tried, we never found a mystery.

Our families also became good friends. We hiked together up the creeks that flowed out of the Sierra canyons and picnicked at Onion Valley. Phyllis's brother, Paul, was in Joan's class. Their father was a geologist and we all, particularly Mama, enjoyed hearing about the uplift and erosion of the mountain ranges that surrounded us.

At the end of the school year, Mr. Oakeshott finished his work in Independence. He had been teaching meteorology in the civilian pilot training program. The family returned to their home in southern California and his teaching job at Compton Junior College.

I was desolate. Phyllis was the best friend I'd ever had. We wrote letters. Hers were memorable and had illustrations along the margins.

She wrote, "When my mom and I were making fruitcake yesterday my cat was watching us from the top of the refrigerator. That's her favorite place to sit when we're working in the kitchen, but she leaned out too far and fell into the fruitcake batter!" Phyllis' illustration made the sticky event very real.

Over the years, we visited each other during summer vacations. On my first visit to Compton, I was amazed at the size of Phyllis' junior high school, envious of the number of movies she'd seen, and enchanted by tales of the Van Johnson fan club she and her friends had organized. We took the bus to matinees every day. It was a different world.

She, in turn, enjoyed her visits to Independence. The summer we were thirteen, the two of us backpacked up the creek to First Pine, a notable landmark about a mile above town. It is the last in a line of stately Jeffrey pines that follow the creek down from Seven Pines. We called it "First Pine" because it was the one closest to town.

Phyllis and I filled our packs with essentials—sleeping bags, a pot and matches, macaroni and cheese for dinner, a can of fruit cocktail, and a box of gingersnaps. All afternoon we played in the creek and moved rocks around to make a dam. We cooked our dinner over a fire at the edge of the creek, and slept on a deep bed of dry pine needles under the tall tree. Phyllis appreciated our valley as much as I delighted in her world of movies.

On a visit when we were in high school, Phyllis brought her climbing rope to teach me how to tie climbing knots and belay. She had learned to rock climb in the Sierra with her cousin. They had climbed Mt. Humphrey, a difficult peak overlooking Bishop. I'm sure Mama was relieved that we were content to climb on the rocks below the waterfall in Pinyon Canyon.

I was fortunate that Phyllis came looking for someone to play with that day during Christmas vacation because I learned it is far better to appreciate and enjoy others than to feel envious of their talents. I have always admired Phyllis's enthusiasm, imagination, and sense of humor. We still write letters and visit. And I still regret that I didn't welcome her when she was the new girl.

More Newcomers

Carol

Joan and I were playing in a favorite spot down the creek with Phyllis on one of the first warm days in April. After a long winter, it felt good to go barefoot again, although our feet would be tender for a few weeks. We liked the different textures—the softness of the lawn, the coarseness of the gravel, the warmth of the asphalt, and the smoothness of the water-polished granite on the creek bottom.

The sun was warm on our backs and quail were calling from the sagebrush as we rolled up our pant legs and waded into a shallow pond next to the creek. The seventh grade boys had made the pond by diverting creek water into a natural depression. They had tired of their project and were off making a bike trail through the sagebrush above town. "The Burma Road," they called it, after the long and winding road through the Himalayas that was used by the allied armies during the War.

We were making the pond deeper when Patsy and Marcia Bateman came looking for us. They lived next door to Phyllis and were in the second and third grades. They took off their shoes and enthusiastically jumped in to help us scoop out the sandy gravel with our hands. We were all having a good time when Mrs. Bateman came striding through the bushes. She looked cross.

A tent sleepover, 1943.
(See Appendix for names)

With her hands on her hips she scolded her daughters, "Patsy and Marcia, you know that you are not allowed to go barefoot down here! We've warned you many times about sharp rocks and broken glass! And you need to remember that there are snakes in these bushes and the water is too cold to be wading!"

Joan and I looked at each other and tried not to smile. We couldn't believe she was serious until she marched Patsy and Marcia home. After they put on their shoes.

I whispered, "I'm glad she is not my mother."

Phyllis commented, "I think she's a good mother, but she is used to sidewalks and parks."

That night at supper I asked, "Mama why are the Batemans so afraid of everything?"

She agreed with Phyllis saying, "They have probably always lived in cities where there are no creeks or snakes. Also, Mrs. Bateman hasn't lived in Independence as long as you have. I'm sure she will get over her worries after she has been here awhile."

Until I heard Mrs. Bateman express her concerns that day, I had never thought about how different our creek and sagebrush must be from a city playground or park.

I said, "Mama, I'm glad we live right here."

Dancing in the sprinkler, 1943.
(See Appendix for names)

In July, Mama took her group of Campfire Girls on a trip to Flower Lake above Onion Valley. She hired a packer to take our gear because we would be staying for five days. Several high school girls went along to help with the cooking. Mr. Bateman hiked in with us, perhaps because Patsy, who was eight years old, was the youngest of the group. Or, maybe because Mrs. Bateman was worried about the hazards we might encounter.

Flower Lake is the second lake in the basin and only two miles from the parking lot in Onion Valley, but the trail is steep. We girls

Campfire Girls on the way to Flower Lake, 1943.
(See Appendix for names)

were walking too fast and were soon out of breath and tired, but we all had snacks in our pockets.

Joan and I munched on Horlicks malted milk tablets. These yummy snacks got Mama's approval because they were made of malt, wheat flour, and powdered milk, with added vitamins and minerals. Mr. Bateman noticed that Joan and I weren't puffing as much as the other girls and thought the malted milk tablets were giving us extra energy. I heard him ask Mama if she thought we might share them with Patsy. We gladly shared. But it was soon evident that it wasn't the malted milk tablets that made the difference, it was the pace. Joan and I knew if you slow down when the trail gets steep, you don't get out of breath. I remember thinking that I already knew many things that Mr. Bateman hadn't yet learned.

Later in the summer, I felt sad when Patsy's family moved back to southern California.

Like Mr. Oakeshott, Mr. Bateman had worked for the army for one year and needed to return to his regular job. I wished they could have stayed longer.

Over Shepherd Pass

Joan

Carol and I shivered with excitement and cold as we watched Daddy and Allie saddle Ginger and the two mules, Jonnie and Dot. We were nine and ten and, at last, were joining our parents on a two-week trip into the Sierra. We had driven up the dirt road to the Symmes Creek trailhead just as it was getting light.

After Daddy and Allie loaded the pack boxes and sleeping bags on the mules, they threw a canvas tarp over each load and tied it in place with a "diamond hitch." The special knots centered the pack and kept the entire load from slipping from side to side or from front to back when the mules were climbing up and down hills. I felt proud that Daddy could tie all those complicated knots. Mama told us, "Allie lets us take the animals without a packer because Daddy knows how to pack and take care of them."

They finished loading the mules just as the sun rose over the Inyo Mountains and touched us with welcomed warmth. We said "goodbye" to Allie as Daddy lifted Carol and me onto Ginger's back. She was a gentle chestnut with a white streak down her nose.

"Hold onto the reins with one hand, and if you need to, hold onto the saddle horn with the other," he told me. "Carol, hang onto the back of the saddle or around Joan's waist. And don't kick Ginger in the flanks because it might make her jump."

He picked up the lead rope for Jonnie and Dot and started up the trail through the sagebrush. Ginger was next and Mama walked behind. We were off to Shepherd Pass and Tyndall Creek.

"Have a good trip. See you in two weeks," Allie shouted.

Before long, we reached the first creek crossing where rocks poked up through the fast current. Daddy told us to stay on Ginger and she would take us across. The horse and mules moved slowly and cautiously through the boulders and rushing water, with a couple of quick, scary stumbles. There were four crossings in all and none seemed easy for Ginger.

From there, the trail left the stream and began to climb the ridge in a long series of switchbacks. Sagebrush and pinyon trees gave way to Jeffrey pines, and soon the white fir and then the red fir appeared. When we finally reached the ridge top, we stopped for lunch and a view of the rugged north wall of Mt. Williamson.

The plan was for one parent and one girl to ride Ginger together, trading off with the hikers, but it worked out that Mama and Daddy did more hiking and we girls rode double. We reached Anvil Camp late in the afternoon. It was tucked into the trees along Shepherd Creek. Daddy unloaded the mules, tied Ginger for the night, and fed them all oats while Mama made supper. It had been a long day.

The next morning, we continued until we reached a small meadow where the trees ended, and we began a climb through a steep rock pile that Daddy called a talus slope. The trail curved around huge boulders. I wondered how Ginger could seem so calm when I was feeling so nervous.

Near the top of the pass, the trail zigzagged in short, steep turns up a loose gravel slope through melting snow patches. I hung on tight to the saddle horn and Carol hugged me around the waist as Ginger scrambled up and up in quick, short steps, trying to keep her momentum. On the summit, we slid stiffly off Ginger and I kissed her nose in gratitude.

A wooden sign announced, "Sequoia National Park, Shepherd Pass Entrance." The elevation was 12,050 feet. We signed our names in a notebook that was in a metal box. Mama took photos and pulled out some candy for a celebration.

While the east side of the pass had been rugged and steep, the west side was broad and gentle. We looked down on the Tyndall Creek basin. Except for a few groves of trees, it was above timberline. Low willows grew along the creek and there were tiny meadows among granite slabs and boulders. Mountains of all sizes surrounded us, up close and far away. Mt. Tyndall rose abruptly to our left, and far to the west were the peaks of the Kaweah Ridge and the Great Western Divide, with names easy to remember—flat Table Mountain, the Milestone spire, and Black Kaweah. Diamond Mesa stood to our right. I knew I would never forget the grandeur of that view.

"Where do we go from here?" I asked.

Pointing toward a dark patch on a hillside above Tyndall Creek Daddy said, "See that group of trees down there? That's Sheep Corral Camp, where we're headed. I'd say we have about two miles to go." And off we went down the gentle slope.

Sheep Corral Camp was in a stand of foxtail pine at 11,600 feet, higher than most trees will grow in the Sierra. Yet here they were, tall trees with cinnamon-colored bark and short branches that curved downward, like a fox's tail. There wasn't much evidence of the rock and log enclosures that sheepherders had built for their animals decades earlier. I couldn't imagine how they had driven sheep and cattle up and over that rugged pass before there was a trail.

Daddy unpacked the animals and took them down to a grassy area where he hobbled Ginger and left them for the night.

The west side of Shepherd Pass, 1943.

"Why don't you hobble Jonnie and Dot?" I asked. "Can't they run away too?"

"Mules always stick around with the horses, so they don't need to be hobbled," he told me. Each morning and evening he checked to be sure they hadn't wandered too far away.

After dinner, Carol and I crawled into our sleeping bag—too tired to sit around the campfire with Mama and Daddy. They shared one kapok bag and Carol and I slept in another. For mattresses, we pushed around dry pine needles to make a flat area. We slept on a canvas tarp with a second tarp nearby to pull over us in case of rain, the same tarps used to cover the mules' packs during travel time.

The next morning, Mama set up the kitchen in a shady spot with the pack boxes stacked sideways for our food. We brought a cooking grate, a coffeepot, two aluminum pots, a frying pan, and a bucket for hauling water from the creek. Nearby were flat rocks that other campers had used as tables. We worried about ground squirrels and mice getting into our food, but we weren't concerned about bears. Although black bears were raiding camps in Yosemite Valley, they were not in the high country this far south.

Tyndall Creek camp, 1943.

Joan and Carol at Labrador Lake, 1943.

For breakfasts, we ate oatmeal, pancakes, or slab bacon, and fresh eggs. The Klim powdered milk was lumpy, and the newly available dried eggs were even lumpier. Lunches were thick pilot biscuit crackers, cheese, salami, dried fruit, and nuts. Dinner was Spam and potatoes, cornmeal mush and Vienna sausages or lentils and rice. But most nights we also had fried fish. A special treat might be a can of fruit or cookies.

Oh, the candy! At home we were allowed to eat it only on special occasions, but in the mountains we usually ended lunch with root beer, lemon, or peppermint hard candy. Mama used it as a treat on hiking days. She knew it was hard to complain when one's mouth was full of sweets.

Tobacco was on Mama's shopping list. During the war years, Daddy rolled his own cigarettes. He pulled a can of tobacco and a packet of thin papers from his shirt pocket and carefully removed one paper. Onto it, he tapped out "just enough" tobacco and rolled it into a tube, licking the long edge to form a seal. This procedure was always careful and deliberate. He brought several empty tobacco cans to the mountains for storing grasshoppers. They had a hinged metal lid and were sturdy and waterproof.

There were many lakes in the area, all above timberline, each one a blue gem in a granite setting, usually fringed with grasses, sedges, and low willows. Most had rainbow trout but a few had brown, golden, or eastern brook. The ponds held only frogs. Golden trout with their vivid coloring and pink flesh were our favorite.

Most mornings, Daddy hiked to a lake after breakfast. Mama, Carol and I joined him after we washed the dishes and gathered lunch. Sometimes we took our dirty clothes down to the creek for a scrub. There wasn't much laundry because we did not take many clothes, just two extra pairs of socks and underpants, an extra t-shirt, and shorts. On our way to meet Daddy we sometimes passed the "swimming" lake where we took quick shivery dips from the tiny sandy beach.

When we arrived, Daddy was casting out his line in long, graceful loops. If a fish didn't strike, he'd move on or perhaps try a different fly. There was no sitting or standing in place with a can of worms for him, although he would sometimes give salmon eggs or grasshoppers a try. He swatted the grasshoppers as he hiked to a lake. Carol and I were good at catching them with a willow branch, the bigger the hopper the better.

Daddy reported on what the fish were biting. It seemed to me they preferred the little drab flies to the big colorful ones lining his fly case. He made his own flies while sitting in his easy chair on winter nights. If the fish heads seemed too big for their bodies, then it meant they didn't have enough food. This was the case when a lake was surrounded by boulders without the plants and willows to attract insects.

After lunch, we might move to a different lake. Sometimes Daddy rigged up poles for Carol and me, but we never had the luck that he did.

Often we left him to fish while Mama and Carol and I took a different route back to camp, one that promised a look at an unfamiliar flower. Mama showed us the tiny catkins of the alpine willow that grew just a few inches above the ground, and told us they were related to the tall willows down at the trailhead and to the middle-sized willows at the lake. "They're like cousins," she said. She pointed out the little pink buckwheats that hugged the ground and the Sierra primrose growing in magenta clusters in rocky crevices.

Back in camp, Carol and I sometimes followed Daddy down to the creek to help him clean the fish. He cut a long slit down the belly and we pulled out the innards and washed each one carefully in the stream. Mama rolled the fish in cornmeal and fried them in butter. And then we ate them, every piece, down to the last morsel.

Daddy lit the campfire before supper. We shifted our positions around it according to the smoke, and on cold nights we stood close to the flames and alternated between our front-side and backside. We talked about the events of the day or plans for the next day, gazing at the flames as they lapped around a piece of pine. Warm and drowsy, we headed for our sleeping bags. Sometimes Mama pointed out a constellation in the black sky above us or we admired the Milky Way, but not for long.

Carol and I found plenty to do right in camp. We climbed on the rocks and poked around the old logs and stumps. One of our favorite activities was collecting pitch from the pines. We went from tree to tree looking for oozing sap and scraped the sticky drops into empty tin cans. When we put the cans over the fire the pitch melted and popped and smelled like turpentine. Our plan was to mold it into shapes, but Mama was nervous about the hot liquid. She finally put her foot down when we got pitch in our hair. "That's it," she exclaimed as she tried to comb it out of my pigtails.

One day, we saddled Ginger and packed up Jonnie and Dot and headed off to Milestone Basin several miles to the west. Soon we turned off on a trail to Lake South America, a big lake above timberline, which resembled the shape of its namesake continent. Daddy told us the fish did well here because the grassy edges attracted many insects. The lake had a gentle grass-lined outlet where trout spawned, and we could spot the orange clumps of roe in the shallow water.

We camped among the boulders in a snug place sheltered by a cluster of whitebark pine. That night we were awakened by yelling, "Get out of there. Go on. Git!" and there was Daddy, a ghost in the moonlight, chasing the horse and mules in his white long underwear. The animals had found the oat supply in camp and were having a midnight snack.

On the return trip to Tyndall Creek, Jonnie would sometimes go ahead of Ginger and the rest of us on the trail, but soon he would come trotting back, his long ears forward and a worried look in his eyes.

Back at Sheep Corral Camp, one of Carol's boot soles was beginning to flap. Daddy told her that she did too much rock hopping and running around for her boots to last. But he had come prepared with pliers and baling wire and reattached the sole, at least for the time being.

Several days later our friends, Joe and Caroline Goff, and Joe's dad arrived. A packer had brought them in over Kearsarge and Forester passes to meet us. Joe was on military leave. His dad was an experienced fisherman and thought he was in heaven in that golden

With the Goffs at Tyndall Creek, 1943.
(See Appendix for names)

trout country. For years afterwards, our family laughed about the high drama at one of the Wright Lakes. After he had hooked a big fish, his pole came apart. He was determined to net that fish and there was a lot of splashing and yelling and swearing, "Goddamnit, git in here! I said git in here!"

Joe and Caroline sang songs around the campfire in their clear melodious voices. Our favorite was "Waltzing Matilda," which our soldiers had learned in Australia.

Too soon, it was time to leave and retrace our steps over Shepherd Pass and back down to Symmes Creek trailhead. The three Goffs were walking out with us and we traded off with the riding and hiking. Carol and I learned that riding downhill could be mighty uncomfortable, and it felt good to walk for a while. It was fourteen miles up and over the pass and down, down, down, the switchbacks, through the willows, across the creek, and into the sagebrush.

The men unloaded the animals while Carol and I said our goodbyes to Ginger, Jonnie, and Dot. We left them in the corral and drove down the rocky dirt road. When we reached the pavement, it felt as though the car was floating. As tired and dusty as we were, eager for showers and clean clothes, we all knew we'd had an unforgettable experience.

Symmes Creek trailhead, 1943.
(See Appendix for names)

The House Next-Door

Carol

It was exciting to get new neighbors. Even though the house and yard next-door were smaller than ours, some large families lived there for a long time. Over the years, the front porch had been closed in and a back porch added.

Our first neighbors were the Kellys. Norman and Warren were the same ages as we were, two and three. We exchanged mud pies and toys through the wire fence. Because of the creek and fishpond, they came to play in our yard only when Mama was outside with us. She was especially fond of little Warren. A few years after they moved to Lone Pine, Warren drowned in nearby Dias Lake. Mama was upset for weeks.

After the Kellys left, an older couple moved in. They were friendly but had no children. One day, when Joan was at kindergarten and I was helping Mama plant petunias in the flowerbed next to the front fence, we heard shrieking from the house next-door. We watched as Mrs. Anderson ran out shouting, "There's a snake in my house!"

Mama put down her trowel, and we rushed to see the snake. She told the frightened woman it was not poisonous and shooed the garter snake out the front door with a broom. It had come through a crack in the living room floor. Those neighbors soon moved away.

Next there were the Brights. Dickie and Sally were younger than Joan and me, and Mama was still nervous about the fishpond and creek when they came to play. She shouldn't have worried because Joan knew exactly what to do when Sally fell in the creek.

Joan yelled, "Mama! Come help us!" as she headed straight for the back gate, planning to catch Sally as she floated out under the fence and into the alley.

Mama had rescued Sally upstream, but she told Joan, "That was an excellent plan."

We were happy when the Feldmans arrived with children both younger and older than we were. The youngest was a toddler named Eddie. He entertained us from the kitchen windows as he chased their cat, and their goose chased both Eddie and the cat. Vivian was in my fourth grade class, but I spent more time with her eight-year-old brother, Gene. He liked to go down-the-creek and out-in-the-sagebrush and to dig foxholes in the alley. During the War, kids dug a lot of foxholes. Vivian didn't seem to like playing outside their yard.

I also liked the older brother, Albert, who was in the seventh grade. He made model airplanes, a hobby for many during the war. I covered our bedroom walls with my models of American, German, and Japanese fighters and bombers. Cereal boxes came with simple balsa cutouts and many fancy model kits were available. Albert had a better model collection than anyone I knew, and he would let Gene and me each select a plane to fly around outside through the sagebrush.

Albert once helped us get the drunken man out of our tumbleweed fort down the creek. We thought the visitor was probably someone from the "Jungle" who had stumbled into our cozy hideout on his way home from the bar at the Independence Hotel. When Albert shook him, he got up slowly and wobbled on down the creek.

Albert was interested in army strength training programs, and he led us in daily calisthenics in their backyard. Their mulberry tree had a horizontal limb at a perfect height for our chin-ups. He challenged us to increasing numbers of push-ups and chin-ups, and when we could meet his expectations he would give us a ride on his bike to the drugstore and buy us a milkshake. Joan refused to participate. She said emphatically, "I do not want to ride anywhere on that bike bar between Albert's arms!"

The Feldmans had two mulberry trees and we had one. Mama loved watching the flocks of migrating cedar waxwings greedily eating the juicy berries, and she sometimes made mulberry pies. We kids preferred mulberry fights. The purple juice made a satisfying mess when you hit someone with a handful of ripe berries. One day Joan was running past our kitchen window with two fistfuls when Mama's voice rang out, "Joan! You get in here and change out of that white blouse. RIGHT NOW!"

Only once did I go beyond the front porch and into the house next-door. There was one bedroom, and most of the kitchen was taken up a by a huge wood range. I couldn't imagine how they could cook in that house during the hot summer months. I don't recall seeing much of Mrs. Feldman—it seemed like she never left the house.

As the years went by, Albert, now in the ninth grade, began taking a special interest in Joan. He did his best to sit next to her when we all sat on their front porch cots reading comic books. She felt uncomfortable and annoyed. When he gave her a fancy cosmetic set for Christmas, Mama became uncomfortable. Both Joan and Mama were probably relieved when the family moved away a few months later, but I knew how much I would miss every one of the Feldman kids.

On moving day, we watched them load a large open truck with sideboards. First they coaxed their horse in and tied him cross-wise just behind the cab. Next came a board barrier to keep the horse in place, then the furniture, followed by the boxes. When the truck was almost loaded, the horse became agitated and wanted out. We all watched in disbelief as he somehow climbed up and over the high sideboards and landed safely on the ground. Mr. Feldman made other arrangements to move the horse.

The family that came when I was in the seventh grade had even more children. They added a second back porch onto the first back porch and stayed for many years. Again, I had more interests in common with the younger brother than with the girl my age. Louis and I built a fine tree house in the tamarisk tree in their backyard. And there were enough kids to have baseball games in the alley.

Joan wasn't fond of these neighbors because Mrs. Muniz thought Joan was meant for one of her boys and made annoying comments and smirks.

"You like my Peter, eh?"

Joan tried to be polite and would mumble something like, "He's OK."

"Maybe someday, eh?" she'd persist.

But I always enjoyed Louis' company and liked the activity next door. Even in a small town where every home is within walking distance, it was nice to have a good friend just over the fence.

The Best Time of the Year

Carol

Daddy was putting our string of multicolored Christmas lights on the spruce tree in the front yard. Mama was making fruitcake. She had already made the English toffee and was trying to think of a new place to hide it. Joan and I wouldn't dare get into it, but Daddy couldn't resist its incredible taste and texture.

Joan and I sat together on the couch looking through the Sears, Roebuck Catalogue and discussing what gift we would most like to have. It was a difficult decision.

Joan said, "I want a Monopoly game, remember when we played it last summer with the Hurlbut kids?"

I turned the page, "I'd like one of these electric motors for my Tinker Toy truck."

Packages that were arriving at the post office quickly disappeared into the garage.

One of the best parts of the holiday was cutting our Christmas tree. We drove north on Highway 395 about sixty-five miles, just past the Mammoth turn-off. The road was icy so Daddy had stopped to put on chains at Sherwin Grade. There were unplowed roads going off into the woods, but he parked at the edge of the pavement so we wouldn't get stuck.

As we walked into the trees, the snow muffled the sound of vehicles on the highway, and I felt like I was in an enchanted forest. It was a silent, white world. The firs were elegant in their snowy coats. Then a scolding jay broke the silence.

Daddy asked, "How do you like this one, Mary?"

And Mama said, "Let's look at that one up the hill," and then, "No, I think the tall one over there is better."

They were red fir, straight and symmetrical, and they all looked perfect to me. After much consideration, Mama found the right tree,

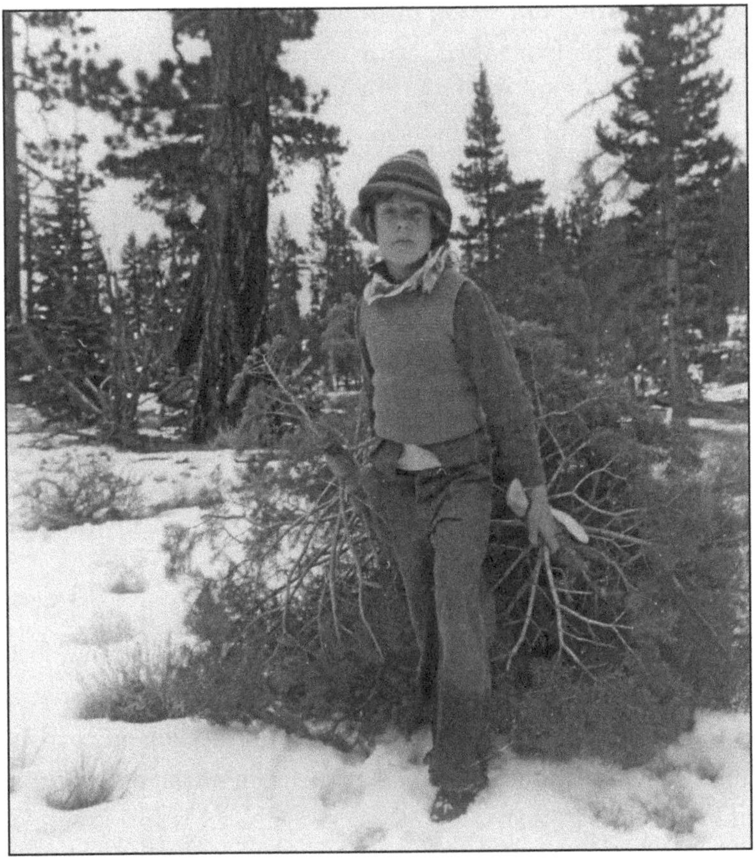

Cutting Christmas trees, 1942.

and Daddy sawed it down. We also cut trees for our aunts and uncles in southern California, which meant going through the selection process many times. Then we dragged the trees through the snow back to the car to load after lunch.

Mama brought chili in one of our thermos jugs, hot apple cider in another, and a tin of oatmeal cookies. We were cold by the time lunch was over and we had tied down the trees on the trailer.

Our 1937 Plymouth had no heater, so it was a chilly ride home for the driver. The rest of us took off our wet shoes and snuggled under blankets. Daddy drove home wearing his fur-lined gloves on his feet. His feet stayed warm in the car, and when we stopped for gas in Bishop, Joan giggled, "He walks like a duck!"

After making a stand for our tree, Daddy climbed into the attic through the trap door in the closet ceiling to retrieve the cardboard box with the Maxwell Coffee trademark on each side. Joan and I unwrapped each precious ornament. There were the red and blue bugles, the little angels, and the delicate glass balls. All were special, even the very odd star for the top of the tree that Aunt Jean had given us years ago. One of her many art projects, it was made from a tin can using tin snips.

When the lights were strung and ornaments hung, it was time for the tinsel. The heavy shiny strips hung straight down from the ends of the branches, and Mama was particular about how each strand was placed on the upturned needles. When we were young she had left that part until after Joan and I were in bed.

The annual school Christmas program was a highlight for the whole town. The lower grades sang, the upper grades danced, the band played, and the audience joined in singing carols. It was a big job for the elementary school music teacher to organize it all.

The program was always held in the Legion Hall. The stage and backstage rooms were cold and drafty, so more than one child went out on stage absent-mindedly wearing a jacket over a skimpy costume. I was one of those kids. Mama and Daddy must have been dismayed when I came on stage for the finale wearing my red plaid coat over my sprite costume.

The Dance of the Sprites was unforgettable. The mothers were responsible for making the costumes, and Mama had made two because Joan and I were both in the fifth/sixth grade room that year. When she went to Lone Pine to buy the white material, Mama chose the wrong fabric. It was wrong only because it was different from the white fabric the rest of the moms chose, and Joan was forever embarrassed. I didn't notice the difference and couldn't understand why it should matter.

The girls in our classroom were thrilled to be Sprites. Barbara Yandell was so enthralled with her costume that she wore it home after the dress rehearsal. It was a frigid and windy day and Barbara lived at the dairy, in the very last house in town. Wanting to appear as a lovely Sprite all the way home, she didn't wear her coat and hat. Sadly, she was sick in bed the night of the performance.

Mama talked for years about the night the younger girls in angel costumes were on the stage singing and holding lighted candles. One of them was so focused on the singing that she didn't notice how close her candle's flame was to the hair of the angel in front of her. The audience held its breath.

Santa Claus arrived at the end of the program, and standing next to the giant Christmas tree, he gave each child a mesh stocking filled with candy, nuts, and an orange. The little children were speechless when they saw a real live Santa.

But Christmas morning was the best time of all. There were presents under our beautiful tree, and our candy dish in its silver stand was on the end table by the couch, each of its three sections filled with a different kind of candy. Mama always made divinity fudge,

Aunt Belle's brown candy, and English toffee. And we could eat all we wanted, even before breakfast.

That evening, in spite of our wonderful day, it was sobering to realize that now it would be a whole year until the next Christmas.

Grandpa DeDecker

Joan

Our Grandpa Frank DeDecker shaved with a long straight-edged razor that he sharpened with a leather strap. I watched this process with fascination and asked him how leather could sharpen a metal edge. He told me, "The leather acts like very fine sandpaper." He used a round brush to lather his face below his eyes until it was completely white. Then he tilted his head to one side, steadied his chin with one hand, and pulled the long steel blade cleanly up one cheek. I was amazed to see how it removed the lather and whiskers and even more amazed that he didn't cut himself.

Grandpa was a short, friendly man who worked as a house painter. One summer, while he and Grandma visited us, he painted our bedroom and the whole outside of our house. Daddy told us that during the Depression his father was sometimes paid with property for his work, but since he couldn't afford to pay the taxes, he usually lost ownership. Still, he managed to earn enough money to "get by" and was always cheerful and hard working. He and Grandma lived next door to Aunt Jean's family in North Hollywood.

One day, when Carol and I were in our fifth/sixth-grade classroom, our teacher called us to her desk and said softly, "The school office called and said you girls are to go right home." We didn't ask why because we sensed that something was wrong. We rushed home and Mama soberly told us our Grandpa DeDecker had been fatally injured while walking along a street near his house. I hugged Daddy and said, "I am so sorry." Carol was unable to say anything. She said later that she just wanted to crawl under the bed.

Soon our family was on the way to North Hollywood. It was a quiet trip. We arrived to find Grandma lying on a bed in a darkened bedroom in Aunt Jean's house. I gave her a big hug, but I didn't know what to say.

Grandpa had been on his way to jury duty that foggy morning when a hit-and-run driver struck him. Daddy went to see his father's body and came back devastated. That night our family slept in Grandma and Grandpa's bedroom, and I'll never forget the sound of Daddy sobbing in the night, "How can I get along without my father?" I had never heard him cry before. It had never occurred to me that adults still needed their parents.

While arrangements were being made for the funeral, Aunt Jean suggested that Carol and I visit our cousin's school. Sydney Ann was in fourth grade. To reach her school, the three of us walked several blocks on busy streets to the streetcar tracks. Carol and I nervously climbed aboard the streetcar, and Sydney Ann helped us figure out how to pay the fare. I was impressed with her confidence, but I wondered if she really could find her way home.

At school, the teacher questioned our presence, but when she read Aunt Jean's note about Grandpa she was kind to us. The number of students in the enormous school was especially noticeable at recess when dozens of boys and girls ran and played on the asphalt schoolyard. Lunch in a cafeteria with trays and long tables was another new experience; the kids at our school all walked home for lunch.

Mama wasn't sure that Carol and I should attend the funeral. It was our first experience with death, and I told Mama that I'd heard stories about children being asked to kiss a dead relative. Mama assured me that wouldn't happen. After telling us a little more about what a funeral was like, she left the decision to us. We chose to stay with a neighbor.

Daddy had to return to work, so late that afternoon we backed down the driveway and waved a final goodbye to our tearful Grandma. I heard Daddy quietly say to Mama, "I hope she will do all right without him."

During the long, sad drive it felt reassuring to hear the subdued drone of our parents' voices and to know we'd soon be home.

Penny Candy

Carol

When I started fifth grade, I was excited about being in the Annex classroom because now I was one of the big kids.

My enthusiasm didn't last long though. Our new teacher was boring, and it wasn't just my opinion. Joan, in the sixth grade and in the same classroom, quickly agreed. We felt that Mrs. Ragle had no patience, no imagination, and no sense of humor. Her favorite topic was Jenny Marie, her talented fourth-grade daughter who was smart, polite, and musical. We all tired of hearing about Jenny Marie, because none of us would ever live up to her achievements.

Joan and I moaned and groaned all year long, but Mama didn't offer any sympathy. She said, "You have been fortunate to have had outstanding teachers in the past, and you shouldn't expect every teacher to be as good. Mrs. Ragle appears to be an unhappy person and you should be understanding and cooperative."

So we tried.

Mrs. Ragle was one of those teachers who taught "by the book" to avoid real teaching. We were supposed to learn everything from the textbook or the workbook. When Joan felt stuck in math, she needed a teacher who could explain how to set up the story problems. Our history workbook had pages of small print sprinkled with a few black and white illustrations. It is no wonder that neither of us can remember much about our studies that year.

Although Mrs. Ragle told us art was her favorite subject, she did not seem creative. At Christmas, we asked to decorate our classroom and were surprised and thrilled when she suggested that we make red and green paper chains.

Joan, always an enthusiastic student, was having trouble staying motivated. Once, when Joan asked a question Mrs. Ragle snapped, "Young lady, if I don't teach you anything else, I hope to teach you not to interrupt!"

At that point Joan's attention began to wane, and she said, "Carol, I'm not going to raise my hand again all year."

I was also developing a bad attitude and didn't work as hard as I usually did. Near the end of the year, Tommy commented, "Carol, you aren't as smart as you used to be."

I didn't want to agree with him and said, "Tommy, it's just because school isn't fun anymore." And I didn't change my behavior.

Mrs. Ragle read to us every day after lunch, always choosing, in my opinion, a boring book. While she read, my challenge was to eat all of the penny candy I had bought at the drugstore on the way back to school after lunch. Up to now, I had liked school and adored my teachers, and never took candy to school. Mama would have been irate had she known, both because she didn't approve of candy and because I was eating it in class.

The next year, Joan moved up to seventh grade in the high school building, and the fifth and sixth-grade classroom had a new teacher. Miss Henke made school challenging. We began with the Norsemen and their explorations. We read books and made maps of their travels. Miss Henke hung our pictures of Viking ships above the blackboard. Next, we learned about the pioneers crossing the prairie in covered wagons. I was captivated by their adventures. Again we made maps and pictures to hang on the blackboard. I paid attention and enjoyed it all.

But as school was getting out one Friday afternoon just before Thanksgiving, Miss Henke told us she would be leaving our school and Independence. She thanked us for our attention and hard work. Her announcement was shattering. For me, she was a stimulating teacher who had reawakened my interest in school.

After school I ran all the way home and asked, "Mama, why is Miss Henke leaving?"

She said sadly, "Sometimes people in powerful positions make foolish decisions, often because they listen to the wrong people." Mama worked in the school principal's office now, and I knew she had more to say about the situation, but she wasn't going to discuss it with me.

On Monday, we met our new teacher, Mrs. Baxter. She probably had lived in Independence all of her life because there were many Baxters in town. Although she was kind and had a ready smile, she was a disappointment to me.

After a few days I asked, "Mama, is Mrs. Baxter a real teacher?"

She changed the subject without answering. Perhaps she didn't know.

I remember nothing about the rest of the year other than Mrs. Baxter reading books to us. It was entertaining, but she had the habit of changing the endings. Evidently she liked happy endings. Once, I'd already read the book, so I knew the Indians had captured the pioneer family and burned down their log cabin. But in Mrs. Baxter's version, the family hid in the root cellar so the Indians didn't find them and went away without burning down the cabin.

The year dragged on, and I started to eat penny candy again in class.

But just before the school year ended, one exciting thing happened. Mrs. Baxter told us that the small elementary school at the Fort was closing, and those students would be coming to our school next year. Getting new classmates was an event.

She said, "They will be coming to visit our school tomorrow morning and will be with us all day. If you can, bring your lunch to school so we can all eat together. And be friendly, the young ones may be nervous about coming to a bigger school. Be sure to invite them to join your games at recess."

We'd always had some Paiute students at our school because a number of families lived in town. Also, some non-Paiute families lived at the Fort, and their children attended the Fort elementary school. All Fort kids came to Independence for junior and senior high.

Mrs. Baxter told us, "Mrs. Bell, the Fort school teacher, is coming too and will be teaching first and second grade at our school next year." She went on to tell us that Mrs. Bell's ancestors had built the first flour mill in Owens Valley on Oak Creek, just above the Fort. But we were a lot more interested in the students.

They arrived during morning recess. Ten kids spilled out of the school bus and ran to the playground. The younger ones headed for the slides. I was disappointed that I didn't see any girls my age, but I watched a blonde boy and a Paiute boy on the swings. I hoped they'd be in my class. Sure enough, they came to our fifth /sixth-grade room after lunch. They would become my good friends in high school.

I learned several things during those two years in the Annex. One was that Mama was right when she said we'd often had exceptional teachers. Another was the fact that the quality of the teacher makes an enormous difference in a student's motivation. I felt I had missed a lot during those years. And I spent the summer wondering who would be teaching seventh grade.

Camp Chaparral

Joan

Carol and I rushed home from our Girl Scout meeting to tell Mama and Daddy all about it, each waving a brochure about Camp Chaparral.

"We've never been to a camp and it's in the redwoods and the school will let us take the school bus and Mrs. Mercer will drive . . ."

Camp Chaparral was expensive. Daddy said they would "think it over." Not a good sign. But Mama soon ordered the required "greenies"—shorts-and-shirts outfits—from the Girl Scout catalog and sewed duffel bags for our gear. Off we went one July morning, heading south on Highway 395, a dozen excited girls and two mother chaperones, one driving our little school bus. It must have looked like a giant yellow beetle waddling down the highway at the wartime speed limit of thirty-five miles per hour. Carol and I were eleven and almost thirteen and we'd never been on such a long trip. It took two days to drive around the Sierra Nevada and into the San Joaquin Valley to the Santa Cruz area.

As we approached Mojave, a small town 130 miles south of Independence, the bus had a flat tire. After some discussion, the moms realized that a City maintenance station was located nearby. Since Mrs. Mercer's husband worked for the City in Independence, the women decided to ask for help. The men at the maintenance garage agreed to repair the tire. It took some time, but eventually we were on our way again, grateful but behind schedule.

It was already dark when we reached Santa Maria, where a relative of Mrs. Mercer lived. Our sleeping bags were handy, and we slept on her front lawn.

On our way again the next morning, we began to see soldiers hitchhiking along the road. Mrs. Mercer told us they were soldiers on leave, returning to Camp Roberts, farther up the highway.

"Couldn't we give one of them a ride?" we asked. After all, it was wartime and "We have lots of empty seats." And "Everyone gives rides to soldiers." And, "Please!"

Mrs. Mercer finally agreed, and soon we pulled over to pick up a young soldier. He was friendly and talkative. When we stopped at a gas station, he bought pop for the girls and a beer for himself. Such a nice guy, we agreed. Back on the bus, the soldier chose to sit next to me. We girls quieted down, the bus slowly chugged along, and then I felt a hand on my bare thigh. I froze, hoping it would go away. I didn't know what to do. I waited, but still the hand stayed on my thigh. Finally, I got up my nerve to get up and move to another seat, and the soldier moved to sit by another girl. One of the girls got up and whispered in Mrs. Yandell's ear. Her head swiveled around and she glared at the soldier.

"You come and sit right next to me," she commanded. He did.

Mrs. Yandell had a whispered conference up front with Mrs. Mercer. She returned to her seat beside the soldier, and we continued on. It wasn't long before we spotted some barracks in the distance and a gate into the complex, and there we let off our hitchhiker.

Late in the afternoon, we reached the Santa Cruz Mountains where the bus wound through the hills, climbing until we saw our first redwood trees and, at last, the turnoff to Camp Chaparral. The director, an older woman called "Bear," greeted our group of tired girls. Mrs. Yandell and Mrs. Mercer assured us they would return to pick us up in two weeks, and then disappeared down the road in the yellow bus.

We were sorted into groups and led by counselors, with names like Mallard, Kinglet, and Cricket, to bed sites called "nests" among the ferns and redwood logs. Carol and I each shared a nest with a girl from Independence. There were paths leading to other bed sites, to the campfire ring, and to the kitchen area. My leader was Robin, a high school girl. She was kind and friendly and we were in awe of her.

Every morning started with a camp gathering at the flagpole led by Bear, and we sat beneath those tall redwood trees and learned many songs. It was my favorite part of the day. After breakfast, we chose an activity. During our stay, I made a lanyard and was pleased with my sketch of redwood bark. There was a swimming hole in the river, but the non-swimmers, which included most of the Independence girls, had to stay in the shallow area. Some evenings there were skits.

The girls my age were scheduled for a long hike one day. The younger girls, including Carol, didn't get to go. There was a lot of fussing around about poison oak and other hazards, but finally we hikers got under way. The flat, wide path that wound through the shady redwoods was far different from the rough, dry, and rocky Sierra trails. And unlike the open mountain vistas that I was used to, the green shrubs and thick forest blocked our view. We saw several kinds of ferns, moss, tall bay trees, and little white flowers. At a stream crossing, we stopped to admire the water skippers skimming across the dappled surface of a pool. Soon it was time for a snack and a drink of water, and then we were told that it was time to go back to camp. I couldn't believe we were already returning from what I considered to be a short walk. What a disappointment.

Each night, before bedtime, we gathered for more singing around the campfire, ending with one of the counselors playing taps on a trumpet. I shivered as those pure and plaintive notes echoed through the forest.

At the end of the two weeks, Mrs. Mercer and Mrs. Yandell reappeared in the yellow bus. It took just as long, two full days, for the drive home. In King City, we stopped at a public swimming pool to cool off, and again spent the night on someone's lawn. We girls were quiet and read comic books and chatted, and no one asked to pick up a hitchhiker.

Desert Country

Joan

During the war years, our family became active in the Desert Peaks Section of the Los Angeles Chapter of the Sierra Club. Most of the members were from the Los Angeles area, and they shared gas ration stamps and car-pooled in order to take weekend trips to the desert. It was a friendly and inclusive group, although Carol and I were usually the only children.

One spring, we climbed Coso and Maturango peaks, located near the desert town of Ridgecrest. This area was soon to be placed under navy jurisdiction and used for gunnery and weapons practice, so our hike was one of the last opportunities to see it for many years.

Our most northerly trip was to the Mono Craters, tall volcanic cones near LeeVining. They were composed of loose pumice cinders and had no trails. For each two steps up, we slid back one. At the top of the highest crater, we looked down on Mono Lake with its white alkaline shoreline. The lake was shrinking because the City was diverting water from the inlet streams into the aqueduct. Coming down the craters made up for the struggle of going up—we felt like deer leaping down the steep slope.

Our most ambitious hike was up Telescope Peak in the Panamint Range bordering Death Valley. It towers more than 11,000 feet above the floor of Death Valley. To reach the trailhead, we traveled beyond the row of historic charcoal kilns on a steep dirt road up Wildrose Canyon.

The road was a challenge for inexperienced drivers in the days before four-wheel drive vehicles. Daddy drove the car of a nervous trip member up a tricky section. The hike was a fourteen-mile round trip on a trail. I learned that at high elevations even the desert gets very cold and different and smaller plants grow there. On top, we looked west to the snow-covered Sierra and the highest point in the country, Mount Whitney. Directly below us to the east was salty and crusty Badwater, the lowest point at 282 feet below sea level.

On Cerro Gordo Peak, 1945.

Through these trips, we began to recognize and appreciate the diversity of the land called The Desert—colorful geologic layers with palettes of pinks, yellows, reds and blues, and canyons so narrow we could almost touch both sides. We visited the deep pit gouged by a meteorite, the natural springs that enabled early travelers and prospectors to survive in that harsh country, and were awed by hills covered with flowers after a rare rain.

By the time we reached our teen years, Carol and I knew that unexpected surprises could be seen on walks up an alluvial fan or a dry wash. Perhaps it was a colorful rock with veins and crystals, a spiny lizard sunning itself, or a delicate-looking lavender flower with an orange spot at the base of each of its five petals. We felt comfortable in the desert lands and appreciated the wild beauty as fully as we treasured the granitic Sierra.

Part Four

CHANGING TIMES
1945–1947

V-J Day at Bench Lake

Carol

The July sun was already hot when we started up the trail to Sawmill Pass. We had hiked the steep hillside before when we led old Silver, the mule, on our Fourth of July trips to Sawmill Lake. But today we were on our way to Bench Lake with the Swan family, each of us riding a horse! The packers were up ahead leading long strings of mules. Each time we reached the end of a switchback, Eddie Swan turned his baseball cap so the bill would shade his face.

It would be a two-day trip over Sawmill and Pinchot Passes with an overnight stop at Twin Lakes. We had planned to take the shorter one-day route over Taboose Pass, but Archie Dean told us, "That pass is too rough for my animals. I haven't been over it since the cloudburst took out part of the trail two years ago."

Mama grumbled, "He just wants more work for his packers," but Joan and I were thrilled to be spending two whole days on horseback. Archie was the new packer in town after Allie Robinson sold his business.

The Swans had brought two of their teenagers. Corky was nineteen and Eddie fifteen. Joan and I were thirteen and eleven. Like his father, Eddie was a fisherman. Joan and I weren't fond of him, and we once put a frog in his sleeping bag. But we idolized Corky. She was wise and pretty and amazingly tolerant of two girls who constantly teased her about her boyfriends. She seemed to have lots of them.

Bench Lake sits on a shelf about a thousand feet above the South Fork of the Kings River. It is larger and deeper than most Sierra lakes. The far shore was edged with talus slopes and cliffs while our side of the lake was mostly flat with foxtail pines and grass. Because we would be staying for two whole weeks, we took our time choosing a perfect camp. We wanted one with good bed sites and a view of Arrow Peak.

After unloading the mules, the packers left for home with all of the animals. Mama and Mrs. Swan set up their kitchen while the men went off to test the fishing.

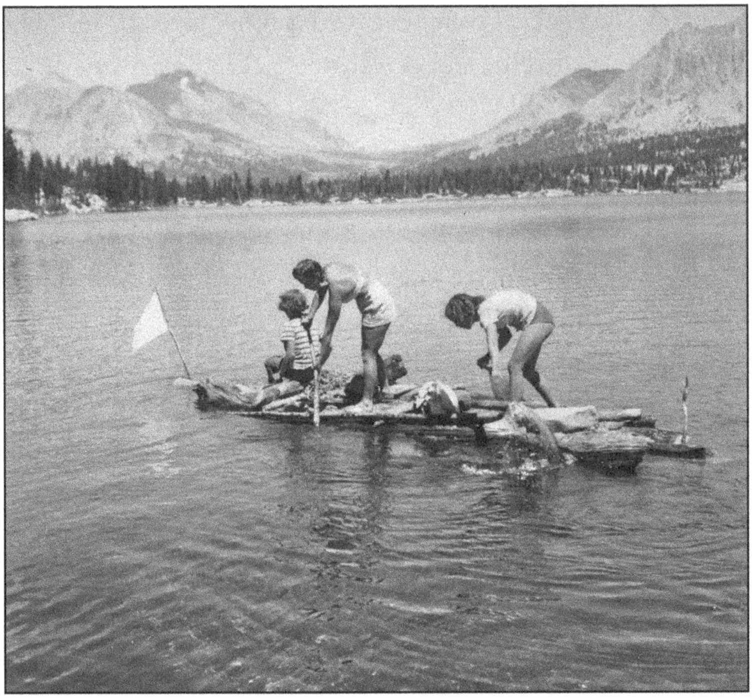

Carol, Corky, and Joan at Bench Lake, 1945.

They returned with exciting news—they had found an old log raft! Mr. Swan said, "After we add some more logs we can paddle out to those islands at the far end of the lake."

While they fished, the rest of us explored. We climbed to Cartridge Pass one day and to Mather Pass another day for views into distant basins. We lounged in the hammock strung between two pines, played cards, and read books. Sometimes we borrowed the fishermen's raft and paddled in the shallow bays. Corky always brought a favorite book to read aloud to Joan and me. That summer it was *Anne of Green Gables.*

After a few days, Art Reyman joined us. He was the backpacker Mama and Daddy had met on their third Sierra trip. In winter, he worked as a carpenter at Lake Tahoe, made woodcarvings, and wrote poetry. When the War started, he had tried to enlist in the army but was rejected because of a bad back. Now he spent every summer climbing Sierra peaks. We all enjoyed his infectious sense of humor. He often visited us before Christmas, arriving with an ingenious wood carving for each of us. One year, he brought me a wooden case to house my insect collection. The lid had carvings of crickets and dragonflies, painted with bright colors. As always, he was ready to make Christmas cookies with Joan and me.

When Art went off to climb Arrow Peak early one morning, he told us, "I'll yodel from the summit exactly at noon."

It looked like a difficult climb. We heard his call and saw him on the 12,958-foot summit, right on time. Art couldn't understand why our family didn't climb more mountains, and each summer he wrote detailed directions for the peaks we would see. Although we did climb a few, Dad preferred to fish and Mama was engrossed with the alpine flowers. By now she could identify many of them, but she found endless new ones.

We thought Art probably knew the mountains as well as the legendary Norman Clyde, the mountain man of the Sierra Nevada.

They both were making numerous first assents. During the war, Clyde was well known for finding military planes that had crashed while crossing the Sierra in winter storms. He often guided rescue parties to the site. We sometimes ran into him, and this year, when we met him near the top of Pinchot Pass, he said, "Mary, I have a plant to show you. Maybe you can tell me what it is."

Joan and I watched with fascination as he held his enormous pack upside down and gave it a good shake. Out came sooty pots, bags of food, books, extra boots, and dirty socks. And finally he found the flower that had caught his attention. It was a new one for Mama, and she made some notes for its identification at home.

One day, we all hiked down to the Kings River where it was easy to catch small rainbows in the deep pools between the cascades. It was the kind of fishing Joan and I liked because we could expect a bite on every cast.

At the trail junction, we met a backpacker and asked him for news of the War. "I heard something about a new kind of bomb," he said.

We asked questions, but he didn't know the details.

At the end of their weeklong vacation, the Swans hiked out over Taboose Pass. Our family accompanied them to the top early that morning. The sole had come off one of Mr. Swan's boots on our hike down to the river, so he left camp that morning wearing his bedroom slippers. Familiar with the rough trail down the canyon, Dad mused all day, "I wonder how Ned's slippers are holding up."

Art went off to climb more peaks, and our family enjoyed a second week at Bench Lake. When we were fishing at Marjorie Lake, a packer told us the United States had dropped bombs on Japanese cities and perhaps Japan would surrender.

On our last day, we too walked out over Taboose Pass. Archie would bring our camping equipment the next week when his packers were in the Bench Lake area. Taboose Canyon is short and steep,

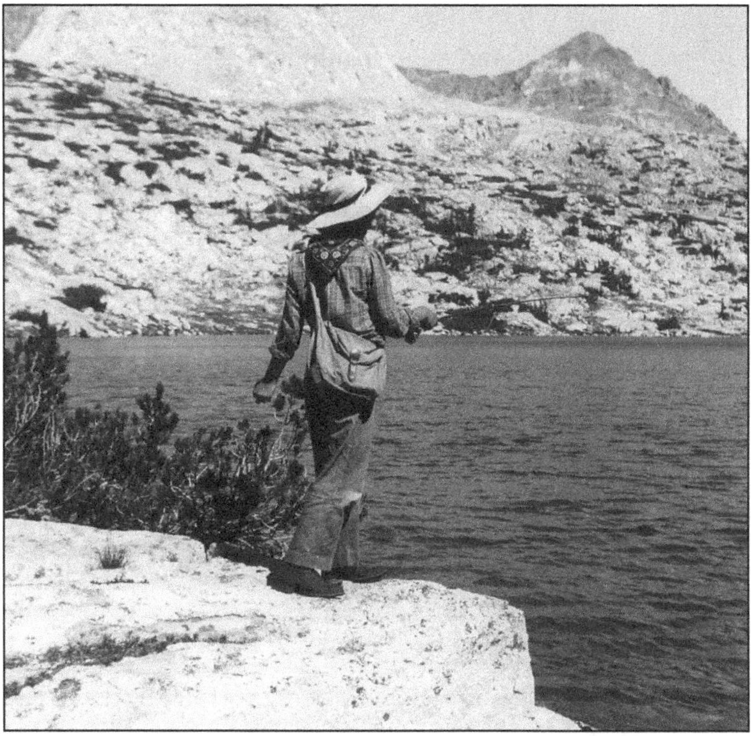

Carol fishing at Lake Marjorie on V-J Day, 1945.

dropping 6,000 feet in six miles. The recent cloudburst had washed away parts of the trail and as we scrambled across the gullies, Mama had to admit, "Archie is right, this route is too rough for his animals."

As we dropped down the rocky canyon, we talked about what we had liked best about the trip. This was the first time we'd been packed into the mountains to spend two weeks at a base camp. Always before, Dad had saddled the horses and packed the mules.

He said, "Well, I liked not having to worry about the animals. Getting packed in here for a base camp was a good idea.

Joan added, "I liked having Corky come." I like her sense of humor, she's always laughing."

Mama said, "What I liked best was having the Swans and Art here for the first week, and then spending the second week with just our family. Both weeks were just right."

"What I liked best was riding that horse for two days and paddling around on the raft and having Art come and hiking down to the river," I said.

It had been a memorable trip, but we were happy to see Sammy Griggs' yellow car parked at the end of the dirt road far below. He was Dad's good friend and often drove us to one trailhead and picked us up at another. We hurried in anticipation of the cold drinks and watermelon we knew Sammy would bring.

Tired and thirsty, we sprawled out on the ground in the sagebrush. I was drinking root beer as I listened to Sammy relate the town gossip. Even in a small town much transpires in two weeks. The Johnsons' dog had died. Old Mr. White ran into a fence on the way to the dump. The electricity was off for half a day.

I was comfortable and sleepy listening to the drone of the conversation as Dad described our trip to Sammy.

"The base camp idea was a good one . . ."

"Those big rainbows in Bench Lake aren't easy to catch . . ."

"Taboose Pass is as rough as ever . . ."

When he said, "I told Archie to bring our gear to town when it's convenient because I don't want him to waste gas on an extra trip," Sammy exclaimed, "I guess you haven't heard the news? The war is over! And so is gas rationing!"

We sat up and listened as Sammy told us about the atomic bombs at Hiroshima and Nagasaki. On V-J Day, August 15, 1945, we had been fishing at Marjorie Lake, oblivious of the terrible power of the new kind of bomb and the nationwide celebration of the end of the War.

No More War and No More Rationing!

Carol

V-J day was glorious news. No more casualties and no more sad stories on the radio. As a family, we knew we were the lucky ones. We were never in peril, we lost no relatives, and we had plenty to eat. Even as children, Joan and I could feel that our country was united during the War. Everyone pulled together and proudly supported our troops. This was easy to see in our small town with our savings bonds, paper drives, victory gardens, and Meatless Tuesdays.

We were happy to see the end of gas rationing, but shortages of some kinds of food and other items lasted longer. Our family especially welcomed the eventual return of real leather shoes and boots. The wartime cardboard shoes were tolerable for school and work, but they were never satisfactory for hiking.

There was a flurry of activity in Owens Valley. Men returning from the military needed places to live, and there was not enough housing. Manzanar was closing, and the last Japanese internees left in November 1945. Some of the barracks were moved and converted into apartments in nearby towns, but others were torn down for lumber. The officers' quarters were of better quality than the internee barracks, and those units were rented out for some years. Dad bought a building from the pig farm and had it moved to our backyard where he used one room for storage and the other as a workshop.

There was a huge demand for everything—lumber, construction materials, household appliances, automobiles, and tires. Everyone waited impatiently while factories changed from producing airplanes and war materials to making cars and washing machines.

We had driven our 1937 Plymouth throughout the war years. Dad went to Bishop right away to put his name on the list for a new car, but it took time to get to the top of the list. Several years later, after a shopping trip to Bishop, he came into the house and said, "Joan and Carol, you girls go bring the groceries in from the car." As we went out the back door we saw a shiny gray 1949 Ford in the driveway.

The next week, when we were planning to drive up a dirt road to a Sierra trailhead. Sammy said, "Paul, you don't want to scratch up the sides of your new car in the sagebrush. I'll drive you up." And he did.

Changing Times

Joan

As a partial solution to the lack of storage space in our house, Mama ordered a cardboard cupboard from Sears. She assembled and placed it in a corner of her bedroom and joyfully filled it with linens and clothing. Later in the day, she hung a freshly ironed blouse in the cupboard, and as she turned away, the cupboard gave an ominous creak. Then it leaned s-l-o-w-l-y to one side and collapsed.

"Oh, damn it!" Mama exclaimed. "Damn it! Damn it! Damn it!" and she cried in frustration.

"I'm tired of trying to take care of things without enough storage. It's impossible!" She continued on and on.

What had seemed like a roomy house when we moved in ten years ago now felt cramped and crowded. Our only closet was overflowing with clothes for the four of us. As the years went by, Carol and I wore bigger sizes, and as our activities increased, so did the items to be squeezed into our one closet.

Mama's pursuits were also expanding. When she heard the school needed a part-time secretary, she studied shorthand in hopes of getting the job. When she got it, she had less time for sewing, cleaning, and ironing. Instead of making clothing for Carol and me, most of her projects consisted of mending or making canvas bags for our camping equipment.

She was becoming increasingly engrossed in botany. She was thrilled when she purchased a copy of Willis L. Jepson's *A Manual of the Flowering Plants of California*, for the huge sum of eleven dollars. It was the first comprehensive plant identification book of the California flora, and it included many drawings in 1,238 pages, a big fat book! It wasn't long until Mama learned that even Jepson didn't know all the plants she found in the Inyo-Mono area, so she began to correspond with botanists who might have the information she needed. They wrote back, eager to update their knowledge and exchange plant specimens, and in this manner she began numerous botanical-based friendships.

Dad encouraged her and helped with her plant collecting. As we drove a mountain route, Mama scanned the hillsides and road cuts. "Oh, what's that? Stop, Paul, will you, and back up a little," she would say. He was patient and kept a pair of leather gloves under the car seat for dealing with plants such as the Prickly Poppy. He made a plant press for her specimens. Years later, he built a row of cupboards in the garage for her growing collection. Late in her life, she donated 6,400 specimens to the herbarium at Santa Ana Botanical Garden in Claremont, California.

Many evenings after an outing, we girls would go to bed leaving Mama at the dining room table examining specimens with pen and paper, tweezers and handkerchief at hand. She would sneeze and sneeze while peering intently at parts of a flower through her hand lens. Even at the peak of hay-fever season, she couldn't resist going out to gather a perplexing specimen.

During our years at home, Mama's focus was on botany, but she also read the histories of old mines and town sites in Inyo and Mono counties. She identified birds and studied geology. Perhaps it was the interconnections of these topics that led her to become an environmentalist. In spite of her growing range of interests, while we were growing up she was our Mama whose primary concerns were her family and her community.

Dad kept just as busy. In the early years, when he wasn't at his City office, he was usually working in the yard. There were flowerbeds to weed and loads of fertilizer to haul from the dairy. Until I looked at old photos, I had not realized that he had turned an almost barren yard into a lovely garden.

Years before, he had a building moved from the Eight Mile Ranch to our backyard and converted it into a garage. He built a trailer to haul garden supplies and for trips to the dump, and he added a shed to the back of the house for storing our camping equipment.

For years, he made improvements on the house. He painted rooms, added glass windows to the screened front porch, installed a new water heater, and replaced the wood stove with a coal-oil stove that had copper coils for heating water. Dad improved the house and yard so much that the rent for our City-owned house was increased from $18 to $22 a month. He was indignant.

Our parents discussed moving into a larger place, but Dad didn't want to create another garden or continue improving a house he didn't own. Carol and I were spending less time in our yard, and he wanted to do less gardening.

So we had to make the best of it. Mama had always wanted each of us to have our own bedroom. That was impossible, so she had another idea. Why not move Carol's bunk bed to the front porch and turn half of the porch into a tiny bedroom? I would remain in our current room.

We liked our bunk beds in spite of our earlier window wars. The beds had been placed next to a tall window. The bottom half of the window could be raised and the top half pushed down, and we both wanted more than our share of fresh air. The issue was resolved when we measured precisely and Carol scratched grooves in the casing, so in the dark we could each feel whether the other one had exceeded her half.

Carol's bed was moved to the front porch. When I asked, "But how does Carol feel about sleeping out there?" Mama reassured me that this was what Carol wanted to do. Years later, Carol told me how much she had disliked sleeping on the front porch, "Because everyone who came to the front door walked through my bedroom and because it was so cold in the winter." But she considered it better than sharing a tiny bedroom with four doors, one window, and too much furniture. She didn't complain because when she came home from babysitting on cold winter nights she would find that Mama had put a hot-water bottle in her bed.

In spite of its limitations, our house was something we had to live with. We wondered how large families managed in this town of small homes.

The Inscrutable Mr. Storz

Carol

The new seventh and eighth-grade teacher spent the first two days walking back and forth at the front of the classroom, arms folded, looking at us without saying a word. I wondered what he was thinking. Was it, "How am I going to make these kids behave?" Or perhaps, "Why did I take this job in this strange little town?" Possibly it was, "How am I going to teach six subjects to twenty-six students in two grades?" The students were also silent those two days, even ever-ebullient Bobby Bay.

Mr. Storz had a commanding presence. He was tall and slim, wore a dark blue suit and a gray necktie. His gray hair stood up in a crew cut. When he finally began talking, the students listened. There was never a discipline problem in his classroom during his three years at our school. I soon forgot my apprehension about starting seventh-grade in the high school building and having a male teacher after six years with kind and comfortable female teachers. The inscrutable Mr. Storz was a fascinating change.

The seventh and eighth-grades were together in a west room of the high school building with the five tall front windows facing the Sierra escarpment. Mr. Storz said, "That is a stunning view, and to be fair to those of you who'd like to sit by the windows, we will change desks each week. On Fridays, just before the last bell rings, you'll move your desk contents to the desk in front of you."

So we spent the school year rotating around the room and looking forward to our weeks by the front windows. Bobby Bay was the only one who did not rotate. Mr. Storz wanted Bobby's desk within reach of his rubber-tipped pointer so he could tap it to get Bobby's attention. I thought it was unfair, but Bobby said, "I like it because I can see the blackboard better."

In science, we did experiments. Our first assignment was to answer the question, "Can a metal burn?" Mr. Storz brought in a Bunsen burner from the chemistry lab and we all had a turn at holding a narrow strip of manganese in the flame with tweezers. We watched as it caught fire and turned to ash. The empirical answer was, "Manganese is a metal that will burn." We wrote our reports on graph paper and they included: Objective, Materials, Method, Results, Conclusions, and Illustration. I was enthusiastic because it felt like real science.

When we studied the Revolutionary War, we held a Continental Congress with each student representing one of the thirteen colonies. We discussed our grievances with King George III and argued about whether or not we should revolt and go to war. After the war, we studied the United States Constitution and nominated candidates for President. With our posters and banners, we paraded around the school and gave speeches from the front steps.

Mr. Storz thought speaking was important, so we gave endless social studies reports in front of the class. I still remember Bobby's impassioned speech about Teddy Roosevelt leading his Rough Riders up San Juan Hill. Mr. Storz encouraged Arlene to enter a speech contest. After school, he stood under the elm tree behind the school with his arms folded. He listened to her deliver her speech from the back porch in her loud clear voice, over and over again. Although she was the youngest contestant, Arlene won the regional speech contest in Lone Pine.

Mr. Storz did not talk much, but he was an unusually effective teacher. With few words he held our attention. I had not put out much effort in the fifth and sixth grades, but in Mr. Storz' class I sat up and listened. I don't know if he inspired other students as much as he did me, but I believe he influenced the outcome of my education.

Junior high and high school teachers, Mr. Storz with the hat, 1945.
(See Appendix for names)

Snow Banners

Joan

Dad tapped the glass cover, looked carefully at the dial and commented, "The barometer's falling. Looks like we're in for a change." The brass case was round like a clock and designed to look like a six-handled wheel of a sailing ship. Mama had given it to him for a special birthday, and it was something he treasured. After he tapped the glass, he moved the red indicator arrow over the black barometer needle so he could note a change in pressure.

For many years, Dad had observed the direction of the wind and the types of clouds as he watched the storms come and go, so he generally knew what would happen next. Mama claimed the barometer knew when she had just cleaned house. When the pressure fell, the wind blew hard and deposited a layer of fine sand on each windowsill. "Wouldn't you know it!" she would complain.

Before a storm front arrived, the south wind stirred up the dust from dry Owens Lake and blew it north up the valley. The view to the south disappeared in the haze, and we could smell the dust. People who lived closer to the lake, in Lone Pine, Olancha, or Keeler, often had breathing problems. Everyone knew that Owens Lake used to be a real lake with deep water. The silver bullion hauled down from the Cerro Gordo mines in the Inyo Mountains was transported across the lake by boat. After the City began diverting the local streams into the aqueduct, Owens Lake dried up, leaving a shoreline of white alkali.

The strongest winds blew in spring and fall, and on several occasions a shed roof in town tore loose, scattering shingles and pieces of corrugated siding. It wasn't a good time to be on the highway as flying sand could pit the windshield and damage the entire paint job of a vehicle. Large trucks were required to pull off the highway until the wind lessened, especially in the area between Lone Pine and Owens Lake.

Carol and I were accustomed to the wind whipping around our bare legs on the way to school and blowing our hair straight back. Riding horseback on a windy day wasn't at all relaxing because the noise and rolling tumbleweeds made a horse jittery.

The Sierra peaks snagged the storms that blew in from the Pacific Ocean and lifted the clouds, causing them to deposit their moisture on the western slopes. As a result, the eastern side received little precipitation. Owens Valley and the Inyo Mountains were in the rain shadow. Rainfall of any amount was longed for and celebrated in our town that recorded only four to six inches a year. Even a spattering of drops made the sagebrush smell deliciously fragrant. A good winter storm ensured a crop of spring wildflowers, and the desert became a flower garden.

Summers were dry and hot and the temperature often rose to over one hundred degrees. If we were brave enough to cross an asphalt street while barefoot, we had to run to the nearest shade to avoid burning the bottoms of our feet. Carol and I spent the hottest days playing in the creek or reading on our cots on the screened front porch. It was a dry heat and the temperature dropped quickly when the sun set behind the Sierra.

Summer thunderstorms over the Sierra usually took several days to build. Each day, the cumulous clouds appeared earlier and grew higher until Dad looked up at the peaks above town and commented, "Well, it looks like the folks at Rae Lakes are going to get wet this afternoon." Most of the moisture fell in the mountains, and only rarely did the valley get more than a few drops.

One storm was an exception. The thunder crashed nearby, too close in my opinion, but Mama assured me we were safe inside the house. Then there was an even louder boom, and lightning struck a power pole in our alley. The lights went out and the rain came down in sheets. Soon it was over.

As the fall days grew shorter, Dad kept track of the lower temperatures on his thermometer, on the alert for a weather change. Finally, the barometer fell, usually in September, and we had the first storm of the season. When it cleared, we could see a dusting of white on the peaks. Some years it melted, and we continued to have perfect autumn weather, but by late October or early November, winter came to the Sierra.

A snow day, 1944.

With each storm, the snow extended farther down the mountains. After a big system passed, the ground was white from our front door to the top of the peaks. Even the Inyos had a white frosting. Some storms brought a special treat. The following morning, with the clouds gone and the sky a bright blue, the wind whipped the powdery snow from the jagged white peaks and across the sky. With awe and elation, we whispered, "Snow banners!"

Mama's Worries

Joan

Over the years, Mama had stopped worrying about the fishpond and the creek. She knew we were careful about crossing the highway and were no longer fascinated by the rock crusher. As with most mothers, new concerns took their place.

She had long been uneasy about our inability to swim, and like all children, we were attracted by water. Wartime gas rationing made lessons almost impossible for us and other kids, as the closest swimming pool was thirty-eight miles away. So when Carol and her third-grade classmate, Myra Lee, disappeared at the fish hatchery, everyone was worried.

Mama had driven Carol up to spend the night, which was exciting because Myra Lee's family lived in the fish hatchery tower. The next morning, the girls had read books on the lawn for a while, then played around the ponds and fed the fish. After climbing on the granite boulders below the parking lot, they couldn't think of anything else to do. So they set off to walk the two miles across the desert to Independence to see if Barbara could play, forgetting to tell Myra Lee's mother. When Mrs. Pollet couldn't find the girls, she became frantic and considered having the ponds dragged. Finally, she drove to our house to ask if we'd seen them. About then, Carol and Myra Lee strolled through the front gate wondering what all the fuss was about. Myra Lee was not allowed to play with Carol for a long time, which Carol felt was unfair. She said it was equally Myra Lee's fault.

The next summer, Mama took a group of Campfire Girls to Flower Lake to camp for several days. We hiked two steep miles above Onion Valley while mules carried our food and gear. Before we left the parking lot, Mama had given us a talk about "staying together" on the trail and "not running ahead." But the girls were slow hikers and Carol was impatient. The rest of us arrived at Flower Lake to see Carol and Marilyn Kemp on a waterlogged raft. The wind had already blown them to the middle of the lake. Too late, Carol thought to take off her new shoes. She attempted to throw them to shore, but one had landed in the lake. I've never known if Mama was more upset about her non-swimming daughter being on the unstable raft or the loss of a precious shoe. Years later, when I asked that question, she gave a little snort and said, "Both! Those real leather shoes were the best we'd seen since the beginning of the War."

It was time Carol and I learned to swim. As soon as school was out the next spring, Mama organized a group of mothers to take turns driving a carload of us to Keough's Hot Springs for lessons. It was the closest pool, but not ideal. The class was too large and the water too warm. I didn't learn to swim until many years later. Carol learned to dogpaddle in the City sand traps, the ponds designed to settle sand from the creeks before the water entered the aqueduct. Local people sometimes used the ponds to swim or fish ignoring the "Keep Out" signs.

Mama never would have admitted her worry about the men who lived in the "Jungle." It was located across the creek from the cemetery and consisted of a half dozen wood and tin shacks. Most of the men were old prospectors or World War I veterans with pensions. During the day, they walked uptown to the Independence Hotel where they could order a sandwich or a drink at the bar. In winter, they sat near the big iron stove and played poker with the new City employees. Experienced employees refused to join the old experts. A few of them rented a room in the hotel during the coldest months. In spring and fall, they sat on sunny benches on the sidewalk in front of the hotel, talking and watching the townspeople go by. On hot summer, days they walked to the shady park near the courthouse.

Mama was in a bit of a bind because she wanted us to respect these men. She would say, "You are not to go down where they live and bother them." But she was also a little wary because they came and went, and she didn't know them all. One was called "Free Wheeling" because his arms swung convulsively when he walked and his legs weren't much better. Mama said he had damaged his nervous system by drinking "canned heat" (Sterno) during Prohibition. She knew him well enough to stop to chat, and he sometimes visited the Antons who lived across the side street. I've often thought the Jungle living situation was better than many present-day alternatives. The men had independence and privacy in their tiny homes, and they also had a kind of clubhouse in the hotel bar, friends, and a town to observe.

Mama protested loudly against the caves we dug down the creek and out in the sagebrush. Inspired by the foxholes from World War II newsreels, we turned them into "caves" by putting boards across the top and shoveling gravel to camouflage the boards. We "had" to light candles, we told Mama, "so we can see," and we hauled down cups and water and snacks. She was afraid they might collapse and we would suffocate. To tell the truth, we discovered the caves were great fun to build and stock with supplies, but after they were completed we lost interest.

There were new worries during our high school years as we began to date and go to parties. Mama had a strong moral compass, but she wasn't good at discussing the delicate topic of sex. After Carol started going out with Boyd, Mama frequently reminded her that drinking alcohol "can lead to behavior that one wouldn't normally engage in." Boyd came at the beginning of his junior year, sent by his mother to finish high school away from his city school. He lived across the street with the Williams family and was in Carol's class. When we saw him smoking behind the school hedge, we wondered if he would be a bad influence. Actually, he was friendly and enthusiastic and a good addition to our school.

A different kind of concern, during our high school years, was the lack of cultural opportunities in Owens Valley. Would the high school classes adequately prepare us for college? College! It was clear to us by now how much our parents valued education. When Dad had graduated from high school in 1925, he was expected to go out and get a job. Likewise, Mama's family could not provide her the encouragement or financial support needed to attend college. Times were hard in the late 1920s.

As was true of most of their local friends, our parents didn't have college degrees, but they had the habits of educated people. They read the newspaper, listened to the news on radio, used the library, supported the town's children, and were active in their community and the valley. When Mama said she didn't want to pressure us to attend college, we just smiled to ourselves and thought, *not much!*

Mama probably had worries that she didn't share with us. But she never nagged, and never made us feel guilty. I think she empathized with our love of adventure but also wanted us to be safe. Because our parents were strict and fair, we always knew our limits, except for Carol's occasional lapses. And she said she did only what she felt was logical and reasonable.

Winnedumah

Carol

Winnedumah is a tall granite boulder standing upright on the crest of the Inyo Mountains. From Independence, almost ten miles away, I always thought that it looked like a peg pounded into the ridge top.

According to Paiute legend, the rock is named for Winnedumah, a Paiute Medicine Man and brother of the great Chief Tinemaha. When shot with an arrow during a battle with invading Indians, Winnedumah turned to stone and remains on the Inyo crest to watch over his people.

Winnedumah had intrigued Mama for almost ten years before she declared, "It's time to hike up there for a closer look."

She talked to local folks and learned that Barrel Springs, in Mazourka Canyon, was the best place to start because we could follow an old mining trail for the first few miles. She and Dad studied the topographic map to select the best route from there. After they announced their plan, Mama said, "Let's invite the Noyes to go with us."

The Noyes family had come to town at the beginning of the school year. Mr. Noyes was a high school teacher. His son was in my fifth/sixth-grade classroom, and his daughter was in high school. They had come from Maine and felt that Owens Valley was at the end of the earth. They had never seen sagebrush before. Joan and I were fascinated with their Maine accent.

Our family befriended them, invited them to dinner, and took them on occasional outings. Mr. Noyes and the kids were enthusiastic about the hike, but Mrs. Noyes was definitely not interested in taking a closer look. She said, "Why would I want to hike way up there when I can see Winnedumah from town?"

We set out on a warm April day with lunch, snacks, and what we thought was plenty of water. Each of us carried a canteen, and Dad and Mr. Noyes carried two. The Inyos have no streams and few springs, so we would have only the water with us.

Above Barrel Springs, we followed the trail up several reddish hills and over ledges of broken and twisted rocks. These folded and faulted layers have long attracted prospectors, and we saw test pits and tunnels, scraps of metal, wood, and rusty pipes. We followed bits of the old trail for several steep miles until it ended at the top of a ridge. From there, the route we chose proved to be a good one past hillsides and ravines with ancient-looking pinyon trees and great piles of enormous granite boulders.

By noon, we realized we had not brought enough water. Hot and thirsty, we were looking for a shady lunch spot when we spotted a snow patch on the north side of a boulder pile. It was about the size of our fishpond, plenty to fill our canteens now and also on the way back.

Seeing Winnedumah up close was worth the effort. It is one smooth, solid and stately rock, said to be eighty feet tall. As we rested in the shade of a pinyon tree, we marveled at the chances that such a gigantic rock would arrive at its present position, not only upright but exactly on the crest of the Inyos.

"I wonder why it doesn't tip over," Joan said.

Mr. Noyes replied, "That's what I was wondering. It must extend underground a very long way to hold up what is above ground. Maybe what we see is like the tip of an iceberg."

Our family hiked to Winnedumah many times, but it wasn't until later trips that I realized it was a hike through history. Looking down on Owens Valley, we could see the aqueduct and other evidence of recent water-collection actions of the City. Prospectors had searched the canyons for valuable minerals for more than a century, and the

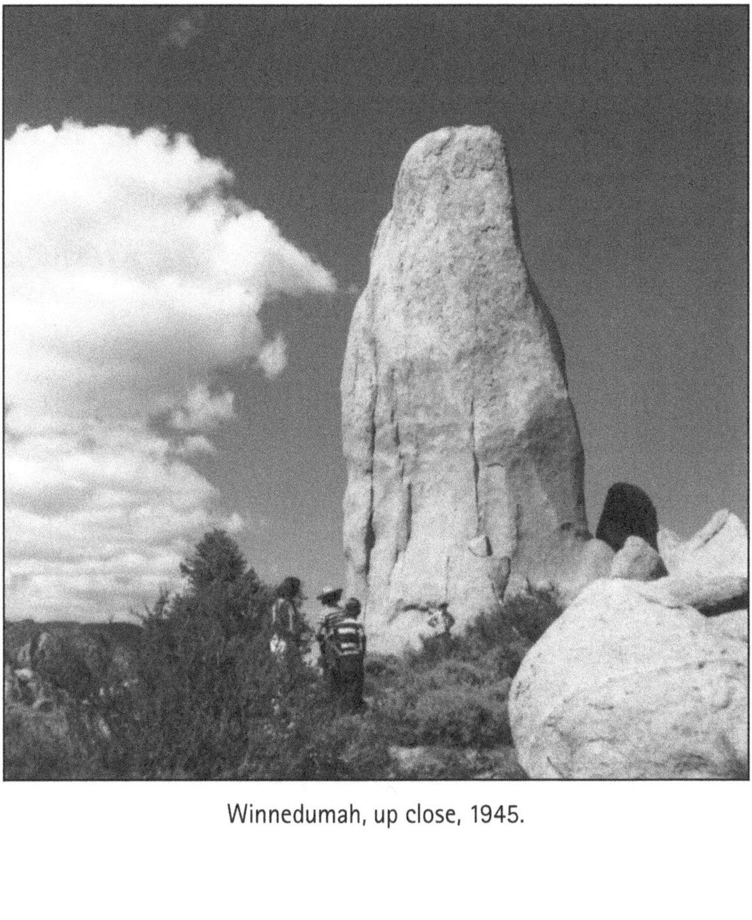

Winnedumah, up close, 1945.

Paiutes had collected pine nuts from these groves of pinyons for hundreds of years.

Over the years, our hikes to Winnedumah began to feel like a pilgrimage. Just as that finger of granite is the Medicine Man of the Paiutes, it is also a spiritual symbol to others who live in Owens Valley—to those who know and love the land of the Paiutes and to those who need to hike up to the crest for a closer look.

Dinner Club

Joan

Mama was setting the table for Dinner Club. I couldn't see how she would fit twelve people around it, even with all of the extra leaves in place. I helped her spread the white linen cloth over a soft fabric pad and set out the silverware while she arranged the candles and flowers. The cloth napkins were carefully ironed. The roast in the oven would be served with mashed potatoes and gravy and green beans. Others would bring the salad and dessert.

Dinner Club was a monthly social event that had begun two years before we moved to Independence. Dad and Mama had often been invited to substitute for absent members, but when the Savages moved away, our parents were asked to take their place. The group limited itself to six couples because no more could be squeezed into their homes.

Well before the guests arrived, Carol and I ate our supper, gathered our books and games and moved into our parents' back bedroom for the evening. It was also a special occasion for us because we loved spreading out on their double bed.

As the guests placed their coats on our bunk beds, most of them stuck their heads into the back bedroom to tell us "hello." We considered them to be our friends too. The woman who brought dessert usually brought Carol and me a serving.

After dinner, the women washed the dishes while the men smoked cigars and told jokes in the living room. The leaves were removed from the dining room table and two card tables were put up in the living room to make three tables of bridge. Carol and I could hear them bid their hands. We wondered what was so funny about "five no-trump" or "seven hearts," because those words were always followed by gales of laughter. There were prizes for the winners, but Carol and I had fallen asleep by then.

After our parents joined in about 1938, the Dinner Club membership changed remarkably little, and for the next thirty-eight years only three couples were replaced with new members. The group seemed to represent a cross-section of the town. The husbands worked for the City (as engineers, mechanics, or office workers) or the County (as a highway patrolman, county supervisor, or sheriff), while three owned local businesses—the hardware store, the grocery store, and a gas station. Most of the women stayed at home until their children were grown, after which some of them took jobs—as schoolteacher, school secretary, librarian, or store clerk. After forty-three years, the aging group sadly disbanded in 1976.

All the couples had children and were involved in school and civic events. All but Dad and Mama, and one other couple, were members of the Eastern Star or Masons. Most attended the local Methodist Church and were Republicans. Still, they all got along and treasured the friendship and stimulating conversation.

The town people had many social events. Right after they moved to Independence, Dad and Mama began playing cribbage and card games several nights a week with other young couples. Children were taken along and put to bed at the home of the hosts. Mama joined the Junior Garden Club and Women's Softball Team.

For many years, a group of local men held a monthly poker party and one night invited Dad to fill in. With unusual luck he was the evening's winner, and they invited him to join the group, "so they could get their money back."

During our high school years, a woman named Rita Herron organized and directed musical revues held on the Legion Hall stage. It was a welcome outlet for people who liked to sing and dance in costumes to live music. They were always in need of men for the couples' numbers, and any man was fair game. Dad was uninterested in these activities and his comments were not positive, to put it mildly. While Mama had no interest in participating, she felt these programs were good for the community. I rehearsed for a group dance number for one revue, but it turned out we would be gone on a mountain trip during the big event. I wasn't disappointed.

It could be said we DeDeckers were a bit unusual. No other family in town went to the mountains for all of their vacations. And unlike many families, we had no relatives in Owens Valley. Carol and I wished we had cousins and aunts and uncles nearby, but Mama said she felt it was just as well we didn't. She knew how fast gossip went through town. Although they loved their families in North Hollywood, our parents enjoyed their distance from the complications of extended-family life.

They enjoyed socializing with friends, and Dinner Club was a highlight of their social life.

Our Creek

Carol

I knew we were lucky to have a creek in our backyard. On summer days, we cooled off in the chilly water. In the fall, when Grandma DeDecker visited, she sat by the bank in a comfortable chair to enjoy the sounds of the birds and flowing water. She always held a fishing pole, and my job was to keep her hook baited with worms from Dad's worm box. In winter, we watched lethargic fish move slowly beneath the ice. In spring, when the water was diverted for cleaning the channel, we joined the neighborhood kids with gunnysacks to collect stranded trout for dinner.

We treasured the line of locust trees planted close together on each side of the creek—their clusters of sweet white blossoms in the spring and their leafy shade in summer. One year, Joan and I built tree houses. She wasn't too enthusiastic about the project, so I suggested that she take the best tree and hoped she would develop a greater interest.

"Joan, come look at this tree! It has four spreading trunks so you can have a wide floor and it will be easy to build because it's close to the ground."

She said, "Well, I'll think about it."

I continued, "And these boards are just the right size, you won't even have to saw them."

My tree had only three spreading trunks and I had to build higher up. That wasn't easy.

Dad kept our portion of the woodpile well stocked, and he let us use his tools as long as we remembered to return them to their proper place. We sawed boards and hammered nails. Our trees houses were on opposite sides of the creek, so we communicated with messages stuck in a tin can that we pulled back and forth with a string and pulley.

During my pirate years, my tree house was a brigantine. I pounded telephone pole spikes into the tree trunk to climb up to the crow's nest. Pirates did not interest Joan, but I never tired of being aloft, wearing my cardboard sword and eye patch.

One day, when I was out riding our bike, I stopped to browse through the junk piled in the sagebrush behind OK Kelley's garage. Things that he wasn't quite ready to haul to the dump stayed there for a few years. Some old cars had been there as long as I could remember. A pile of thick rope caught my attention. I rushed into the garage where OK was working under Mrs. Bell's car.

"Mr. Kelley, what are your plans for that rope out in back?" I asked.

He looked up, "That's the old Onion Valley ski tow rope that we just replaced. It's too thick for most things, but I hate to take it to the dump."

"I think it'd make a good swing," I said hopefully.

He put down his wrench and agreed, "Well, yes, it would. If you want some of it, I'll cut you off a piece when I finish with these brakes."

I could hardly believe my good luck! I had been wishing for a swing for a long time, ever since Joan and I had spent most of a day with the Gates kids on their swing. It was a long rope with a tire tied to the end. The Gates family lived at the very west edge of town, four blocks above our house. The creek flowed through their backyard before it got to ours. We had spent the afternoon jumping off a stump and flying across the water, taking turns with the girls our ages and their younger brother and his friends. As I soared back and forth over the water, I kept thinking that we needed a swing. We had plenty of trees but no rope.

Now we would have a rope! I hurried home to look at the trees along the creek. One locust just outside our back fence had a high limb reaching out over the alley. It wouldn't be as nice as swinging over a creek, but the dead-end alley would do.

After lunch, I went to check on Mrs. Bell's brake job. Her car was off the hoist and OK was sharpening a knife. We estimated how much rope I would need, and he cut a little extra. It was too heavy to carry, so I had to drag it home. I stopped to rest several times.

After work, Dad helped me get the rope over the locust limb, and I crawled out to tie the knot. He found a gunnysack in the garage to fill with rags for a seat and helped me cut off the extra rope. We didn't have a stump for a launching pad, but Dad suggested, "Maybe you could use the oil drum." He kept the 55-gallon barrel behind the garage for use when he worked on his outboard motor. We rolled it out the back gate and stood it upside down next to the wire fence.

Then I climbed up the fence, stepped onto the drum, grabbed the rope and sailed grandly across the alley.

It was a perfect swing! That old rope never broke, the knot held, and we and our friends and neighbors enjoyed it for years.

A Horse Named "Lady"

Carol

At breakfast on a Saturday in September, Joan announced yet again, "I wish we could get a horse. I loved riding for two whole days on our trip to Bench Lake this summer. Virginia has one and she says they are easy to take care of. All you need is a corral."

"And lots of hay," Dad commented as he stirred his coffee.

"But we could feed it lawn clippings," Joan persisted. "And we have such a big lawn."

I was wildly enthusiastic, but I left the lobbying to her because she was more persistent and seemed to have more influence on parental decisions. It was not just because she was a year older, but also because she was considered to be the more sensible daughter. We were twelve and thirteen at the time. Dad listened to her sales pitches with little comment or expression, so I didn't have much hope it would ever happen.

One December morning when I ran into Allie at the Post Office he asked, "Has your dad had any luck in finding a horse?"

I thought his question was about our trip next summer and replied, "We haven't made plans yet, but I think we'll be going to Tyndall Creek."

By Christmas day, I'd forgotten about Allie's comment, but under the tree was a note that read, *"Merry Christmas Joan and Carol! We have asked Allie to find a horse for you."*

A horse! I was too excited to sleep that night.

The next week, Dad built a hitching post behind our back fence and began work on a corral just down the alley on the vacant lot behind Doc Wolf's backyard.

Soon Allie came by with a horse named "Pard." Joan took one look at Pard and wailed, "But I don't want an old horse!" He looked so old she thought he might fall asleep beneath her. A few weeks later,

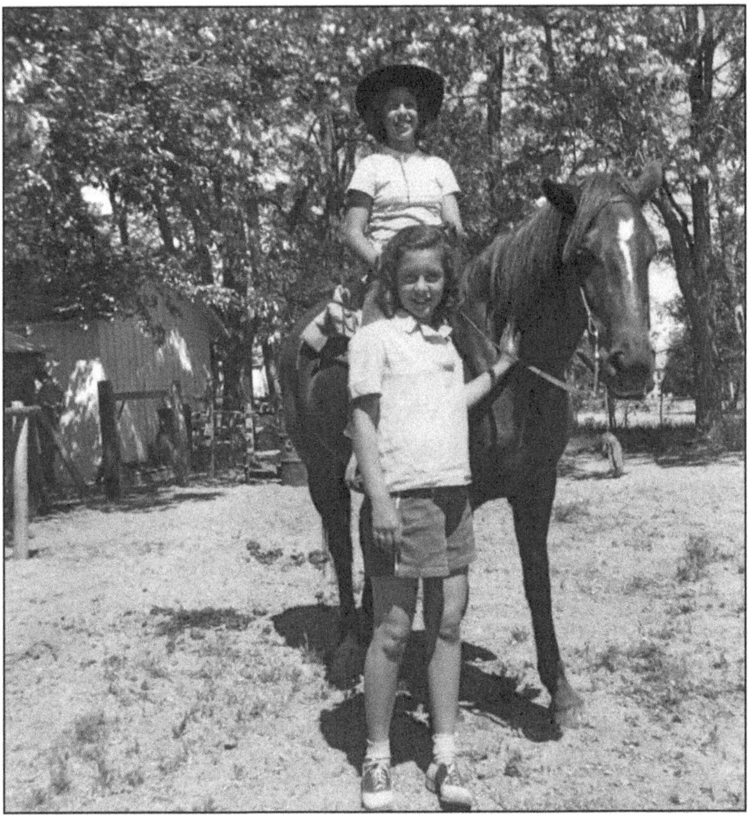

Our horse! 1946.

Allie rode over on wild-eyed "Smokey." Joan said, "I'm afraid to even climb on him." Finding the right horse would be more difficult than we thought.

In February, Allie brought us a tall horse. She was handsome, calm, and friendly. Joan proclaimed, "This one seems just right for us." We named her "Lady."

With the horse came responsibilities. Joan and I were to take over the mowing of our lawn and to feed some of the clippings to Lady. At first, it took both of us to push the hand mower. Together we carried the washtub down the alley to the corral and dumped grass into the manger. It was hard work, but we were too happy to complain. We took turns feeding and watering Lady twice a day. I loved sitting on the edge of the manger to watch her eat and listen to her chomping. I learned not to get too close in case she sneezed. Once, I was late to school because I had to run home and change out of my alfalfa-speckled white blouse.

Over the months, we began to know and understand Lady. She was brown with a white blaze on her face, energetic yet steady and easy to handle. Her eyes were brown, and her nose was soft to kiss. Because she was a tall horse, it took awhile for me to master the art of grabbing her mane and swinging on for a bareback ride.

Our friends lined up for rides from the corral out to the rock crusher. With a timid novice, Lady would walk slowly out, but once there, she would spin around and run all the way back to the corral. Our friend would be clinging to the saddle horn yelling, "Whoa! Whoa!" She seemed to know exactly who would tolerate such behavior—and that was almost everyone.

Joan and I wondered how Art, who happened to be in town visiting, would fare when he rode off to the rock crusher. We tried not to laugh when he and Lady came flying back to the corral.

He never asked for another ride, but sometimes we'd tease, "Hey Art, want to take a ride out to the dump?"

"Thanks, but not today," he would say.

In July, Mama planned a trip to the mountains with Lady.

"Let's go over Kearsarge Pass and spend a week camping in Vidette Meadows. I'd like to invite Mrs. Mullard and her two children. And shall we also invite Phyllis and her brother?" Dad and Mama had met the Millard family on their second Sierra trip and had exchanged letters and visits. Phyllis was my fourth-grade best friend.

Mama planned the food and equipment carefully. Archie would pack our gear, and we would walk the seven or eight miles. She told us all, "We need to go light because we'll have only two mules for the eight of us." Mrs. Mullard didn't fully understand "going light" and arrived with a huge cosmetic case. It looked like a small suitcase.

Mama was dismayed but said, "We'll have to squeeze it in somewhere."

Joan commented, "I think Mrs. Mullard is much too pretty to need so much beauty stuff."

We left from Onion Valley and took took turns riding Lady over Keasarge Pass and down to Vidette Meadows on Bubbs Creek. We had a wonderful week camped on the edge the lush meadow. Lady didn't wander far because I had hobbled her and also because we fed her oats at lunchtime. We six kids were all between the ages of twelve and fourteen. The girls played gin rummy while the boys fished in Bubbs Creek, and we all played endless games of horseshoes with the rusty shoes we collected along the trail. How Lady must have enjoyed hanging out in the meadow for a week and coming into camp for lunch.

In September, Lady needed new shoes. Joan and I took her to a local rancher who lived in town.

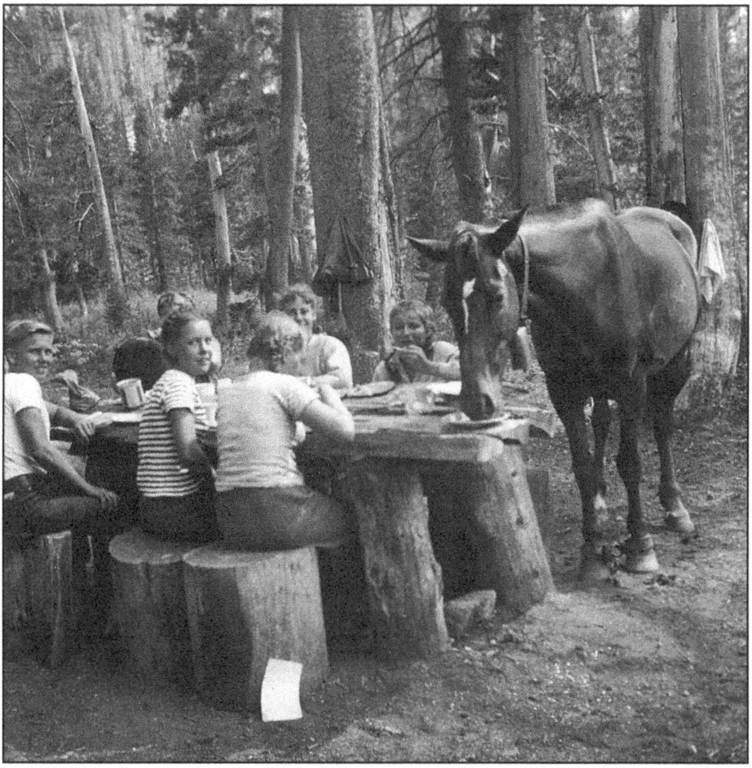

Lunch at Vidette Meadow, 1946.
(See Appendix for names)

When he finished the shoeing, he looked at Lady closely and said, "Well, it looks like she'll foal in about three weeks."

"WHAT?" Joan and I responded in unison.

Joan had commented several times that summer, "Lady's mammary glands look swollen, I wonder if she is pregnant?"

But I had asked, "How could Lady be pregnant?"

I rushed straight over to Allie's house to tell him the glorious news. I banged on his front door and evidently woke him from a nap.

"Lady is pregnant!" I exclaimed.

Allie didn't look happy. He said slowly, "I suppose your dad wants his money back?"

What an odd question, I thought, as I replied emphatically, "Oh no! No, he does not!"

Dad didn't say much when we made the thrilling announcement, but he got busy building a maternity corral in the back corner of our yard where the rabbit hutches used to be. Terry Elliott's horse, Molly, had come to live in the corral with Lady behind Doc Wolf's house. Because the two horses were not the best of friends, we thought we should separate them for the birth.

We put Lady in her new corral one afternoon, and that night the colt was born. The boy next door was the first to see him. Louis woke us at daylight pounding on our front door. We all ran out in our pajamas to see Lady calmly licking the wobbly colt's soft coat. We named him "Billy" after Mt. Williamson, our favorite mountain.

Lady enjoyed the attention and snickered for a treat whenever anyone went out the back door. She also leaned over the fence and trimmed the grape leaves on the arbor. The next morning, she lay on the ground groaning in distress while little Billy jumped happily back and forth over her prostrate body. We were all worried. There were no veterinarians in Owens Valley so Mama called one in Los Angeles.

He was terse and emphatic, "Lady is bloated from eating too many grape leaves. She will either recover or she won't."

We watched and waited. Lady soon recovered.

Lively and curious, Billy entertained us in the backyard. When we went out the back door he rushed over to see us. He tolerated our hugs and liked to suck on our fingers. When we were out riding Lady, he pranced along at her side. He was a handsome chestnut with a wide white blaze on his face.

Dad was a good sport about providing for two horses, hauling more hay and later arranging for Billy's castration and training. Although we were good at taking turns on Lady, Joan and I couldn't wait to have a second horse to ride.

Meanwhile, more kids in town got horses and more corrals were built on Doc Wolf's vacant lot. I rode with my friends—Terry on stately Molly, Diane Passage on little Buttons, Janeane Bodell on old Sabrina, and Elsie Lockridge on unpredictable Babe. We went out in the sagebrush, up the creeks, and down to the Owens River. I must confess that we spent some time playing cowboy in the pastures

Billy's first outing, 1946.

between town and the aqueduct. There is something satisfying about rounding up cattle with your friends.

We all loved our horses even though they were imperfect in different ways. Molly was not friendly with the other horses and was quick to put back her ears and kick. Buttons liked to roll in water, even with a saddle on. Sabrina was so old she couldn't gallop fast or far. Babe would buck Elsie off for unexpected and unwarranted reasons. Lady was impossible to catch when she was in a pasture.

Once, Joan, Janeane, and I spent most of a morning trying to catch Lady in a field near Aberdeen. Janeane's family had recently moved from Independence to Aberdeen to manage the run-down restaurant and resort on the highway, fourteen miles north of town. We occasionally rode out for a weekend visit. On that visit, we chased Lady around and around the pasture for two hours until Mr. Bangs, the caretaker at the nearby Aqueduct Intake Station, came out.

"I think you girls could use some help. Let's get her into the corner and then slowly work her between the south fence and that high berm."

He stayed with us, and we followed his instructions. When we caught Lady, she was probably as tired as we were. It was a long fourteen miles back to town that afternoon.

After more chasing experiences, Elsie's dad took us out for a lesson on horse catching. He strolled to the middle of the pasture with a burlap nosebag of oats and waited. Before long, one horse came in for some oats, then another. Soon a dozen or so, including Lady, were milling around. Mr. Lockridge talked to them, calmly sharing the oats, and quietly slipping a rope around Lady's neck. Although I never liked being in the center of a snorting greedy bunch of horses, this technique worked every time.

Billy had a lazy life in the corral with Lady until he was old enough to break. Dad hired a local cowboy to train Billy when he was two.

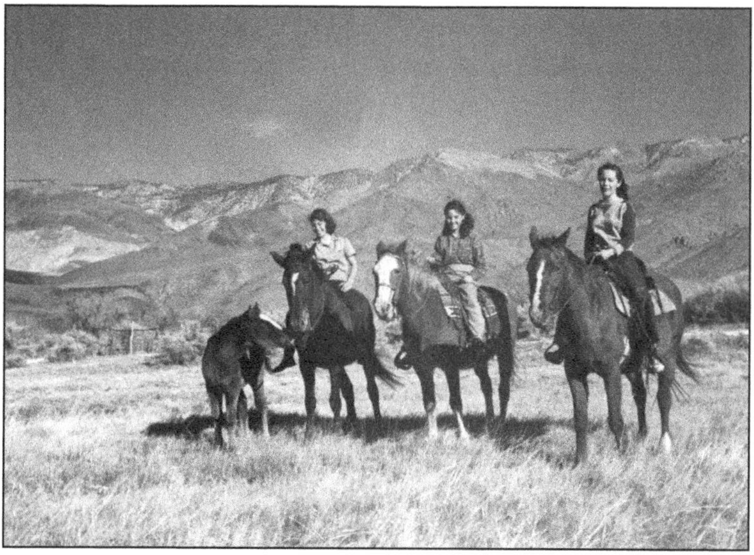

Riding at Aberdeen, 1947.
(See Appendix for names)

He was smaller and calmer than Lady and easier to train and ride. And unlike his mother, he happily came to us in a pasture whenever we arrived with oats.

Joan and I could finally take long rides together.

One day, Dad and I were at the corral sitting on the hay bales we had just unloaded from the trailer and talking about the horses—the work, the expense, and the joy of riding.

"What Joan and I like about having horses is that we can ride through the sagebrush all day in any direction from this corral without coming to a single locked gate."

Dad nodded, "Yes, it's almost like being in the Sierra, except there you come to cliffs and lakes. But it is the same feeling of freedom."

"I'm so glad you got us a horse that Christmas. And I loved raising a colt. Having horses has been the second best part of my life."

Looking curious, Dad asked, “What is the best part?’

I didn’t even have to think when I replied, “Our trips to the mountains, of course.”

And he smiled.

The John Muir Trail

Carol

Art called out to Joan, “Time to get up. What are you waiting for, a mule?”

Dad was starting the campfire because the morning was chilly. Mama was cooking bacon over a kitchen fire. She somehow carried a slab of bacon and an amazing supply of fresh eggs in her backpack. Corky was collecting firewood, and I was getting water from the creek. But Joan was having a hard time leaving her warm sleeping bag.

“Hey, you sack artist, rise and shine,” Art called again.

“But it’s way too early, and it’s cold!” she objected as she turned over and pulled the sleeping bag over her head. Art did his best to make sure that we set off by eight a.m.

I was thirteen the summer we took our first long backpack—two weeks on the John Muir Trail. Corky Swan, now twenty-one, had arrived in Independence from North Hollywood on the Greyhound bus with her new backpack and new hiking boots. She was bubbling with enthusiasm. Art had joined us in Tuolumne Meadows.

The trail began down in Yosemite Valley at 4,035 feet and climbed east to Tuolumne Meadows at 8,600 feet. Then it turned south and followed the Sierra crest, ending on the summit of Mount Whitney, a total of 212 miles. Our plan was to do the 135-mile stretch from

Tuolumne to Bench Lake and go out over Taboose Pass. To do this, we would hike eleven miles every day with no layover days.

Beginning a trip was a simple matter in those days. Few people went to the mountains and permits were not required. Even fewer people backpacked, and lightweight equipment was not available. We carried army surplus sleeping bags and nylon tarps that had been used as life raft covers during the war. The blue side was for when an enemy plane flew over and the yellow side for an allied plane.

We had a strange assortment of packs. Joan's and mine were homemade. Mama carried a war surplus molded-plywood pack frame whose original purpose had been to transport a rocket launcher. Art made his pack of wood, canvas, and leather. Dad and Corky had brand new Trapper Nelsons, one of the few commercial packs at that time. All were heavy and so were our sleeping bags. But we didn't carry much else except food. No tents or air mattresses, stoves or fuel.

In those days, everyone cooked over a fire. Water filters were neither available nor necessary. We used our tin cups to dip water from any stream or lake. Bear barrels had not been invented because bears were rarely seen.

From the trailhead in Tuolumne Meadows, the John Muir Trail makes a gradual ascent to the top of Donohue Pass, following Lyell Creek as it meanders over granite slabs and through broad meadows of shooting stars and gentians. The sights and sounds helped me forget the weight of the pack on my back.

At lunch, we stopped by a stream, dipped our bare feet in the cold water and relaxed on the grass. We ate salami, cheese, crackers, dried fruit, and candy bars.

As I munched on my Almond Joy, I said, "One of the things I like about our lunches is that we have a different kind of candy bar every day."

Joan was sprawled out among the flowers and added, "What I like about this lunch is resting in the shooting stars and gentians."

Art said, "Don't get too comfortable because it's time to get going."

While we rested on Donohue Pass, we admired the view in all directions. To the south were the lakes, peaks, and passes that we would encounter. They looked far away.

After three days and twenty-eight miles, we were at Devil's Post Pile National Monument where the road touches the John Muir Trail.

When we picked up the box of food we had left at the ranger station, Mama asked the ranger, "Is there any place we can buy first aid items? In just three days of hiking, one in our group has developed terrible blisters, and we've already used our entire supply of Band-Aids and moleskin."

He told us, "The closest store is in Mammoth and you could probably hitch a ride. That's about an hour's drive. But let me ask my wife if we can help you."

Thanks to his kind wife, we left Devil's Post Pile with tincture of iodine, boxes of Band-Aids, and plenty of moleskin. She said, "I keep a good supply. You aren't the first hikers to arrive with blisters."

Corky had made the mistake of bringing new boots. In addition, her feet had been affected by polio when she was young and so no boots fit her well. She dreaded long downhill sections of the trail, and some days she was desperate enough to wear Art's size twelve tennis shoes with toilet paper stuffed in the toes. Every step of the trip was uncomfortable for her, but she never complained.

We took long baths in the hot springs before leaving Devil's Post Pile with very heavy packs. We had added food for the remaining twelve days of the trip.

Joan moaned when she picked up her pack, "Do we really need all this food?"

Mama laughed, "Before we get to Bench Lake you'll be wishing for more." And she was right.

Art had been over the John Muir Trail many times and had good camping spots in mind. He chose places near timberline where we had sweeping views of the canyons and peaks. Usually we were at our destination by mid-afternoon, and when we dropped our packs we experienced a pleasant floating sensation.

Our first activity in camp was to look for a flat bed site with dead pine needles. Sometimes we moved the dead needles from under other trees to make our bed more comfortable. After we washed our socks and hung them to dry in the sun, we might take a dip in a nearby stream or pond. Books were too heavy to carry, but we often played cards. Dad had brought his fishing pole but had little time to use it, and we greatly missed our fish dinners.

After dark, we sat close to the fire with tea and cookies while Art played his harmonica and recited Robert Service poems. He had memorized many poems. I often requested, *The Ballad of Blasphemous Bill*. Mama's favorite was *Lucille*—about a flea on a polar bear. But since every day was strenuous, we were early to bed. We admired the stars only briefly before falling asleep.

When we came to the Duck Lake trail junction, Art went off into the woods to find a small food cache he had left earlier in the summer. That night after dinner he grandly presented a can of pineapple for dessert.

As I was relishing my pineapple chunks, I said, "Art, I had been wondering all day why you kept talking about Pineapple Junction. I looked and looked, but I could never find it on the topo map."

He chuckled, "It's not often that I can fool you girls."

We hiked on and on, some days dropping thousands of feet to cross a deep canyon, like the headwaters of the San Joaquin and Kings rivers. The next day, we would climb over a pass into the next basin.

While we regretted the elevation loss and steep climb, the view from each pass was exhilarating.

There were so few people on the trail that we always stopped to chat with the fellow hikers we encountered. We met the occasional packer with a string of mules taking a group of men to a good fishing lake. They tended to have large camps in wooded areas close to a creek or lake with big umbrella tents and folding chairs set up around the campfire ring. Once, we saw a family with burros. One burro carried a basketful of little kids, with the adults walking and leading the animals. Another time, we passed a Boy Scout troop. We felt sorry for the scout leader who was puffing along behind and trying to keep

On the John Muir Trail, leaving Muir Pass, 1947.
(See Appendix for names)

up with his energetic boys. There were also a few groups of men with backpacks and fishing poles and a few solo men who were climbing peaks, but no other families and almost no women or girls.

One day, we met the legendary Norman Clyde on the trail. That night he joined us at our campfire on Palisade Creek. He and Art had never met, but they knew of each other as mountain climbers from the notes they left in summit registers. They were competitors in the number of first ascents and the conversation that night was a bit tense and strained. Mama said later, "What was not said that evening was more notable than what was said."

Our family agreed that Art was right. For years he had been saying, "Backpacking gives you freedom from those animals. You can camp in high basins without the need to consider grazing. You can take knapsack routes that have no stock trails. And you don't have to chase after horses and mules at dawn."

Mama added, "I especially like the simplicity of living with only what we have in our packs."

We became dedicated backpackers, and would hike the rest of the John Muir Trail from Bench Lake to Mount Whitney next summer.

On our last day on the JMT, we hiked over Mather Pass and down to Bench Lake to meet the rest of the Swan family. They had been packed in for a week of fishing and to meet up with us. The nine of us hiked out over Taboose Pass with Dad teasing Mr. Swan about hiking that rough trail in his bedroom slippers two years ago. "Ned, tell us again how long those slippers lasted."

My feet were sore when we neared the bottom of the pass. My nose was sunburned and the tops of my ears were peeling. I had a hole in the seat of my brand new Levis, and I couldn't stop thinking about a bath. But I already knew how much I would miss the flowers in the meadows, the campfire camaraderie, the quiet nights, and all the rest.

On Taboose Pass with the Swan Family and Art, 1947.
(See Appendix for names)

After two weeks of rocky trails, broad vistas, and the Milky Way, our house seemed different. At breakfast I said, "This house always feels strange when we get home from the mountains. The linoleum floors feel too smooth, the walls are too flat, and the ceilings are too low."

Mount Whitney in the Moonlight

Joan

Art had always wanted to climb Mount Whitney in the moonlight. None of our family had been there, even in the daylight, and we quickly agreed that a moonlight hike would be an unusual experience. We would go on the next full moon, the Saturday night of Labor Day weekend in 1947. Art suggested we arrive on the summit in time to greet the sun on Sunday morning.

Whitney is the highest of the ten 14,000-foot Sierra peaks, and the only one with a trail to the top. It is a massive mountain. Glaciers have carved the east face into a spectacular series of pinnacles while leaving the west side broad and sloping. Even with a trail, the twenty-two-mile round trip and elevation gain of over 5,000 feet is a challenging undertaking.

We packed quick-energy food and what we thought were enough warm clothes, and drove from Lone Pine up the steep road to Whitney Portal where the trail begins at 8,360 feet. It was a pleasant day as we climbed up a long series of switchbacks through sagebrush, manzanita and pinyon to Mirror Lake at 10,640 feet. It is an alpine gem in a setting of pines, rock gardens, and granite slabs, and we spent the afternoon lazing around the shoreline. It was one of those typical

Sierra summer days—the sun was too hot and the shade was too chilly. After supper, Carol and I dozed in our sleeping bags while the others talked around the campfire. When Art called, "Time to get going," it was hard to climb out of our cozy nests.

We wore the clothes we always took on mountain trips, a T-shirt, a long-sleeved flannel shirt, and a sweatshirt. For this trip we added a jacket. Experience told us we would warm up as we hiked, but we had never hiked at night at this elevation. In the thin Sierra air, the temperature plummets after sundown, and we were used to sitting around a campfire and then jumping into our sleeping bags. It hadn't occurred to any of us to bring a warm hat, and we would soon use our extra socks as mittens.

Off we went about 11:00 p.m., each with a supply of lemon drops, raisins, and nuts in our pockets and a canteen of water. The moon was already overhead, and it was surprisingly easy to see without our flashlights. Soon we were above timberline and admiring the stark beauty of the high granite country.

In spite of our exertion, we never warmed up enough to feel comfortable. When we stopped to rest the cold quickly penetrated our bodies and we felt an urge to move on. The only way to get a little warmth was to keep hiking, and because we were in good shape from our recent Muir Trail trip, we didn't need to stop often. But I was too cold to fully appreciate the moon's glow on Lake Consultation, now far below us, or the moonlight and shadows on the granite spires above.

By the time we reached Trail Crest at 13,600 feet, the water in our canteens was frozen solid. There we turned north towards the summit of Whitney. The trail stayed just to the west of a series of pinnacles. Between each pinnacle, we looked down the v-shaped "window" several thousand feet. Even in the moonlight, the drop took my breath away. The last half-mile was up the broad, sloping west side of the mountain where the trail wound through granite slabs and boulders.

Finally, we could see the top and the stone hut that had been built in 1909 for research purposes. When we got there, I opened the door and found it was full of ice, just as we'd been told. A few feet beyond, a sign read "Mount Whitney 14,495 feet." We had arrived.

But we had arrived early, and I was too cold to enjoy the 360-degree view. Only a slight brightening of the sky above the Inyo crest signaled that dawn was approaching, and I felt it would be a hopelessly long time before sunrise. Art had brought along a few sticks of wood and we huddled around a tiny fire in a sheltered spot. I sat in that bit of warmth, hugged my knees and dozed off.

Several other hikers joined our summit party, and someone said, "The sun is about to rise!" We all turned to the east in greeting while in the west the moon was setting. Everyone seemed excited and cheerful, but to me it seemed a timid and heatless sun. I walked around a little and then laid down on a flat rock, my back to the sun, and fell asleep while listening to the drone of voices. The others seemed to be suffering less, or just didn't complain as much.

Finally, the sunshine grew warmer. Someone woke me, we all signed the register, and Mama took photos. I felt only partly awake and a bit dazed.

The others wanted to climb Mt. Muir, a short side-trip on the way down. At 14,015 feet, Muir was one of the pinnacles we had passed along the trail.

"I don't want to climb it," I told Mama.

But she encouraged me saying, "It's on the way down and the walking will warm you up. But if you don't want to climb Muir you can wait on the trail."

I dimly remember the scramble from the trail up Mt. Muir and that it didn't take long. Then we continued on to Trail Crest where we stopped for a rest in the sunshine. Art took a portrait of the DeDecker family before we began the ten-mile descent to Whitney Portal.

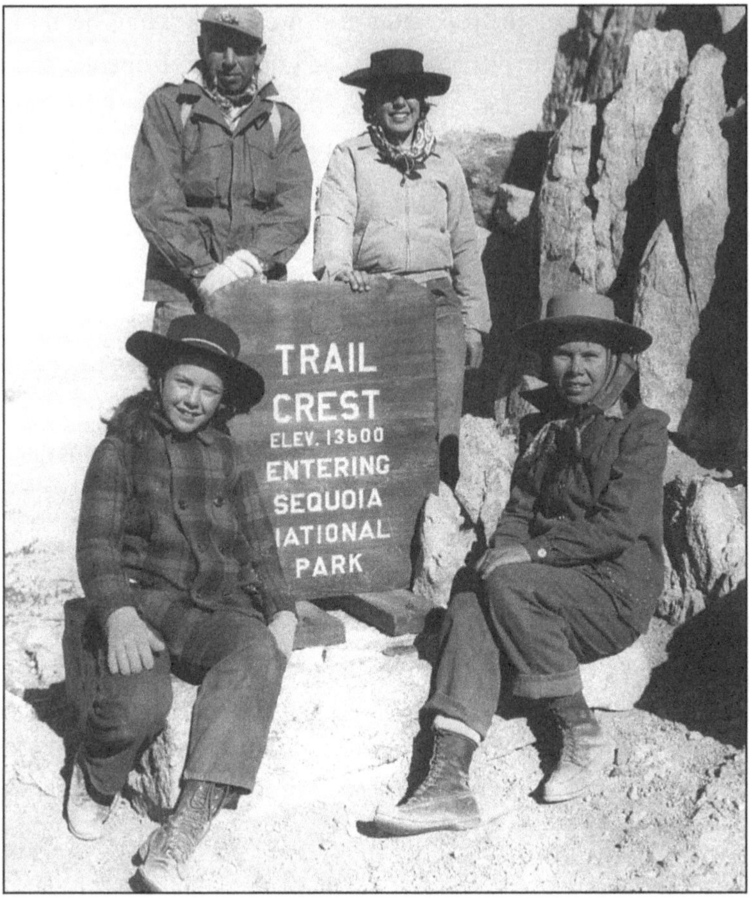

Our family on our return from the Whitney summit, 1947.

It wasn't until years later that we learned about hypothermia, the condition in which the core body temperature drops—leading to confusion and other dangerous symptoms. Only in retrospect did I realize I had been experiencing two of the symptoms, drowsiness and confusion.

Eventually, I felt warm and more alert and began to appreciate the sights along the trail. All of those people going up Whitney! We saw some amazing scenes—a man with cooking pots tied to his belt loops, women with toeless shoes or wedgies, men wearing motorcycle boots. Hikers draped over a rock and suffering with altitude sickness would ask, "Have you been up to the summit already?"

"What time did you start?"

"Are we almost to the top?"

We wondered how many of them would make the summit.

We made a quick stop at Mirror Lake to pick up our gear and then continued down to the trailhead at Whitney Portal.

As we began the drive down into Owens Valley, the late summer heat seemed unusually warm, causing me to comment, "Never have I felt so cold and so hot on the same day."

Part Five

HIGH SCHOOL DAYS
1947–1949

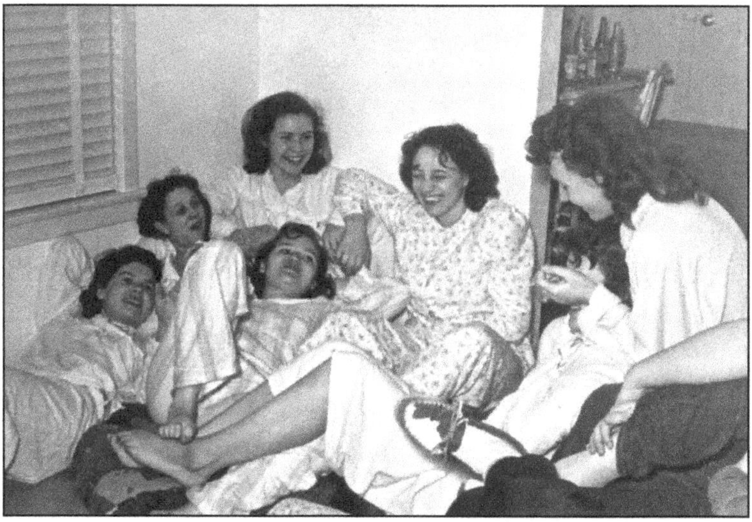

High School Memories

Joan

Owens Valley High School was a sheltering and friendly place. Located on the east side of town, the building had a combination of charm and simplicity, a big box with a hip roof and tall multi-paned windows on all sides. The wide entry sidewalk was flanked on each side by rose bushes and lawn. Four broad steps led to an arched façade over the front entrance. In cold weather, the arriving students gathered on the school steps and entry porch. In warm weather, they lounged on the lawn.

Glass-paneled doors opened into a hallway with the principal's office on the left, where Mama worked, and the library on the right. Straight ahead was the auditorium with a stage and seating for about eighty people. There were three classrooms off each side hall.

The high school was part of a complex that also contained the elementary school, tennis courts, a woodshop, a gravel field with a baseball diamond, and the boys' locker room. A few elm trees provided some shade and greenery. Only the entry areas of both schools had lawns. By the time I graduated four years later, there was a new elementary building, gymnasium, and administration building.

Looking back at those four years, the first teachers who come to mind are Mrs. Loundagin and Mrs. Wilder, who taught at Owens

Owens Valley High School, 1947.

Valley High School for many years. In a way, these teachers *were* the school for me.

Mrs. Agnes Loundagin taught typing. The room was furnished with small tables, each holding a typewriter and an instruction booklet. We chose a seat and sat facing Mrs. Loundagin, who stood straight and serious next to her oak desk. Above her hung a large chart of a typewriter keyboard showing the alphabet letters, numbers, punctuation marks, and symbols. Our typewriter keys were covered with black caps. No hunt and peck in this class.

First, we learned to sit erect. Next, we learned the correct finger positions on the keyboard. "Eyes always on the chart," she said as she tapped the chart with her long wooden pointer. And we began our exercises.

View of Kearsarge Peak from the high school, c. 1942.

FR, FV, FR, FV for a while. Then JU, JM, JU, JM. Next we advanced to FR, FT, FG, FV, FB, FG and to JU, JY, JH, JM, JN, JH. Each class began the same way; we practiced the keyboard positions like piano scales. Soon we picked up speed, following the exercises in our booklets, and then began typing the alphabet. Faster and faster.

Mrs. Loundagin believed in accuracy before speed. She allowed no erasing, and it was years and years before Wite-Out correction fluid was invented. If you hit the wrong key, it was an error. If you hit the wrong key, but very lightly, it was still an error. We soon learned that if it was light enough, it could be successfully typed over with another key if Mrs. Loundagin wasn't standing behind you. She was tough, but fair, and occasionally gave us a tiny smile of encouragement. Every few weeks, we had to change typewriters; the Royals were our favorite and Underwoods the second best.

I also took government from Mrs. Loundagin. She taught by chapters, and we wrote out the answers to the questions at the end of each chapter. I remember almost nothing about that class, although I assume some of the content must have stayed with me.

Mrs. Loundagin was known as an excellent sewing teacher, and yet I never took sewing. "You don't need to spend time with sewing at school when I can teach you at home," Mama said. True enough, but I didn't learn at home because neither Mama nor I had the time. Near the end of high school, I wanted to sew a corduroy shirt for a boyfriend. Because "I knew it all," I didn't want to ask Mama for much help. All I had to do was follow the pattern directions. By the time I finished, I had learned how to "go with the nap" of the corduroy and that no shirt can use two left sleeves. I also learned to buy plenty of fabric.

Later on, I sewed for my own family, always learning by the mistake-and-rip method. Mrs. Loundagin would have saved me no end of grief.

Mrs. Mabel Wilder was my all-time favorite teacher. She wore rayon print dresses on her rounded frame. Her long graying hair was braided and pulled in a twist firmly pinned around her head. She was sober and down to business but had a good sense of humor. When she smiled, a dimple appeared on her right cheek, but we did not dare to mention it. She had grown up in Manzanar, which was then a prosperous orchard and farming area with its own elementary school. In 1921, she became one of three teachers at the Independence high school and for several years drove students with her from Manzanar.

Her specialty was math, and when a student didn't understand something she was always willing to go back for review. She carefully explained the meaning behind the geometry theorems with frequent use of the chalkboard because she wanted us to understand. Her patience was amazing, and she expected and received our full attention.

In English, Mrs. Wilder felt we should read a Shakespeare play. As we struggled, she helped us understand the meaning of the strange language in *The Merchant of Venice*.

She wanted us to know the history of Owens Valley High School and spent several weeks telling us the story while we took notes. For homework, we wrote up the notes in narrative form. We learned about the early years when the high school consisted of a handful of students, with teachers and subjects added as enrollment increased.

When our class put on a play, Mrs. Wilder assigned the parts. I don't remember the plot, but I do remember that Lorna got the plum female lead, and I played a bossy, unpleasant woman.

Mama was unsympathetic when I complained, and she told me, "Lorna needs more recognition and support in her life and you have plenty of both."

Carol's junior year class, 1950.
(See Appendix for names) Owens Valley High School yearbook

One year, there was no qualified physics teacher, so Mrs. Wilder took on the class. She put on demonstrations to illustrate some of the principles, and we did experiments. That's when I realized students learn far more by doing than by just reading or filling in blanks.

Teachers and principals came and went, but they generally didn't stay more than a few years. If they were single, the lack of social activities in town was a problem. If they had families, they wanted more opportunities for their children than our town could offer. Principals wanted to advance to larger schools. In spite of the turnover, on the whole, we had good principals and teachers. Mrs. Wilder and Mrs. Loundagin were the school pillars; each taught for decades and each served as principal.

The Year We Played Football

Carol

For the first time in its history, Owens Valley High School had a football team. I was in the eighth grade that year, but because the seventh and eighth grades were taught in the high school building, we all felt like we were in high school.

The new school principal was also the boys' PE teacher. I wondered if he had visions of becoming a great football coach. Although it was a six-man team, the eleven boys from the tenth, eleventh, and twelfth grades were not sufficient for a scrimmage. The four ninth-grade boys were too small to play, but all the others were drafted regardless of their interest in the sport. The mother of the brainiest boy in the high school commented, "The last thing I ever expected was that my son would be needed on a football team."

The playing field behind the high school was watered until there was a bit of grass among the weeds and gravel. The boys were expected to call the new principal "Coach," which reinforced my opinion that the football year was more for the coach than for the boys or the school.

Our first game would be against Ridgecrest, a town about 100 miles south of Independence. The team left for the game with handsome new uniforms, black pants and a big black OV on the front of their orange shirts. They had plenty of spirit and some amount of confidence. The school bus had room for the team, cheerleaders, a student cheering section, a few teachers, and the band. I was the flute player.

As we began the long ride, Mr. Blaisdell, the new science teacher asked, “How many of you can whistle loudly?” A few of the students could, and the rest of us were eager to learn. Perhaps hoping to enhance our cheering section, he showed us where to put our two little fingers in a V on the end of our tongues and said, “Blow softly at first until you get the hang of it.” By the time we had practiced all the way to Ridgecrest, we were LOUD. It must have been an unpleasant two-hour ride for the non-whistlers. Some were trying to do their homework.

When we reached Ridgecrest High, we realized right away that it was a far larger school than ours. Their football field had green turf and expansive bleachers. Our home field had neither of these amenities, and our busload of supporters filled a tiny portion of the visitor section.

It was one of those sparkling crisp and clear autumn days, and we were bursting with enthusiasm. Our tiny band played with gusto. Then their sizable band played. We cheered and whistled when our eleven players ran onto the field in their dashing new uniforms. Then we watched in stunned silence as their forty-four players ran onto the field. It seemed like that line of tall boys in blue and silver would never end. Mr. Blaisdell said in a low voice, “This doesn’t look good.”

The game was a disaster. The ride home was silent and subdued. No one whistled.

We also lost games to Big Pine, Lone Pine and Trona—but no loss was as traumatic as the Ridgecrest debacle.

Not surprisingly, Owens Valley High School’s first football season was also its last for many years. That spring the coach announced, “We won’t be able to have a football team next year because of an insurance problem.” That might have been true. We all knew that Tom, our best player, had two false front teeth, but I always suspected the coach might have accepted a reality lesson—one that the football boys had probably been aware of all along. Our school was just too small for football.

Happily, for the coach, we were competitive in basketball, a sport not so dependent on numerous players. He could take pride in having a winning team composed of our indefatigable football players. He said, "I believe we would all agree that our boys enjoy basketball more than football."

Other Lessons from High School

Joan

Of course, there was a lot more to high school than classes and homework. We had special events, such as the Sadie Hawkins Day dances when the girls invited the boys. The Girls Glee Club and the band often performed at PTA meetings or other local programs.

In my sophomore year, we had a school newspaper, *The Cub Reporter,* and I was the editor for a semester. As the year began, the new principal, Mr. Riley, announced to the students that he knew deer season was at hand, and he wanted the boys to know there would be serious consequences if they cut school to go hunting. Deer season arrived, the usual boys went hunting, and nothing happened. I pointed this out in my next editorial. Then I got nervous about whether Mama's job could be in jeopardy, or if Mr. Riley would scold me. I kept waiting for repercussions, but nothing happened. I'm still not sure what lesson I learned. Was it President Truman's, "If you can't take the heat stay out of the kitchen," or "Keep a low profile," or "Have the courage of your convictions?"

That same year, my friend Dee and I ran for school cheerleaders. Dee, a junior, was athletic and limber, far more able than I to do the leaps and moves. Mama sewed outfits for us, black knee-length jumpers lined with orange, and with a large orange OV on the bodice. We wore white long-sleeved blouses and saddle shoes. Our cheering section was small but enthusiastic.

During my senior year, I spent some time volunteering in one of the elementary classrooms. Mrs. Crispin was a talented third-grade teacher and welcomed the assistance. She asked me to help Peggy Ann learn her spelling words. Peggy Ann had no clue about how to approach a spelling word, and I didn't have much of a clue about how to help her. It made me wonder if I really wanted to become a teacher. The other careers offered to girls at the time were secretarial work and nursing. Mama told me, "You can do better than be a secretary," even though she herself was one, and I had no interest in becoming a nurse. In looking up career possibilities in the school library, physical

Cheerleaders, Dee and Joan, 1949.

therapy popped out, but it sounded similar to nursing. I didn't have a real concept about what any of these jobs entailed or what other possibilities existed.

My favorite school event, by far, was the annual trip to Los Angeles to attend the California Scholarship Federation conference. To be a member of CSF, a student needed to maintain a high grade point average. Usually four or five students qualified each semester. The organization held a one-day spring conference at a different high school each year. Mrs. Wilder planned the trips and did all of the driving.

The conference took most of a Saturday, but we spent several days seeing sights in Los Angeles. When we attended the first operetta of my life, *Song of Norway,* I was so entranced I felt as though I was floating. Next, we saw a movie screening of *Hamlet* with Lawrence Olivier, memorable in a different way. Always we visited colleges—Occidental, Redlands, Pomona, University of Southern California, and University of California, Los Angeles. Over the years, we toured a bakery, steel factory, plant nursery, the Huntington Library, and Palomar Observatory. We stayed in hotels, ate our meals at restaurants, and were busy every minute of our four-day trip with new and rewarding activities. For small-town students it was an exciting time, and I am forever grateful for those experiences.

Although the school board and PTA donated funds for the trips, we students also raised money by cooking several dinners for the local businessmen's group. We set up tables in the auditorium, peeled potatoes, washed lettuce, served the meal, and washed the dishes. Mrs. Wilder was chief cook and she tolerated our varying degrees of cooking ability. Mary Cole was the only one of us who had cleaned and cut up a chicken, and Mrs. Wilder repeatedly complimented her. She herself made fantastic biscuits using Bisquick. One of our guests couldn't get over those biscuits and came to the kitchen asking for the recipe. "I'll have to get it to you later," Mrs. Wilder murmured, not wanting to give away her secret.

On the 1947, trip we visited a former schoolmate, Douglass Elliott, who had returned to Los Angeles after attending school in Independence during the War years. We remembered Doug as a super student. His father had served as an officer during the War and was now the Dean of Law at the University of Southern California.

Their family invited our group to their new home. Doug's mother, chatting non-stop as she always did, served juice and crackers to us students. Then, holding a stemmed glass in one hand, she turned to Mrs. Wilder and said, "We're having martinis. May I serve you one?" I looked in fascination and horror at the goblet containing a clear liquid and two tooth-picked green olives. During our school classes, Mrs. Wilder had frequently mentioned her opposition to liquor and told us that she still believed in Prohibition. It seemed unthinkable that anyone would ask her if she'd like an alcoholic drink! With ice in her voice, Mrs. Wilder firmly replied, "No thank you." We didn't stay long.

In the spring of my senior year, we became aware that Mrs. Wilder wasn't feeling well. She missed some days of school, which she had never done before, and the rumors flew. On our spring CSF trip to Los Angeles, Mrs. Loundagin went along to help. Sometimes Mrs. Wilder sat down for a while to rest. She didn't say anything, but it was easy to see the pain on her face. In a few minutes, she would determinedly stand up and say, "It's time to go."

Soon she stopped teaching, and we were told she had cancer. The word "cancer" was said in kind of a hushed voice as though it was some kind of secret. She had surgery but "nothing could be done," and her sister came to take care of her. One afternoon, Mary and I made arrangements to visit. Propped up in bed, she smiled and seemed happy to see us. She asked some questions about our coming graduation. Then her sister told us, "Mrs. Wilder needs to rest now." She never returned to school. How I missed her.

From Mrs. Wilder I learned about some of the qualities of an outstanding teacher—high standards, flexibility, a willingness to take on new challenges, patience, dedication to her students, and a sense of humor.

Earning Money

Joan

How I loved my job as a "soda jerk" at Kings Pharmacy. Mr. King hired me in June after my sophomore year. The soda fountain was the kind now seen only in the movies. It stood along one wall of the drugstore. All of the kids in town were familiar with the selection of candy bars and penny candy at the end of the counter. The pharmacy was against the back wall and the newspapers and magazines were arranged near the front door. The rest of the store was filled with items in glass cases. Carol and I had spent many hours poring over the ones that held gifts. Should we splurge and get the set of pretty juice glasses for Mama's birthday, another ashtray for Dad?

By watching and helping an experienced employee, I learned how to make sodas, milk shakes, malts, root beer floats, and sundaes. I marveled that the milkshake container didn't fall off the machine, and I learned to quickly wash the glasses and spoons and to keep the marble counter sparkling clean.

The customers would wander in and sit on the stools at the counter and visit with one another while I filled their orders. Milkshakes and malts were popular, and so were sodas. My own favorite was a cherry phosphate, made with cherry syrup and soda plus some ice. I tried to be a combination of friendly and businesslike, as Mr. King often stood watching from the pharmacy counter.

Ice cream was a nickel a scoop, and Mr. King showed me how to pull the metal scoop along the edge of the ice cream carton to make a hollow scoop. I knew it was not right, but I didn't have the courage to say anything and continued to make full scoops. Mr. King caught me disobeying his orders and gave me a sound scolding. A few days later, he raised the price of a cone to seven cents a scoop. The kids would look at me with big eyes and protest, "But I only have a nickel." That was too much for me. I gave them a full scoop for their nickel and told Mr. King to take it out of my paycheck. He didn't, but I thought to myself that it was no wonder no one liked him.

Every morning when I swept the oiled wooden floor, I couldn't help but notice the constant supply of empty liquor bottles in the backroom wastebasket. I mentioned this to Mama and she commented, "I don't think Mr. King is a happy man."

As a teenager, it was hard to find even a part time job. Mr. King preferred older girls for work in the drugstore. Our best bet was babysitting. Parents didn't go out a lot but when they did we were available. Carol and I charged the going rate, twenty-five cents an hour.

We liked to sit for Jack and Virginia Fair because their two little girls were always tucked into bed and asleep by the time we arrived, leaving us time to catch up on our homework. They later had identical twin girls. I remember how impressed I was one night when I was babysitting for them. They rushed home, Virginia nursed both babies, and she and Jack returned to their social event.

Little Patrick was a memorable baby. His mom asked me to put him in his highchair and feed him mashed peas, but he didn't seem to like peas. It was a trial for both of us. My experience with babies was limited. When Patrick was a toddler, Carol learned to watch him carefully after finding him in the bathroom filling his mother's cowboy boots with water. Carol didn't know much about toddlers either.

Part Five

Each high school summer, Carol and I felt desperate for work. Mama and Dad didn't discuss finances unless we asked, and they never put pressure on us to earn money. We knew it would be difficult for our parents to pay our college expenses.

We found plenty to do each summer, but it didn't include earning money.

Rainbow Girls

Carol

One winter day, the chatter among the girls at school was about a new organization coming to town. It was called "Rainbow Girls." Joan and I listened.

"It sounds like a club for high school girls and I like to be in clubs," Joan said as we walked home through the sagebrush.

"But what's the club supposed to do?" I asked.

"Well, you memorize things, and there are the colors of the rainbow, and there's music, and I think it would be fun," she said with uncertainty.

That night we asked Mama about it. She'd already heard the news and said, "Hmmm." And then, "It's an organization for girls who want to be Eastern Star members when they are older."

"But what do they do?" Joan asked.

Mama said, "I'm not sure. Grandpa Foster belongs to the Masons, which I think is a very old social organization that came from Europe and had something to do with the stone masons who built the medieval castles. It's for men only. The Order of the Eastern Star is somehow related to the Masons. I think both groups work to promote good character and community service and are based on teachings from the Bible."

"Yes, but what exactly do those clubs do?" I repeated.

Mama said, "It's all rather secret, so I really don't know."

Knowing her disinterest in the Eastern Star and Masons, we didn't expect her to be enthusiastic, but to her credit she said, "You girls can decide whether you want to join."

I thought she was probably torn between her desire to support local organizations and her disinterest in that particular one. She always participated in community activities. She had joined the Junior Garden Club just a few weeks after moving to Independence. Before I started school, she occasionally took me along to afternoon meetings. I was never sure just what that group did, but I thought it was about card parties and making decorations for dances. They never talked about gardening. There was also a Senior Garden Club for the older women, and perhaps they talked about flowers.

During her first years in town, Mama had played on the Women's Softball Team. Their games were with the high school girls and the women from Lone Pine.

The Order of the Eastern Star was the one organization in which Mama had no interest even though most of her friends were members. She didn't ever give her exact reasons, but we were old enough to interpret her comments when they seemed vague, and we knew she felt it wasn't "worthwhile." Dad likewise had declined to join the Masons even though many of his best friends were members. Meetings of both groups were held on the second floor of the Masonic Temple that was located on the highway, just north of the courthouse.

Small town kids long for anything new and different so, of course, Joan and I joined Rainbow Girls. Mama went to Lone Pine to get fabric at J. C. Penney for the formal gowns she would make for our initiation ceremony. She chose red-checkered cotton fabric for Joan and green for me. The Eastern Star women from Bishop came to help with the event. They had established a Rainbow Girls group in Bishop some years before and knew all about it.

Our group of about twenty included girls from both Independence and Lone Pine, and we welcomed the opportunity to make new friends. The Eastern Star women were always gracious and helpful. Music was an important part of the meetings, the part that I enjoyed the most. We sang church hymns accompanied by Miss Lawrence on the piano. And although it was a positive experience overall, my enthusiasm waned.

Joan liked it better and progressed through the ranks to the top position before she finished high school. She was conscientious about learning her lengthy parts, although she would often fall asleep in the bathtub while practicing her lines. Everything that is spoken at a meeting is memorized ritual.

I didn't like the secret rituals or the memorizing. None of it made any sense to me. And I didn't like wearing the formal dresses. I especially objected to the manner in which they voted on girls who wanted to join. It was a secret ballot and if two members voted against an applicant, she was rejected with no discussion. The secrecy didn't seem right to me.

After three years, I had used up all of my patience and was looking for a tactful way to quit Rainbow Girls. That wasn't easy with the group of over-enthusiastic Eastern Star women who were my mother's good friends.

When I realized that Elsie felt the same way I said, "Let's make a plan."

At the next meeting, I excused myself to go to the restroom. A few moments later, Elsie excused herself too. We had always been intrigued by the fire escape on the back of the building, so down we went.

"This long dress is a nuisance when sliding down a slippery tube!" I whispered.

Elsie said, "Long dresses are always a nuisance. But I feel better already!"

We retrieved the bundles we had stashed in the lilac bushes, changed into our Levis and headed down towards the pastures near the aqueduct for a bonfire.

We felt happy and free as we went leaping down Market Street to the pastures east of town.

After the last street light, we stumbled along the dirt road by the light of the stars and a sliver of moon. "I think we should have brought a flashlight," Elsie commented.

Of course, our mothers soon heard of our escapade. Mama only said, "You must respond politely to the notes you are receiving from the Eastern Star women." Elsie's mom probably said the same thing. Their notes assured us they would welcome us back at any time. When we didn't return, they wrote to ask if I would play a flute solo at the next meeting.

I was both polite and honest when I replied, "I am no longer playing the flute because I have taken up the tuba. I'm playing it in the high school band, and I'd be happy to play a tuba solo at the next meeting."

The response was a polite, "No thank you." Again, Mama didn't say much.

The Rest of the JMT!

Carol

We were eager to hike the remaining portion of the John Muir Trail the summer I was fourteen. Art was off climbing peaks, but Corky joined us with her usual enthusiasm and better-fitting boots. It would be a shorter distance, only seventy-eight miles, and our packs would be lighter because Dad had arranged with Archie to leave a food cache at Tyndall Creek, our halfway point. We anticipated a leisurely trip.

But we had never hiked up Taboose Pass from the Owens Valley side before. It was a grueling 6,000-foot climb on that hot July day with packs containing enough food for a week. The rough trail seemed to go straight up. In the afternoon, we saw a group of college boys resting on the rocks.

They asked as we passed, "Do you want to buy a can of peaches? Or beans?"

Joan laughed and said, "No thank you. Our packs are already heavy."

Just above timberline, Mama sat down. "I'm too tired to walk another step," she said.

This was a surprise to Joan and me, as our mother always seemed to be able to go on forever. She took off her pack in a grassy patch not far from the trail and crawled into her sleeping bag. We found enough twigs to make a tiny fire, and Dad made her some chicken noodle soup. There were some flat spots nearby, and we slept right there that night. With no wood for a campfire, we went to bed early and enjoyed the starry sky.

In the morning, after her long rest, Mama was completely recovered from her exhaustion.

She said, "We should have realized that a 6,000-foot climb and seven miles with a full pack was too much for one day."

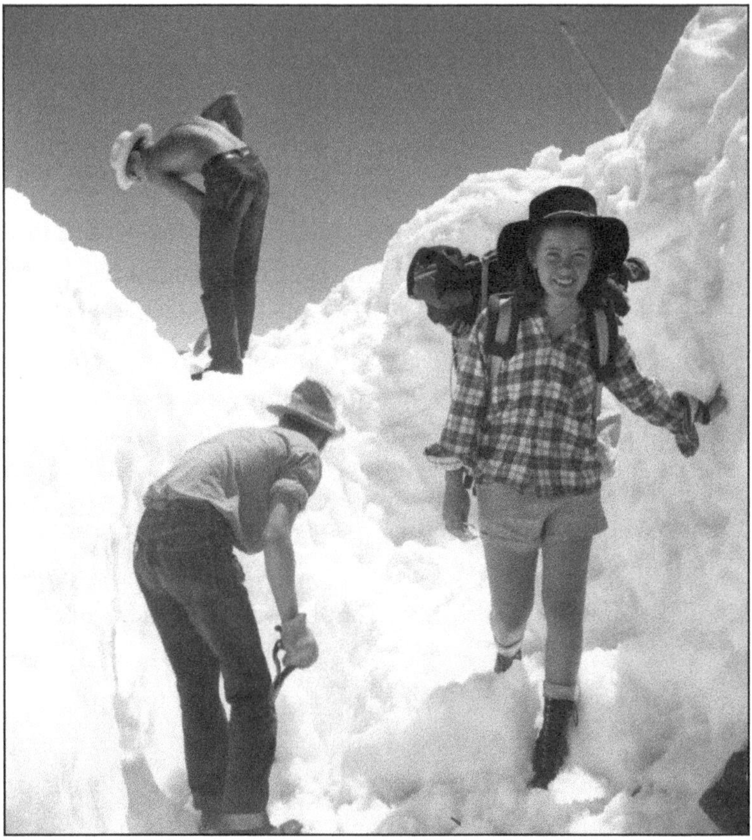

Joan on Glen Pass after a heavy snow year, 1948.

Part Five

After Taboose Pass, the trip was easy. We visited some of our favorite places—Bench Lake, Lake Marjorie, and Twin Lakes. We had time to play cards, read, and fish. Mama found new flowers and made notes and took photos.

Mama had told us last winter that the Inyo County supervisors and local merchants were promoting the construction of a road across the Sierra. It would begin in Independence, climb to Onion Valley, and cross the crest at Kearsarge Pass. From there, it would drop down to Bubbs Creek and into the San Joaquin Valley.

As we were approaching Bubbs Creek at the end of our first week, we talked about the proposed trans-Sierra road. We tried to imagine a highway here and vehicles whizzing past, but we couldn't bear to even think about it.

"It would put Independence on the map," the merchants had said.

Mama commented in indignation, "Yes, it would give them more business, but a road would bisect the Sierra wilderness and completely change this area forever."

Corky said, "Those County supervisors need to hike up here to see for themselves the beauty of these peaks and lakes and meadows. If they did, they might forget about that road."

Soon, we began anticipating the treats we would find in the food cache waiting for us at Tyndall Creek. We had put in extravagantly heavy items because Archie and his mules would be taking our cache all the way to Sheep Corral Camp.

I said, "Mama, I keep thinking about those two big cans of pineapple juice you put in the cache and those boxes of candy bars."

But as we climbed higher above Bubbs Creek, we saw the extensive snowfields on the north side of Forester Pass. Just after Dad said, "I'm beginning to wonder if Archie was able to get over the pass," the hoof prints in the snow suddenly stopped. We saw our food boxes on a granite ledge next to the trail. Archie had taken them as high as he could.

We drank the two cans of pineapple juice before dividing up our new food supply. The snow and our heavy loads made it slow going to the top of the 13,200-foot pass. From there, it was six miles down to Tyndall Creek. By the end of the day, it was Dad's turn to look exhausted. Feeling responsible for the unintended location of the food cache, he had carried far more than his share.

Several days later, we took a side trip to the Wallace Lake area, one of Dad's favorite fishing spots. On earlier trips, he had caught big rainbows in the two large and deep lakes in that basin. It was off the John Muir Trail a ways, so the lakes didn't have many visitors.

We planned two layover days in that basin and the first morning Mama said, "Let's climb Mt. Barnard today."

Corky was enthusiastic, "I've always wanted to climb one of the high peaks."

Mt. Barnard was one of the twelve Sierra peaks over 14,000 feet. We packed a lunch and left Dad to fish.

From our camp, it was a 2,500-foot climb up a talus slope, considered a "walk-up," with incredible views from the summit. Years later, we learned that Mt. Barnard had been resurveyed, and its height was reduced by about twenty feet.

Corky was not pleased with that news. She said, "Barnard was a 14,000-foot peak the day we climbed it, and today it is only 13,990!"

Another day, we hiked to Tulainyo Lake. At 12,802 feet it is the highest lake in the Sierra. After an especially heavy winter, it was still covered with ice in mid August. Corky, Joan, and I sunbathed on the boulders near its shore.

As we approached Mount Whitney from the northwest, we could see what a grand and imposing granite mountain it was, with its

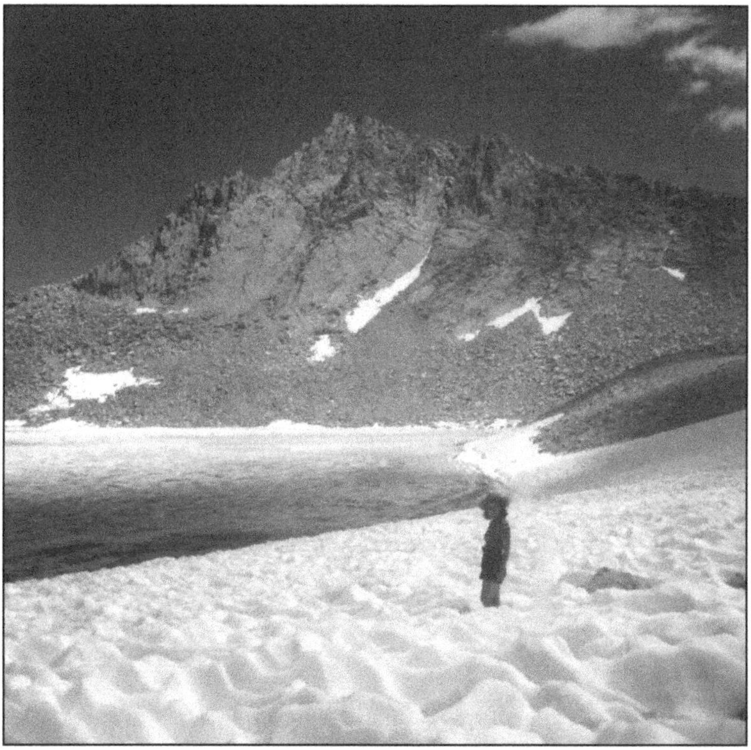

Mama at Tulainyo Lake, ice-covered in August, 1948.

sloping west side and sheer cliffs and pinnacles on the east. In contrast to our frigid moonlight climb the previous year, we enjoyed a warm and leisurely look from the 14,495-foot summit.

Joan said, "This time I can enjoy the view. It makes me shiver to think about our moonlight trip last fall." And from the highest point in the United States, she looked at that glorious scene for a long while.

On the way down from the summit, we climbed 14,015-foot Mt. Muir. It was the tallest of the several spires south of Whitney and an easy scramble.

At its summit, Joan said, "You would think that John Muir would have a more impressive peak than this pinnacle named for him."

Mama agreed, "Yes, but the trail is a lasting tribute to him.

Corky said, "I feel proud to have hiked the John Muir Trail! And to have climbed three 14,000-foot peaks on this trip—without getting a single blister!"

The Wider World

Joan

Although we lived in a small isolated town and were seldom far from home, we knew we were part of a wider world through books, newspapers, magazines, radio, phonograph records, and movies.

When we were very young, story time came after supper. Carol and I would get ready for bed and climb onto the couch to listen to stories and poems read aloud by one of our parents. Often, these were from *Childcraft*, the set of five orange books that had been a splurge for our family. The first volume, *Poems of Early Childhood,* became worn with use and we knew much of it by heart. The next two books were filled with illustrated stories. The remaining volumes were for grownups, with topics about raising children.

We also chose our own books on our weekly trips to the library. When we began school, we participated in special events sponsored by the librarians. The annual "Book Week" included a parade down Edwards Street with students dressed as their favorite book character and awards for everyone. There was a summer reading program with little orange booklets entitled, *Books I Have Read*. We filled in the blanks for author and title. In the lines for "What I think of this book," I wrote, "It was a good book because Mr. Bear didn't eat Danny." Mama made sure we filled up those booklets. In the summer after her first-grade year, Carol won the prize for the most books read.

Dad checked out Steinbeck's *The Grapes of Wrath* and was so impressed he asked Miss Margrave to order copies of *Tortilla Flat* and *Cannery Row.* She never got around to it even though he reminded her several times, and he finally commented to Mama, "They are way too earthy for her." Miss Margrave was of the opinion that it was fine to read fiction that revealed or built character, but nonfiction had more lasting value.

Mama read a great deal, but as time passed the subject was usually about local history or native plants. Much of her evening time was spent writing letters to family and friends. Later, she wrote articles for newsletters about her various interests. She longed to buy an encyclopedia, but she and Dad never made that investment, partly due to the expense and partly because they couldn't figure out where to keep so many books.

In our early high school years, Mama made us a list of novels she had especially liked as a teenager, such as *Tess of the d'Urbervilles* and *Jane Eyre.* Reading was the ideal thing to do on a cold, blustery winter day, with feet propped up next to the coal oil stove in the dining room.

We subscribed to the *Los Angeles Times.* Carol and I sprawled on the living room rug with our after school snacks and caught up on the activities of Prince Valiant, Li'l Abner, Daisy Mae, and the Bumsteads. The weekly *Inyo Independent,* published in Bishop, kept us up on events in all of the valley towns. The social column was an important feature. There we read that DeDecker relatives from North Hollywood were in town for Thanksgiving, or the DeDecker family had returned from a two-week pack trip into the High Sierra.

We all pored over the photos and articles in *Life* magazine. Dad never missed the Captain Hornblower stories in *The Saturday Evening Post,* and we all enjoyed the cartoons.

During the War, the radio news kept us informed. Every night, Mama and Dad sat near our new Zenith upright, listening intently to the latest about North Africa, Italy, England, Germany, the Philippines, and places I'd never heard of, such as Guam and Guadalcanal. Information came thick and fast and was hard to sort out.

On Sunday evenings, we all listened to the radio comedy shows. Dad sat in the armchair shining his work shoes. Carol and I were on the rug polishing our black-and-white saddle shoes, and Mama darned socks on the couch. I loved to hear Dad laugh and Mama chuckle as Dennis talked to Mr. Benny about his worries; Rochester and Jack discussed a trip in the Maxwell to the races at Santa Anita or a train trip to Anaheim, Azusa, and Cucamonga; Jack played his violin or made a trip down to his vault; Don Wilson did the Jell-O ads; and Phil Harris interrupted from the band. It was over all too soon, and it would be a whole week until the next program.

Two small matching doors on our handsome radio opened to the record player. On winter days, we stacked it with Marais and Miranda songs, Gilbert and Sullivan's *H.M.S. Pinafore,* or selections from classical music, while we worked on a jigsaw puzzle on the card table.

During the War, Carol and her friends played records of military songs like *Anchors Aweigh*, *The Caisson Song*, and *The Marines' Hymn*. Their favorite was *The Army Air Corps Song.* They climbed onto the dining room chairs singing, "Off we go into the wild blue yonder, climbing high into the sun." And yelled, "BOMBS AWAY" as they jumped off.

The first movie I saw was *Snow White and the Seven Dwarfs* at Grauman's Chinese Theater in Hollywood. Mama took me to see it when it came out in 1937. We waited in a long line in a foyer that had floor-to-ceiling mirrors. I was terrified when the Wicked Queen descended the castle stairs, but Mama squeezed my hand and I got through it. I loved the dwarfs, Snow White, the music, and everything else about it. I still have the framed drawing of Bashful that Mama bought for me.

Independence did not have a movie theater and going to Lone Pine was a big event. First, we had to convince Mama that it was a good idea.

"It's supposed to be a really good movie, and Debbie said her Mom liked it a lot."

Mama in turn had to convince Dad. He usually, but not always, said "no."

At that time, newsreels came before the main movie feature. They were a source of information about the War and the political scene. In high school, Carol and I occasionally went to a movie in Lone Pine with a boyfriend. But I never saw enough movies to be a part of those great conversations my friends had about *Tarzan* or *Flash Gordon,* or *The Last Days of Pompeii.*

The Alabama Hills were a favorite setting for western films, with Indians hiding in the unique rock formations and swooping down to attack the cowboys, or vice versa. We often caught a glimpse of Mount Whitney in the background. When *Gunga Din* was filmed, we drove out with visiting relatives to see how close we could get to the action. Not very close, but close enough to see a lot of extras and horses milling around in an open area amid swirls of blowing dust.

We did not have a telephone, much to my dismay when I became a teenager. A few other families did. Dad said there was no place in our house to put one, and he and I had numerous heated discussions.

I pointed out the perfect location. "Let's put it here, right in this corner, where there's already a chair, and the phone would be on the wall, out of the way."

"Why do you need a phone when everyone in town lives just down the street?" he asked. "Just walk down and talk to them."

His comments made me angry, and I wouldn't give him the satisfaction of bringing it up again because I knew he wouldn't change his mind.

I suspect that Dad and Mama had many conversations about getting a telephone. She may have finally put her foot down, which rarely happened. But when she did, Dad listened. After we had both left for college, the phone was installed in the very location I had suggested. But before that, our emergency communication source was the City telephone in Dad's office. It was to be used only for something important. Gradually, more people in town got their own phones, at first four-party and then two-party lines. If you picked up the phone to make a call and someone was talking, it meant the line was busy and you should hang up and try again later. Even though it was considered rude, it was hard not to listen.

We first saw television at Aunt Jean's house in North Hollywood. We had come for a visit and Aunt Jean, Grandma, Sydney Ann, and Clinton were clustered on the couch and floor focused on the glowing screen. They were watching a wrestling match. Aunt Jean said apologetically, "That's the only program we can get right now."

I didn't even have to look at Mama to know what she thought when we had traveled so far to spend time with their family. "I think the reception's pretty good, don't you?" Aunt Jean asked as we stared at the flickering screen.

It would be many years before TV came to Independence and even longer before it came to our house.

Lee and Leslie

Joan

Dad referred to Lee and Leslie as "the girls"—two women in their mid-thirties who came to town to open a feed store. They were slim, had short dark hair, and wore Levi's and western shirts with pearl buttons. People liked these friendly women and felt fortunate to have a store in town that specialized in ranching supplies and sporting goods. It saved many shopping trips to Bishop. Carol and I liked to check out the saddle blankets and admire the handsome leather saddles. We always felt welcome to look over their merchandise. It was where we bought our levis and a bridle for Lady's colt. They carried the new Trapper Nelson backpacks and other camping items.

Lee and Leslie knew a lot about softball and soon began coaching the local women's team. It was composed of high school girls, some of their moms, and other young women. Carol and I both played. We practiced on summer evenings and had frequent games with the Lone Pine and Big Pine teams. Martha Austin, Lorna's mother, played third base and helped schedule the games.

I definitely needed to improve. I could run and catch the ball, but somehow couldn't hit it. Lee told me that my timing was off. She patiently threw ball after ball to me, explaining just when and how to swing the bat. It worked! I was thrilled and began to enjoy rather than dread being at bat. I also didn't have the knack for throwing the ball very far, and Lee had begun to help me.

Leslie was an experienced catcher and helped Carol in that position. Carol had saved her money to buy a catcher's mitt. Leslie showed her just where to squat behind the plate and how to keep runners from stealing bases. We were all improving.

Then, unexpectedly, Lee and Leslie quit coming to our practices. One night at supper, I commented that I'd be glad when they returned.

Dad said, "They're gone. Didn't you know?

"What do you mean, they're gone? They can't be! Where did they go? Just like that?" I asked.

Dad replied, "Yes, they're gone. They closed the store and left."

At baseball practice the next day, I asked Lorna about it. As always, she knew what was going on.

"My mom said some of the town people thought Lee and Leslie were a bad influence on us girls. They didn't want them around."

"But why?"

"Just because," Lorna said smugly. "My mom knows all about it, but that's all I'm supposed to say."

Mama provided a little more information. She told me that some local people felt that two women shouldn't live together. Her explanation didn't help me at all, and I gave her several examples of local women who lived together. She said, "You're right, there are some who do, but most of them are sisters or relatives."

Mama never used the term "lesbian," and neither did anyone else. Still, I got the message that it wasn't okay for two young, single women to live together. Both Mama and I were uncomfortable. She didn't volunteer more information, and I didn't ask more questions. But I knew an injustice had been done.

The story of Lee and Leslie still makes me feel a mixture of sadness and anger.

Halloween Pranks

Carol

In our town, Halloween night provided an excuse to get rambunctious. Perhaps it was a tradition left over from the late 1920s when the high school principal, Norman Clyde, was so annoyed by Halloween pranks that he shot his pistol at a carload of boys. They were speeding away from some mischief. A bullet hole was found in the side of the car, so Mr. Clyde resigned. He spent the rest of his life climbing mountains and ultimately became a legend and icon as the "Mountain Man" of the Sierra Nevada.

Two decades later, the kids were still dumping outhouses on the high school lawn, putting old wagons and car parts on the roof, and running girls' bras up the flagpole. But on the Halloween night of my sophomore year, they got carried away and hauled in more items than ever before.

While the boys were transporting outhouses, other kids were soaping store windows Uptown. We generally weren't selective, but that year King's Pharmacy was a special target. The students didn't like Mr. and Mrs. King for numerous reasons. One was because the minute they finished their sodas and root beer floats, Mr. King would tell them to "Move along, move along," fearing that his soda fountain would become a teen hangout. And as Joan had learned, Mr. King insisted on her serving hollow ice-cream scoops. Also, other girls who worked there complained, "Mr. King tries to squeeze us against the counter."

That October, Mr. King made a big mistake. He announced to the business community, "Those kids won't get the best of me this Halloween!"

The pharmacy was on the corner of Edwards and Market streets, the building that today houses the post office. As we soaped the Edwards Street windows, Mr. King was washing the soap off of the Market Street windows. When the Market Street windows were clean, he went around to wash the Edwards Street windows again—while we re-soaped the clean Market Street windows.

Joan said, "I would feel sorry for him, but I keep remembering how rude he was to his young customers."

We were having a very good time because Mr. King couldn't keep up with the dozen or so of us. He was tired and angry, and Mrs. King didn't come out to help him.

When Joan and I went home, after our soap bars were used up, other kids took over the soaping, and the older boys were planning to put an old car body on the pharmacy roof. I never knew just how that was accomplished or when Mr. King went to bed.

The next morning, the lawn in front of the high school was a sight! As soon as the bell rang, our principal announced a student body meeting on the lawn in front of the school. He stood on the top step to give his lecture.

"I don't know who was responsible for this mess on our school lawn and for the destruction of private property, but this sort of behavior will not be tolerated." He went on and on and ended with, "And you have been disrespectful to a businessman in our town. You will all help clean up after school today, and you will all stay one hour after school for the rest of the week to pull weeds and rake the schoolyard."

Arlene protested, "But Mr. Riley, I wasn't even in town on Halloween night."

"Well, I can't tell the sheep from the goats so you will be treated like the rest of the students, Arlene," Mr. Riley spoke decidedly.

Somehow, the outhouses disappeared and the car was removed from the pharmacy roof. We all worked after school to clean up the school grounds. Dad and Mama, and other parents, didn't say much about the incident, and Mr. King wasn't any nicer to his young customers.

As the following October approached, the Independence businessmen told Mr. Riley, "Get those kids off the streets and out of town this Halloween."

So the teachers and parents planned a hayride and party at Onion Valley for the junior high and high school students. It was Anna Kelley's idea and she and her husband, OK Kelley, contributed the food and offered the use of their ski hut.

We rode up the steep, winding road on piles of hay in cattle trucks. There was enough daylight for an energetic treasure hunt. We ran in teams from the waterfall on Robinson Creek on the south side of the valley to the stream from Golden Trout Lake on the north side, and then back to the tall pine that stood in the middle of the ski hill.

After all of that running at 9,000 feet, we were ready to retreat to the warmth of the ski hut for chili, cider and donuts. We bobbed for apples, played games, and each class put on a skit.

For my junior class, Bill Hopper and Mary Drew played an eloping couple. Although their plans had been carefully made, for some reason the young man couldn't make it to the meeting location. He had no way to get a message to his beloved without letting their secret out so he sent her a cantaloupe (can't elope).

For the evening finale, Mrs. Wallace, our music teacher, led us in a sing-along.

We returned to town feeling that it was the best school party ever, and that night there was no mischief in Independence.

Annual Halloween parties at Onion Valley broke the outhouse tradition. Mr. King had lost a battle, but had won the war. Although the high school students, the town businessmen, and Mr. King were happy with the party in Onion Valley tradition, Mr. King never learned to be kind to his young customers.

Ski Days at Onion Valley

Carol

Joan's first day on skis didn't turn out well. She went with her boyfriend, Roy, to Onion Valley where Vic Taylor and OK Kelley ran the rope tow. It was a poor snow year, and the cover over the rocks and brush was skimpy. Vic and Roy took Joan a short distance to where the snow was better for a lesson. They showed her how to turn, and told her to always try to fall sideways. But as they started down, the sagebrush poking through the snow flustered her. She fell forward and twisted her ankle.

They came home early. Roy helped her hop through the front gate and down the walk to the front door.

The x-ray showed it was a sprain, and it took awhile to heal. Joan didn't mind her ankle problem as much as Roy's attitude. He was the best skier in town and had a natural grace at the roller skating rink and on the dance floor, but he was not sympathetic about Joan's ankle.

"She should have followed directions," he said when explaining what happened.

Some months later, Joan told me, "I should have paid more attention to Roy's crummy attitude."

Joan was a sophomore, and Roy was her first boyfriend. He was a senior, the student body president, handsome, and excelled at everything. So it took her awhile to realize that he wasn't always a kind person.

Our first skis were army surplus that someone had given us. They had been used by the Tenth Army Mountain Division during the War and had knobs on the tips to anchor the mountaineer's sealskin climbers. The heavy wood made them inflexible, and they were far too long for us. But we were happy to have them. Joan was the first to try the new sport of skiing.

After she sprained her ankle, Dad told her, "I'll put metal edges on those skis and hopefully they will work better for you."

They did work better, and we took turns with them until we got a second pair.

Vic, who worked for the City as a hydrographer and snow surveyor, and OK, who ran the OK Kelley Services, set up the rope tow every winter. They used an old Model A engine bolted onto a twelve-foot toboggan. The Onion Valley road was never plowed, so they drove up as far as they could and then pulled the toboggan the rest of the way on foot. In unusually heavy snow years, they set up the tow down by Seven Pines.

In Onion Valley, they anchored the toboggan at the bottom of the ski hill and ran the rope up the hill, through pulleys mounted on poles, to a tall pole at the top. It was a good hill, but Onion Valley didn't always have enough snow to cover all the rocks.

When the lift was operating, I rarely missed a weekend. I often had a Saturday night babysitting job for Jack and Virginia Fair. When they apologized for staying out until 2 a.m., I said, "That's not a problem for me, I've finished my homework, and earned enough to pay for two days of skiing!"

I loved standing outside our front gate watching the sun hit the top of Mt. Williamson while waiting for Anna to come by in the OK Kelley Services tow truck. Our house was her first stop as she drove

Onion Valley ski hill, c. 1948.

through town picking up the ski kids. We sat on the back of the truck and hung onto the towing frame as we bumped up the dirt road in the frigid air. Anna drove as far as possible. After a storm, we sometimes walked the last mile or so carrying our skis.

When Vic started the engine, we grabbed the towrope and hung on. He had mounted a safety gate at the top of the tow to trip the electricity in case anyone forgot to let go.

As we waited in line one day, Joan said, "The best thing about a tow is getting to the top of the hill so quickly. But the worst thing is that it rips our sweaters and gloves."

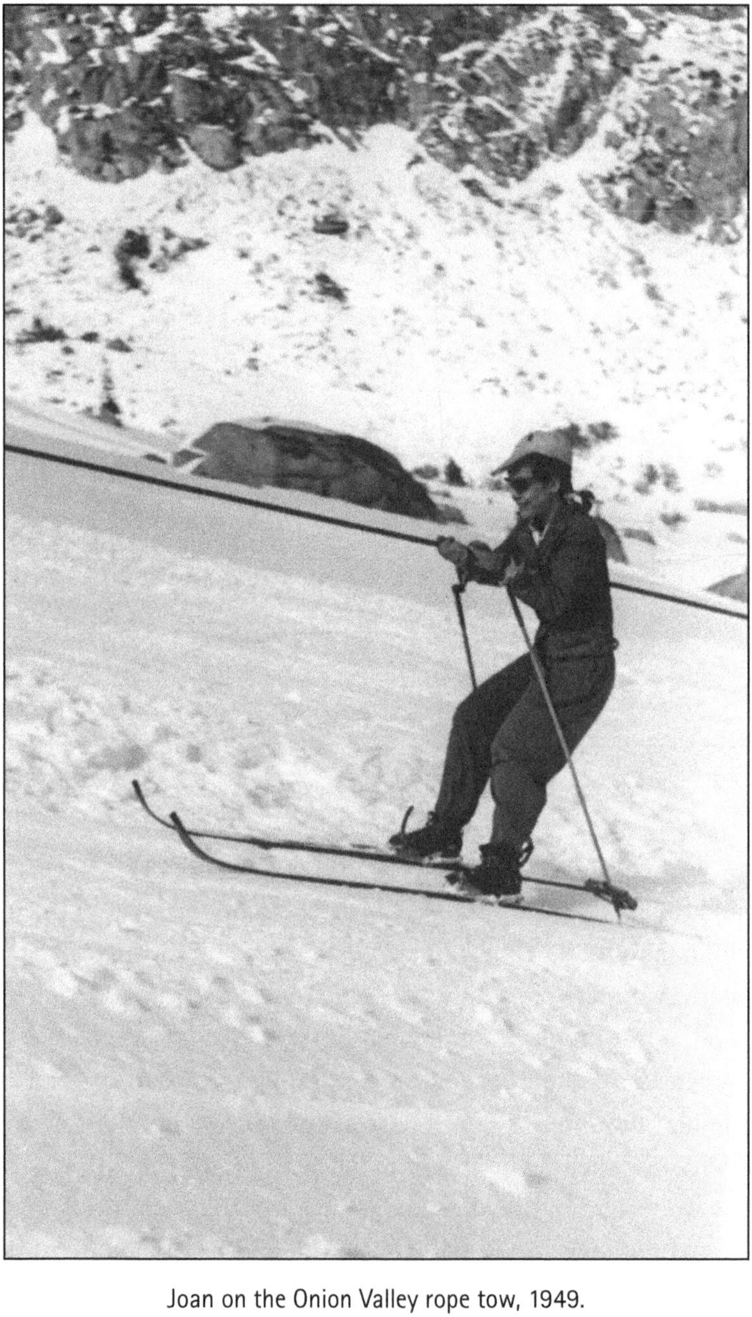

Joan on the Onion Valley rope tow, 1949.

Dickie Little, in line ahead of us, said, "Hey, the Sports Shop in Bishop is selling grippers now. They really work. Watch this!" He clamped his metal gripper onto the rope zipped up the hill.

We found that they did reduce the wear and tear on our clothing, but even with a gripper attached to our belt, our arms ached by the end of the day.

Our regular group included a few adults, a few kids from the high school, and a few from junior high. Vic's son, Ronnie, was in elementary school. Occasionally a skier from southern California showed up. Vic, Roy, and Ronnie were beautiful skiers, but most of us needed some instruction. However, age and ability didn't matter. We were all just skiers, although the boys skied faster and looked for the steepest slopes. It was challenging for me to follow Jimmy Tyler on his routes through the rocks and trees.

We all yelled at Dickie as he wallowed in a snowy hole, "Cover up your sitzmarks!" But he never did.

We ate our sack lunches in the sun on the ski hut porch, enjoying the splendid scenery—the frozen waterfalls and the snowy peaks and pinnacles surrounding Onion Valley.

The Taylors and the Kelleys had built the two-story ski hut where Anna sold hot drinks and snacks on ski days. They later operated it as a summer store for hikers and one summer as a restaurant. Sadly, an avalanche originating in Robinson Basin destroyed the hut in the early 1960s. As the slide tore down the slope and crossed the creek, it had gained so much momentum that it continued uphill all the way to the hut.

In late afternoon, Vic shut off the motor, and we all walked down to the vehicles, the long shadows causing a quick drop in temperature. When the snow was deep enough, we skied down the canyon a ways, following the horse trail.

We considered that last run to be the perfect end of an already perfect day.

Part Six

ENDINGS AND BEGINNINGS
1949–1951

Meeting Mrs. Sperling

Joan

Mrs. Sperling and Mama met by chance in the women's shower room at the Glen Aulin High Sierra Camp. Either she or Mama asked, "Where are you from . . .?" and the conversation went from there.

Our family was backpacking through Northern Yosemite on our way to Tuolumne Meadows. Mrs. Sperling had spent a week at the backcountry tent camp with her husband and young daughter. It was the summer before my senior year, so soon they were talking about colleges.

Mrs. Sperling had attended Pomona College, and she felt it would be a perfect fit for Carol and me because it was a small liberal arts college in the Los Angeles area. As our two families hiked out together the next day, Mama got a pep talk all the way to Tuolumne Meadows. I listened as I followed them up the trail.

That autumn, Mrs. Sperling invited us to visit her family in Pasadena. From there, Mama took me to Claremont to visit Pomona College. We toured a women's dormitory, a classroom building, the student union, and walked around the Quad, a large grassy area with oak and sycamore trees. It was a beautiful campus.

After lunch in a dining hall, I had an appointment with the Dean of Women. She was polite, professional, and asked questions such as, "What are you looking for in a college education?" and "Why do you

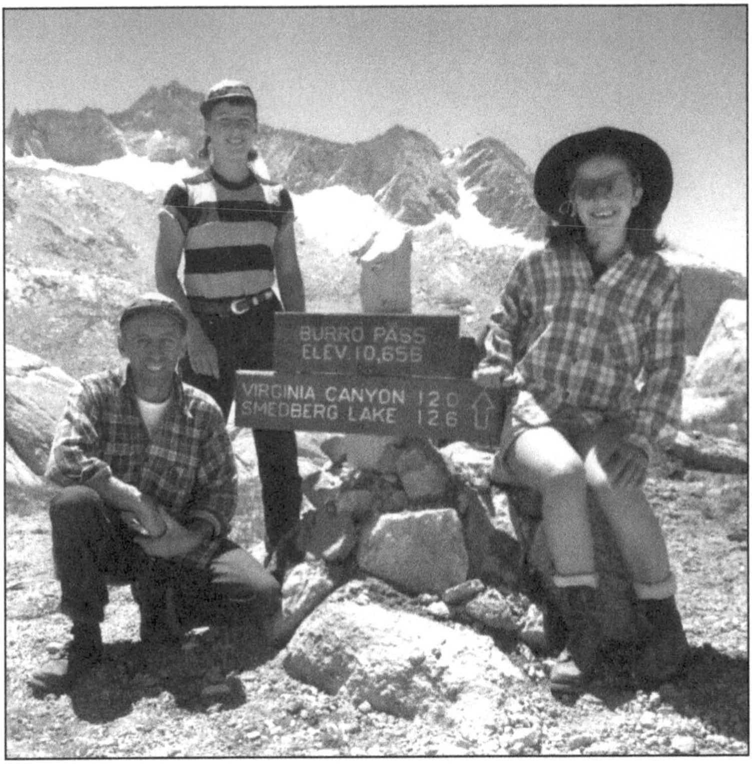

On Burro Pass in northern Yosemite, 1949.

have a special interest in Pomona?" I had no idea how to respond. I felt overwhelmed by these questions and by all that I had seen that morning. Dean Walton could not have been impressed with me.

Mama and Dad had told me they would pay my college tuition and room and board. I knew it was a big commitment for them, but one they had saved for and wanted to make. I also considered Chico State in northern California. It was far less expensive, but getting there on public transportation would be difficult. Mama and I agreed that I would be happier at a small college than a big university, so I applied to Pomona, Occidental, and Redlands, all liberal arts colleges in the Los Angeles area. Because I had an interest in several subjects, a liberal arts approach seemed a good one for me.

I was sure that going to college would be a totally different experience from anything I knew, both academically and socially. I was thrilled to be accepted by all three schools, but I decided to attend Pomona. I was apprehensive about whether I would succeed.

Mrs. Sperling had done an excellent job of selling her alma mater.

The City Boy

Joan

Of course we'd heard about Bill, as word of any newcomer spread quickly through town. The sensitive antennae of the town matrons quickly tuned in whenever an available man appeared. We already knew Bill was an engineering student at the University of Southern California and had taken a temporary surveying job with the City.

It was a perfect autumn day, with golden cottonwoods and a cloudless sky, when I first met him. The annual City Picnic was held at Manzanar that year. Dad drove our family the six miles south from Independence and turned into the parking area. An attendant came to greet us and Dad said formally, "Bill, I'd like you to meet my family. This is my wife, Mary . . ." Each of us gave Bill a polite, "Hello" and each of us got a friendly smile and, "Glad to meet you," in return. As we entered our parking spot, Carol giggled while I scrunched down in the back seat.

We knew Bill was a "City Boy," or "Flatlander," from Los Angeles and at age twenty-two was far too old for us. The local men had been giving Bill advice about fishing, hunting, and mountain trails. The social aspect was up to the town women. Bill was totally caught up in the new outdoor activities and told me later he had "forgotten all about women."

The fact is that Bill had already checked us out. His landlady had told him Carol and I would be playing flute and clarinet solos at the next PTA meeting. So Bill had attended the meeting in our small high school auditorium, oblivious to the snickers and knowing looks of the town folk. He was evidently surprised by our appearance because on his recent hike to Winnedumah on the Inyo crest, he had noted in the hikers register that the DeDecker family had made the hike several times in the last few years. Girls who liked to hike! He was intrigued. Having spent a year living in a fraternity house, he had learned that the last thing sorority girls were interested in was the out-of-doors.

When he saw us in person, we appeared feminine and certainly not brawny hikers. Still, we were young, only sixteen and seventeen.

A few months later, when snow covered the Sierra, Bill invited Carol and me to go skiing at Mammoth. We accepted. Bill came to pick us up in his '37 Chevy coupe. It lacked glass in the window on the passenger side, but Bill had come prepared with blankets and a sleeping bag, and we headed north on Highway 395. The snow began to fall heavily on the steep grade above Bishop, and the road was closed at the Mammoth turn-off. Still determined to take us skiing, Bill turned the car around, tied a rope to the rear bumper, and pulled us down the road on our skis. But not for long as the cold wind froze our fingers and stung our faces until we could hardly see.

On our way home, Bill treated us to hot cocoa at a roadhouse called "Tom's Place." As we dropped in elevation it stopped snowing, and Bill suggested he might try some duck hunting, "If you two don't mind." He pulled into a favorite place along the Owens River, left us in the car wrapped in the sleeping bag and blankets, and went out with his shotgun for an hour. No luck, and soon we were back home.

We ran inside and reported on our trip, "Bill's car doesn't have glass in the side window."

Mama commented, "So it was a little chilly?"

I continued, "And he stopped to go duck hunting!"

Dad laughed and shook his head.

Later that week after supper, Carol and I were doing our homework at the dining room table when there was a knock at the door. Waving a mitten in the air Bill asked, "Has anyone missed this?" In he came, chatting with Mama and Dad and offering to help us with our advanced algebra.

At about 10:30, after Dad had gone to bed, Bill cheerily asked Mama, "Oh, by the way, what time do you like your guests to leave?" Without batting an eye she responded, "Oh, about an hour and a half ago." Bill was out the door in a flash.

Old Time Dances

Joan

I never missed an old time dance—the two-step, four-step, polka, waltz, varsovienne and schottische. It was a community activity that was the rage up and down the valley during the late forties and early fifties.

In Independence, the dances were held once a month in the Masonic Hall with live music supplied by local people, including Mary V. Phillips at the piano and Fred Rood on the violin. Fred also called the square dances. Dad was one of the local men who ran the event for a year or two. He loved to dance. On three-by-five cards, he wrote down the order of the music pieces for Fred and let us know when it was time to stop for refreshments.

Everyone partnered with everyone else regardless of age, and the floor was a colorful scene of men dressed in western shirts and bolo ties and women in full skirts that swirled as they moved.

Those who knew the steps taught them to newcomers. Dad was smooth and graceful and I liked being his partner. Roy, my boyfriend, was as good at dancing as he was at skiing and roller-skating. I was impressed with some of the older women, although gray-haired and a bit stout, their steps were elegant and light-footed. A bachelor from Lone Pine always attended. He struggled to learn the correct steps and was poorly coordinated, yet the women patiently encouraged him.

About ten o'clock, we set up tables and sat down to enjoy cakes and pies. Then everyone helped put the tables and leftovers away and danced until midnight.

Carol came with us if she didn't have a babysitting job. She felt there was no activity better than skiing, and dance nights usually provided opportunities to earn money to pay for two days on the Onion Valley rope tow.

After Roy left for college, I attended with Mama and Dad, and in my senior year I talked my classmate, Mike, into going with me. One Saturday evening, he and I were sitting out a difficult dance, one I didn't know, when Bill the City Boy appeared at the entrance.

"Uh-oh," Mike said.

Bill came up to me and asked, "Would you like to show me this number?"

"I'm sorry, but I really don't know this one. It's tricky and I just haven't learned it yet," I replied with a sweet smile.

Bill went on to dance with other women, but when he asked me a second time, how could I refuse?

Tuba Tunes

Carol

Mr. Hilliard, our music teacher, had discovered an old tuba in the high school basement and brought it to band class one day. It looked dull and dusty.

"Would any of you like to learn to play this tuba?" he asked.

"Oh yes, yes, yes!" I couldn't help but shout.

Mr. Hilliard smiled, perhaps pleased that someone wanted to play the old instrument. I smiled too, relieved that no one else spoke up. I had always enjoyed playing the flute, the instrument I had chosen in the fourth grade, and I was surprised that I had made the decision without any thought. I suppose I was drawn to that tuba because it was the exact opposite of a flute. Next to the piccolo, the flute is the smallest woodwind, and it is the highest-pitched. The tuba is the largest brass in a band, and it is the lowest-pitched. It seems that I was ready for a dramatic change.

"Carol, I'm glad you are interested. I'll figure out the fingering and give you some lessons next week," Mr. Hilliard said.

The tuba sparkled after he cleaned and polished it.

During the first lesson he said, "The important thing is how to hold your mouth and lips. When you blow into the mouthpiece, your lips vibrate and that makes the sound. Another important thing is to breathe from your abdomen, not just your mouth, because it takes a lot of air."

After a few more lessons, I discovered that the tuba was easy to play. It had only four valves. A flute has seventeen keys! Also the music seemed easier—slower and without trills. The deep resonant tones made it worth the chore of lugging it home to practice. I wasn't sure how the neighbors felt about it. Louis said they could hear it in their kitchen on the far side of the house next-door.

In addition to new and different music, the tuba also stopped the invitations for me to play the flute at PTA meetings and various other events in town. That was a good thing because I didn't much enjoy solos in front of an audience.

By the end of the school year, I was playing the tuba well, and the band was practicing the "Triumphal March" from Verdi's *Aida* for the high school graduation. Joan's class would be the first to graduate in our brand new high school gymnasium. Previous graduations took place in the Legion Hall because the high school auditorium was too small. The town had been waiting for years for the new gym, which also would be used for basketball games, student dances, and music programs.

That year there were eight seniors. The four girls were all outstanding students—all had been in the Honor Society every high school year. None of the four boys were exceptional scholars, but they were loyal classmates involved in school activities and sports. All eight would be missed in our little school.

Most of the graduates had some part in the program, sang in the glee club, or played in the band.

Bill was the band drummer, but he didn't play that night because he was recovering from the measles and was barely well enough to attend his graduation. He said, "I feel fine, but the bright stage lights hurt my eyes, so I'm going to watch the ceremony from the hall."

June sang in the glee club.

Lorna gave the "Welcome."

Joan gave the class address, "Owens Valley High School, Past to Future."

Dr. Myron Hesse, a much-admired principal at our school during the War, came to town to give the inspirational commencement address, "Let Go All Lines."

Mary presented the class gift—a rosebush.

Mr. Riley presented the class to the school board.

And the President of the Board presented the diplomas.

The class marched out to the rousing recessional played by the school band with an unusually loud tuba.

We Say "Goodbye"

Joan

There were eight students in my senior class of 1950. We'd given up wishing for more or different classmates by this time, and we were like a family—Bud, Jimmy, Lorna, June, Bill, Mike, Mary, and me.

Bud helped his dad run a packing business out of Onion Valley. On one of our hikes over Kearsarge Pass, we ran into him. Riding a horse and leading a string of mules, he easily passed us as we slowly puffed up the trail with our backpacks. He shook his head in disbelief and said, "You guys are crazy." It was inconceivable to him that we would walk when we could ride a horse, our own horse!

From the first day in kindergarten, Jimmy was the self-appointed class authority for every new teacher. He knew all about everything, and the rest of us would roll our eyes and wait for the new teacher to get tired of listening to him. He did not seem to share his mother's high ambitions for him, and he had no interest in sports. During high school, Jimmy found every excuse to go to the library where he could read *Popular Mechanics.*

Lorna was the other veteran of our kindergarten days, always way ahead of me in social connections, skills, and athletics. She knew how to use power and pressure, but for the most part we got along. She liked the older boys, and I remember sitting with her on her front lawn while she gave me advice about how to "get" a boy.

After graduation, she enrolled in a nursing program at the University of California, Berkeley.

June and her little brother lived with their grandparents. Her grandma was the high school custodian. June and I had good times together in junior high, alternating between her grandma's exciting *True Confessions* magazines and verses from Longfellow's *Hiawatha*, which Mr. Storz required us to memorize. Besides being a good student, June had the best voice in the glee club and always sang the solo parts.

Bill came to our school in third grade. He was a tease, but also a friend. His favorite activities were fishing and hunting, and he was in the group of Boy Scouts who spent two weeks on an annual summer pack trip in the Sierra.

In our freshman year, Mike came to live with an aunt and uncle in order to get away from a "bad situation" in San Francisco. At first painfully shy, Mike gradually warmed to our teasing and attention. He did well in basketball and made a real effort in his classes. I enjoyed his company and wry sense of humor. In our senior year, Mike was not happy when a much older college guy named Bill came to town and began to show an interest in me.

Mary lived with her large family at Kearsarge Station east of town, where her father worked for the narrow-gauge railroad. They were the last family to live there before the train route was abandoned. Mary was a fine student and yet quiet and unassuming. We both knew she wouldn't have the opportunity to go to college, but we didn't talk about it. I didn't know how to tell her I was sorry without sounding patronizing.

We seniors lined up by the front doors of the new auditorium in our black gowns and mortarboard hats. To the strains of *Aida,* we slowly walked through the gym and onto the stage where we turned to face our family and friends. Our school years had lasted so long, yet now seemed to be over too soon.

Our Last Family Vacation

Carol

That summer, after Joan's graduation, we planned what we all knew might be the last family vacation with just the four of us. We all agreed that we should return to Sheep Corral Camp on Tyndall Creek, but this time we would take a different route.

In late July, we backpacked in over Kearsarge Pass to Bubbs Creek and through Center Basin to Junction Pass. This route to Tyndall Creek was abandoned years ago after the construction of Forester Pass, and the trail was no longer maintained. Dad and Mama had been over Junction Pass before, but it was new and dramatic country for Joan and me.

At Sheep Corral, we enjoyed the familiar views of Mt. Tyndall and Diamond Mesa to the east, and the Great Western Divide and the Kaweahs to the west. Each day, we hiked to a favorite lake to fish.

Bill walked in over Shepherd Pass to spend the weekend with us. He left Independence after work on Friday. Even if he hadn't lost the trail in the dark, the 6,000-foot climb and eleven miles each way made it a long trip for a weekend. We expected him to arrive late Friday night. Joan slept lightly and when she saw a light in the direction of the pass, she woke Mama.

"I need the flashlight to go meet Bill, I can see his light coming down from the pass," she said excitedly.

Dad and Mama on the way to Kearsarge Pass, 1950.

Looking south from University Peak towards Mt. Tyndall and the route of our last family vacation, 1950.

Mama sat up and looked toward the east. She laughed, "Go back to bed, Joan, that's the morning star." We teased Joan about the "morning star" for the rest of the trip.

After Bill's visit, we went on to Lake South America and over Harrison Pass, a knapsack route with no trail. Boulder hopping down the steep talus was not easy with a backpack. On the trail below Lake Reflection, we met a group of fishermen on horseback.

When Joan and I stopped to chat, one of them asked, "Are you here by yourselves?"

"Oh no," we replied, "We're with our parents. They're not far behind us."

Other questions followed, "Do you like backpacking? Or do you just come along to please your parents?"

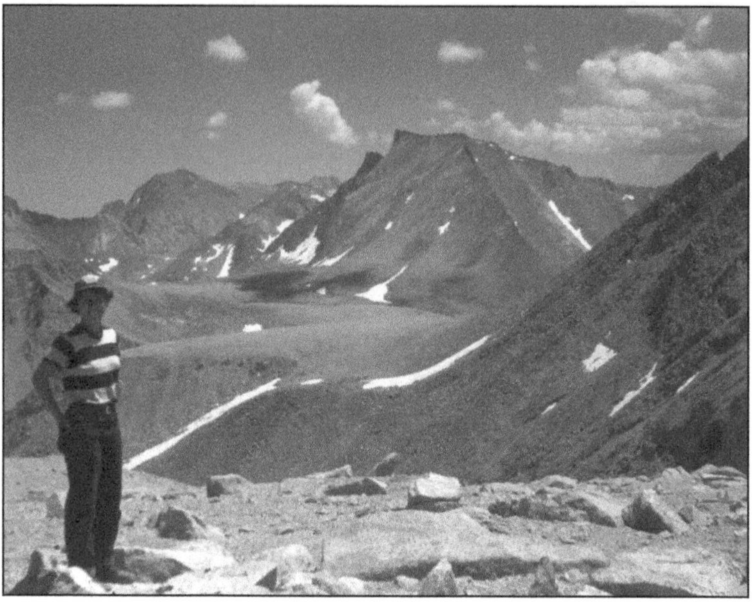

Carol on the summit of Junction Pass, 1950.

We looked at each other and smiled. "We absolutely love backpacking!" Joan said.

"This is our family vacation, and we've been doing this for years," I added. "I'll bet your kids would like it too, if you invited them.

It was hard to explain to these men, who probably always left their wives and daughters at home, how important backpacking was to us. We treasured the early trips with horses and mules when our parents were introducing us to the Sierra. The backpacking that followed was even better because of the simplicity and freedom of living for days with only what we carried. How could we put into words the impact of wilderness trips on our lives when we were just becoming aware of it ourselves?

On our last night around the campfire, we talked about our favorite trips and our favorite places in the Sierra.

Dad said, "I like the deep lakes like Wallace and Wales, South America, and Labrador, where the golden trout live."

Mama was quick to say, "What I like best are the high granite basins and alpine flowers. My favorite flowers, of course, are Sky Pilot (*Polemonium*) and Alpine Gold (*Hulsea*) that grow above 13,000 feet."

I didn't need to think about it, "My favorite thing is the view from the top of a pass or a peak."

Joan added, "I have no favorite lake or flower or place. I love it all! How can I possibly choose?"

At the time, we valued the experiences we had with each other and the knowledge that we shared an appreciation for it all. But Joan and I didn't know then how lucky we were to have been introduced to this sort of family vacation. And none of us knew that the beauty, the vastness, and the solitude of the wilderness would be embedded in our hearts and minds forever.

A Frog Hunt

Joan

Just before I left for Pomona College, Art stopped by for a visit after his summer in the Sierra.

I don't know if it was his or Carol's idea to go frog hunting. I'd been told by my Grandpa Foster that frog legs were tasty, and he'd proudly shown me the rows of canned frog legs packed in glass jars right below the canned peaches on his back porch shelves in North Hollywood.

The next evening at dusk, Art, Bill, Carol and I piled into Bill's old Chevy and headed out to the ponds where the Owens River had once flowed. We turned off the Kearsarge road onto a bumpy route through the pastures, bouncing over cattle guards and through the sand and brush.

When we stopped at a willow-lined pond, we could hear the frogs croaking among the cattails. As car doors slammed, it became suddenly quiet. We had a gunnysack and were each armed with a flashlight and a long-handled gig. The frogs had resumed their croaking as we waded into the shallow water. Our flashlights began to pick up the shine of frog eyes just above the water surface.

"There's one!" Carol called out, and off she splashed. "Ah! I got him!" followed. "Let's get him in the sack."

Spearing just one frog was enough for me, both the spearing part, aiming right behind the head, and the putting it in the sack part. Yuck! It gave me a strange feeling in the pit of my stomach. Why hadn't I thought more about this process beforehand? I was demoted to holding the gunnysack of half-dead frogs and commented frequently, "I think we have enough now," while the other three hunted with enthusiasm.

When satisfied with the catch, we drove home in the heavy warm darkness, scratching our mosquito bites. Mama and Dad had gone to bed.

Bill, Art, and Carol dumped the frogs into the kitchen sink, admiring the big ones while they sharpened their knives. Some frogs still had enough life in them to jump out of the sink and across the kitchen floor.

"Oh no, you don't," Carol yelped, going after the escapees.

I reacted to this noisy, gory scene by deciding to take a bath to rid myself of the scent and slime. I was beginning to relax in the warm water, even forgetting the mosquito bites, when someone opened the bathroom door.

It was Bill's idea to throw a frog into the bathtub with me, but Carol did the deed. I screamed and grabbed a towel yelling, "Stay out!" as the other three doubled over with laughter.

The next night, Art and Carol rolled the frog legs in flour and fried them for supper. I managed to sample one, with little enthusiasm—just enough to agree that it tasted much like chicken. It was my first and last frog hunt.

Mt. Williamson

Joan

Just as Winnedumah kept watch over us from the crest of the Inyos from the east, Mt. Williamson was our guardian on the west. A massive mountain and the second highest Sierra peak, it looks even higher than its 14,375 feet because it stands a little forward of the crest. In contrast, Mount Whitney, just five miles to the south at 14,495 feet, sits back from the crest, so from Owens Valley it looks lower than it really is. Williamson is grand and well-formed, the peak that everyone in town admired and could name. It was "our" mountain, and Carol and I had even named Lady's colt Billy in its honor. Every morning, when the sun rose over the Inyos, it first lit the highest crags of Williamson with a rosy glow, the light gradually working itself down until lower crags also greeted the new day.

Even though we'd been up Whitney twice, Carol and I had never climbed Williamson. It had taken Dad and Mama two attempts to get to its top. The first was from the west in 1945, when the weather became too stormy to continue. The following summer, they joined Art and another friend to successfully climb it from the south.

Mountain sheep lived in small groups in isolated areas high in the Sierra. Fred Jones was living in town while studying the sheep as a graduate project. He invited our family to join him on a weekend hike to check out the herd up George Creek on the south side of Williamson.

He also invited a new physical education teacher, Ellie, from Lone Pine. Dad said he'd seen enough of that part of the mountains to last him for a while, but Mama, Carol and I were eager to join him.

On a cold November day 1947, we slowly made our way up George Creek through brush and partly timbered hillsides. It was difficult for all of us, but seemed to be even more so for Ellie. At an afternoon rest stop she said, "I'm at the end of my rope." Fred thought for a moment before replying, "Well, that rope is always longer than you think it is." Carol and I exchanged worried glances, but soon Ellie stood up and continued on.

Fred told us what tracks to watch for, what shrubs the sheep favored, where they spent each season, and why their numbers had declined from a once much larger population. In 1948, his research was published as the first baseline study of mountain sheep. He must have taken many cold Sierra hikes, and I'd guess that he didn't have companions on many of them.

We camped at timberline at the base of a steep talus slope. The next morning, we awoke to see a herd of six mountain sheep looking down on us. The sighting made the trip worthwhile, and I hoped it did the same for Ellie.

In the summer of 1950, we learned that a group from the Desert Peaks Section of the Sierra Club planned a climb up Williamson on Labor Day weekend. Carol and I asked to join them, and we invited Bill.

At dawn, we three in his Chevy met the Los Angeles group at the highway turnoff, then we all drove up the rough road right to the base of the mountain at about 6,200 feet. Our hiking route was much like the one we had traveled with Fred, through the brush and jumbles of boulders. We camped near timberline.

The next morning, we climbed up a long steep slope of unstable and sliding talus and finally reached the broad upper plateau. It wasn't as steep and the rocks were stable. This kind of surface is visible only on the highest Sierra peaks in places that haven't been glaciated, including Diamond Mesa, Barnard, and the east side of Whitney.

It was afternoon before we reached the summit.

From the top of a mountain, it is always exciting to recognize the nearby peaks. Each side looks different from a new location, and from the top we had the extra dimension of height. Instead of looking up, we looked across or down. We talked about which side of a peak would be easiest to climb or looked impossibly rugged. Our old friend Tyndall was close by, and so were Russell and Whitney, as well as countless peaks in the distance.

"Let's eat. I'm starving!" Bill announced.

Carol and I got out our rations, meager for two reasons. When we had packed our food we were in our "lose weight" mode and forgot

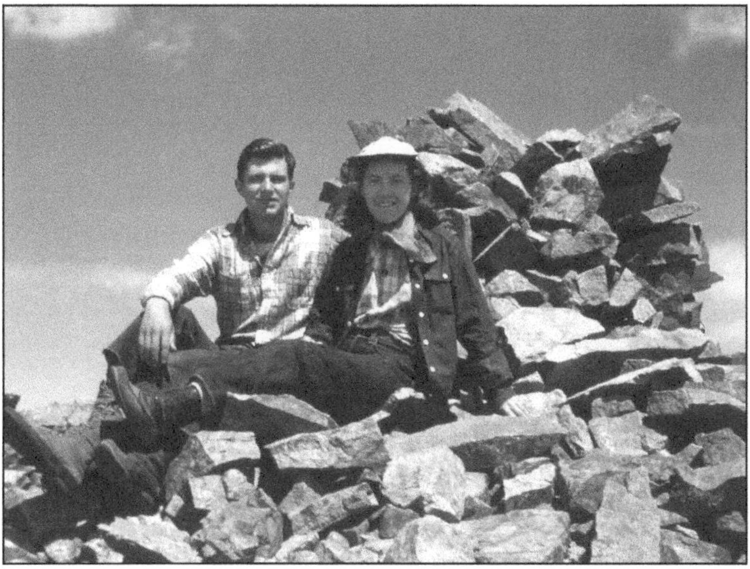

Bill and Joan on the summit of Mt. Williamson, 1950.

to consider that Bill was not part of our decision. It was also meager because we had eaten part of it on the climb.

"Is this *all?*" protested Bill. "Is this *all?*"

I felt guilty. Bill was always such a good sport and never complained unless he was hungry.

It was a long way down, with an overnight stay where we'd left our packs. As I picked my way around large boulders or dug in my heels and let sliding gravel carry me, I thought again about how much easier it is to hike on a trail than to travel cross-country. I was pleased that with the exception of Mount Whitney, there were no trails up the Sierra peaks. The view from the top is one's exhilarating reward for the extra effort. It is a different experience from being a member of a crowd on Whitney. The winter snows will wash away our footprints on a mountain, just as the tides wash over them on a sandy beach.

I've always felt great satisfaction about reaching the summit of our special Mt. Williamson. It was like shaking hands with a long-admired friend.

The New Science Teacher

Carol

Mr. Block came to Owens Valley High School at the beginning of my senior year. It was his first teaching job, and he arrived with great enthusiasm to teach biology and physical science. Right away, I liked his approach to teaching and his sense of humor. We were often out in the schoolyard or in the hills observing some significant aspect of science. Mrs. Loundigan, the principal at the time and a strictly "by the book" teacher, must have often wondered, "Where are they going now?"

One day, our physical science class was discussing sound waves and Mr. Block asked, "Have you ever noticed that the sound of a car horn changes after the car has passed? Let's go outside and I'll show you what I mean."

We students were standing on the corner across the street from the school and Mr. Block asked a student, "Bill, will you drive by the school fast and with one hand on the horn?" Bill Aseltine was one of the few kids that had a car. He drove by—loud and fast.

"As the car approaches, the sound waves are bunching together so the arrival time of successive wave-fronts is reduced," Mr. Block was saying. "And after the car has passed, the sound waves . . . "

He was interrupted by Mr. James, the history teacher, who was marching down the front steps. "WHAT'S GOING ON HERE?"

"We're learning about the Doppler Effect," Mr. Block smiled.

The next week, we were laying out the solar system on the playing field behind the school. How could I ever forget the spatial relationship of the sun and its planets with Bobby's smile beaming in the center, Tommy as Mercury, Rita as Venus, Boyd as Earth . . . ?

In biology, we read about van Leeuwenhoek, the Dutch scientist of the 17th century who, with his handmade microscopes, was the first to observe the single-celled organisms in pond water. He called them, "cavorting beasties."

"Bring your lunch tomorrow and we'll all go down to the Owens River during noon hour to get some pond water," Mr. Block announced.

We collected numerous samples and, back in the lab, we took turns with the microscopes observing the many "beasties."

In early November, Mr. Block passed around the announcement of a national science contest. He said, "This Westinghouse Science Talent Search is an annual national contest which some of you might want to enter."

We had never heard of the contest although this was the tenth year it was being held. There were three parts to the entry—a science project and report, a science aptitude exam, and teacher evaluations and scholarship records. "I can help you think of ideas for a project and help you get started," Mr. Block encouraged.

Right away, I began to think about possible projects, and Mr. Block helped me make a choice. It would be about evidence of glaciation in the Sierra Nevada. I looked for information about the last ice age and tried to recall what the geologist father of my fourth-grade best friend, Phyllis, had told us on our hikes years ago. I couldn't remember much about it, so I wrote and asked him questions. Dr. Oakeshott was now Deputy Chief of the California Division of Mines and Geology. He sent references to helpful articles.

An excellent place to see glacial evidence was in the Tyndall Creek basin, just across Shepherd Pass. During recent trips, we had climbed some of the high mountains in that area: Tyndall, Diamond Mesa, Williamson, Barnard, Whitney, and Muir. From the top of those peaks, it was easy to see the glacial cirques, hanging valleys, moraines, and remnants of pre-glacial surfaces. With the camera I had bought, after years of saving, I had taken enough photos from those summits to illustrate a research paper. So the project part was easy enough.

The exam was not so easy. It lasted two-and-a-half hours and had short answers, multiple choice, and math problems. I took it in the home economics room with a monitoring teacher. I was the only one in the school to enter the contest.

With Christmas and the long holiday, I almost forgot about the science contest. Then one morning in February, Mr. Block called me out of Mrs. Baker's English class. As we stood in the quiet hallway he said, "Congratulations, you are one of the science contest winners!"

I was speechless!

A month later, the forty top Science Talent Search contestants in the United States, ten girls and thirty boys, went to Washington, D.C., to attend the Science Talent Institute for five days. We would compete for two scholarships.

The trip itself was a new experience for me. I had never been out of California. Dad and Mama drove me to Mojave, the closest train station, 130 miles south of Independence. It took three nights and four days to cross the country, and I enjoyed the elegance of the diner and sleeper cars. Never had I traveled in such luxury, but I had never been anywhere except camping trips. It seemed as though I was the only teenage girl on a train full of young soldiers on their way to Korea. Some of them didn't have a girlfriend and asked for my address.

On the long train ride, I had plenty of time to worry about spending a week with kids from big city schools. Would they be sophisticated? Intimidating? Brainy? Would I feel like a small-town hick?

In Chicago, I met the eight other students from the western states. They had arrived on several different trains, and we were collected at the station and introduced to each other by a contest sponsor. Like me, they were happy to meet others on their way to the event in Washington, and most of them were as nervous as I was.

It was an exciting and busy week. We stayed in the Statler Hotel and visited scientific research centers, historic sites, and museums. We went to the Capitol, climbed the 897 steps to the top of the Washington Monument, and visited the White House where we all shook the hand of President Truman. Interviews with the contest judges were scheduled throughout the week.

We displayed our science projects in the hotel's Presidential Ballroom. There was a wide range of topics from "A Study of Canned Dog Food in the Feeding of Rats" to "Construction of a One-half Million Electron-Volt Proton Cyclotron." My project display, "Glacial Evidence in the Kings-Kern Divide Area of the Sierra Nevada," was a series of photographic enlargements with overlays to illustrate evidence of Pleistocene glacial activity.

There was also a wide range of students. Some were the brilliant type and some were ordinary students like me, but we all enjoyed getting to know one another. Instead of sophisticated and intimidating, they were a friendly, confident, and lively bunch. We were all sixteen or seventeen years old, and we came from thirty-seven schools in fifteen states. Almost half were from New York. Three students were from two enormous high schools in New York City. Those two schools had strong science programs and competed each year to produce the most science contest winners. I was amused to think that our high school was competing with schools that had enrollments larger than

Visiting President Truman (I'm the one in the ugly plaid dress), 1951.
Westinghouse Science Talent Search photo

our entire town! The two top winners were the brilliant types from those New York City schools.

The ride home on the California Zephyr with the three others from California was even more fun than my trip east. We had become good friends, and we spent the days together in the observation car. We all felt that it had been an unbelievable and unforgettable experience.

As spring came, Mr. Block had us identifying the native wildflowers and shrubs at Grays Meadows and making lists of birds seen in our backyards. Up Mazourka Canyon, just ten miles east of the school, we examined the faults, folds, and fossils in the metamorphosed layers of the Inyo Mountains.

I have often reflected on the science contest and how a student from a fifty-student high school could compete with students in far bigger schools. I've come to know that the teachers are more important than the size of the school. Most of us can recall a particular teacher who changed our lives in some significant way. For me, there were three special teachers. Mr. Storz made every part of United States history fun and recognized a speaking talent in Arlene. Mrs. Wilder made algebra and geometry concepts easy. Mr. Block pointed out the possible to me.

Our school lacked opportunities in some ways. We never had a wide choice of classes, and sometimes the teachers taught subjects far out of their fields. But the basics were solid, and we benefited from having small class sizes, a supportive community, and those exceptional teachers.

I'll never forget the sound of the Doppler Effect and the cavorting beasties that live in pond water.

Easter at Calvert Slough

Carol

Elsie and I were discussing what to do during Easter vacation of my senior year. We wanted a long ride on our horses with a few days of camping. Springtime in Owens Valley was beautiful IF the wind didn't blow. Dad and his barometer assured us that it would be calm and clear.

"It's still cold at Seven Pines so I think we should stay down here in the valley—how about the Alabama Hills or Aberdeen," Elsie suggested.

"Those are good ideas. Janeane doesn't live at Aberdeen any more, but we could go to Calvert Slough."

"That's a great idea!" Elsie agreed.

Joan and I had ridden to the slough with Jeanene during our visits to Aberdeen several years ago. It was a marsh about two miles northeast of Aberdeen, fed by the nearby Owens River, just a mile before most of the river was diverted into the Los Angeles Aqueduct.

There were several routes we could take, but we chose the dirt maintenance road on the east side of the aqueduct, a seventeen-mile ride.

I was riding Billy because we had sold Lady the previous spring. It was a whole year ago, but I was still recovering from that traumatic event.

During our last high school years, Joan and I were too busy with school activities to ride in the winter, so we had put Lady and Billy out to pasture at the Fort. The spring of Joan's senior year, when Mama had driven us out to the Fort to get them, we had been astounded to see that Lady had another colt! Lady looked scruffy and skinny. The colt was still wobbly and too young for the four-mile trip to town, so we had gone home to report the news to Dad.

He had said firmly, "With Joan going off to college soon, we don't need three horses."

I was heartbroken, but I knew he was right. "Yes, Dad. But I would rather sell Billy than Lady. Even though I've known Billy all his life, I still feel closer to Lady. She's been my special friend. I feel like we've grown up together."

"I understand your feelings about Lady, but because of the colt we'll have to sell her rather than Billy. I'll ask Allie to find a buyer."

On the way to the slough that day, I was still feeling guilty for deserting Lady and her new baby. I never saw them again. Allie had picked them up that very week and taken them to a horse auction in Nevada. I never got to tell her how much she meant to me. I didn't get to say goodbye with hugs and kisses on her soft nose. Dad hadn't realized that Allie would take them so soon.

Elsie and I left for the slough soon after sunrise, and we weren't in a hurry. While riding at a horse's pace, we had a long look at the scenery—every snowy Sierra peak and every pass, every canyon and the creeks that wiggled down them, and every ribbon of willows that found its way through the sagebrush to the aqueduct.

At Black Rock, we saw the first of the many lava flows and cinder cones that occur in this middle part of the valley. We'd been looking at them from the highway for years, but many features are not as noticeable from a fast-moving vehicle as they are on horseback.

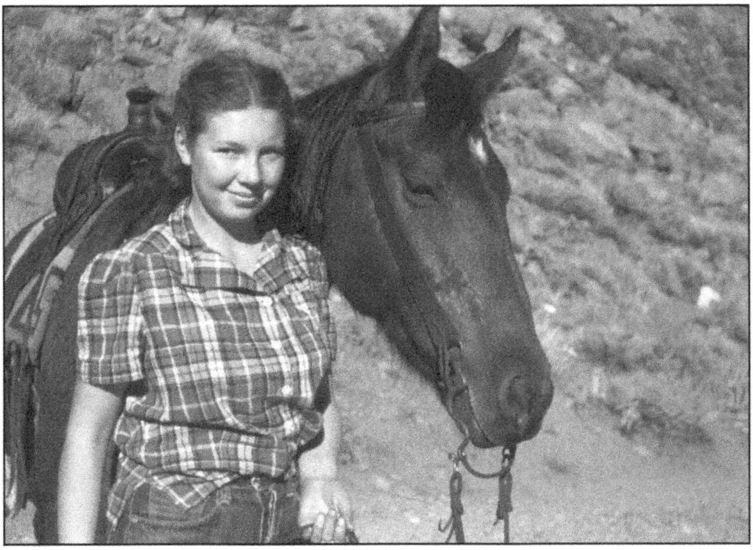

Elsie and Babe, 1951.

When we came to the aqueduct intake, I said, "Elsie, that pasture is where Joan and Janeane and I chased Lady for two hours until Mr. Bangs came out to help us. He lives in that house over there." And I pointed to the caretaker's home and well-kept patch of lawn and flowers under the cottonwood trees.

She laughed, "I remember that story!"

"I'm glad your dad taught us how to catch Lady. His technique with the nosebag of oats always works."

A mile farther on, we arrived at Calvert Slough, a marshy pond with reeds and cattails around the edges. Cottonwoods grew on the higher banks. It in a sea of sage and rabbitbrush, the slough was our special oasis.

We set up our camp under the cottonwood tree next to a corral. Sociable Billy looked over the fence and watched. He seemed to like being close to us, which was not surprising since he had spent his first months in our backyard.

Mama drove out in the late afternoon with our food, sleeping bags, and jugs of water. She welcomed an excuse to get out to explore the dirt roads and to see what plants were blooming.

We fed Babe and Billy their oats and filled the water trough with water from the slough. Then we collected firewood and sharpened willow sticks to cook hot dogs. Later we toasted marshmallows and watched the full moon rise over the Inyos. Around our campfire, we talked about the rides we had taken and the new places we wanted to explore. Also, we discussed how fortunate we felt that our families had moved to Independence. I was beginning to realize just how hard it would be to leave this all behind when I left for college.

The next morning, we took Babe and Billy down to the water and let them nibble the grass for a while before we cooked our bacon and eggs. Then we went off to explore the slough.

"Wow, look at this!" Elsie shouted.

She had found a raft in the reeds. It wasn't in good shape, but we didn't bother to improve it because the water was shallow, never more than waist-deep. We found some pieces of wood near the corral to use as paddles and spent the whole day paddling around through the cattails. When the sun got too hot, we slipped into the cool water.

That evening, we realized how sunburned we were. We were pale from the winter months and had burned more quickly than we'd expected. It was an uncomfortable night as we tossed and turned.

In the morning, Elsie said, "I didn't realize how sunburned I was until I tried to sleep on my back. I hope you brought some suntan lotion because I didn't."

"I didn't think of it either," I groaned.

We were cooking breakfast when Elsie suggested, "Hey, we should try some of that bacon grease on our noses."

She poured some into a cup and said, "But it doesn't look much like suntan lotion, it needs something else."

"I know what it needs!" and I grabbed a spoon and an empty tin can.

After we stirred in some fine dust from the road, it looked just right. We dabbed it on our noses and the top of our ears.

On the long ride home, we talked about horses, the beauty of the Sierra, lava flows, and how much we loved Owens Valley. Camping at Calvert Slough had been fun for us and also for Babe and Billy.

"Elsie," I said, "I'm so lucky to have a friend like you. Not everyone would delight in a dusty campsite and homemade suntan lotion."

A Spring Hike

Carol

Art came to visit in early May, not long before my high school graduation in June 1951. He spent the snowy winters at Lake Tahoe doing carpentry work and often visited us before heading into the Sierra for the summer. Over dinner, he talked about moonlight snowshoeing and hiking in the woods and hills around his home. His enthusiasm for outings in the snow resulted in our plan to hike to the lakes above Onion Valley on the next Saturday.

The Sierra still had plenty of snow, so we didn't expect to go far. Mama, Dad, Art, Elsie, Fred Jones, and I set off early that morning. The snow was patchy in Onion Valley, with drifts and bare spots. The ski hill was mostly rocks and bushes. No one else was there—and we didn't see another human footprint all day.

Although the drifts got deeper as we climbed and the trail was not often evident, the walking was easy on the crusty surface. The creek was mostly iced over and the freezing and thawing had left dazzling ice crystals on the rocks and shrubs. Gilbert Lake looked like an ice skating rink. As we passed Flower Lake, also frozen like a skating rink, I saw the spot where we had camped with the Campfire Girls eight years ago. Snowmelt had collected in small depressions, and my icy bed site looked uninviting.

The snow remained firm, and the stunning view held our attention during the four miles and 2,700-foot climb to Kearsarge Pass. From the pass, we looked down on more icebound lakes.

"That was easy, and the snow is still firm. Maybe we should go a ways up the ridge for a better view," Fred suggested.

We all agreed, and we began climbing the ridge north of the pass. It was easy at first, but as the temperature rose on that south-facing slope, we began to sink up to our knees with each and every step.

"Whew, this is getting to be work, I'm ready to turn around," Mama puffed.

Art agreed, "Yes, we probably should start down, but I think that pile of boulders over there is the summit of Mt. Gould."

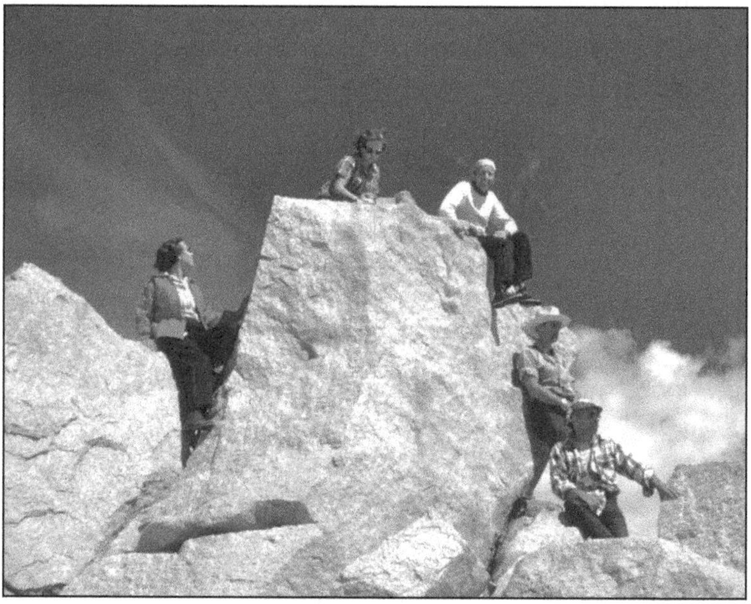

Summit of Mt. Gould, 1951.
(See Appendix for names)

Looking down on the Kearsarge Lakes from Mt. Gould, 1951.

When we realized how close we were, we struggled up the last few hundred feet to the summit of 13,005-foot Mt. Gould. We sat on the enormous boulders for a long while and marveled at how snow enhances an already remarkable landscape.

Our descent was quick and easy—a slide down the steep snowfield to Kearsarge Pass. The snow was soft enough for us to control our speed and also perfect for the snowballs that Elsie and I tossed at Art and Fred all the way down.

That spring hike was a new experience. The soft snow had made the afternoon hiking tedious, but the scene was unforgettable. I was ready to go again. It is probably fortunate that I didn't. We were all competent in the summer Sierra, but none of us realized how unprepared and ill equipped we were that day. We didn't even think about avalanches. We didn't know that spring freezing and thawing lubricates and weakens lower snow layers and can result in slow, but dangerous "wet slab" avalanches.

Our climb to Kearsarge Pass in the early morning was reasonably safe, but we should not have climbed the south-facing ridge to the summit of Gould, or slid back down the steep snowfield to Kearsarge Pass in the warm afternoon.

Understanding the hazards we faced in our carefree innocence that day has enhanced my fond memories of that delightful spring hike in our tennis shoes.

Goodbye to Owens Valley

Carol

Our house on the highway was the only one I'd ever known.

That house and the town, the sagebrush, the Sierra, and the Inyos—all were my home. Leaving Owens Valley would not be easy. I couldn't imagine the world of college.

Mr. Block had graduated from Pomona College, and he influenced my decision to join Joan there. Southern California, with its dense population and frightful traffic, was a foreign landscape. Although Pomona was a school with only 1,200 students, sophisticated classmates were too intimidating to even think about. How would I cope?

The week before I left home, Elsie and I decided to climb Mount Whitney. Mama dropped us off at the Whitney Portal trailhead on that late September morning. The sun was bright, and the air was crisp. Few people were on the trail. We hiked the first six miles and camped at Mirror Lake where we plucked orange gooseberries from the low bushes around the lake and napped on the grass in the sun.

When the sun went down, the temperature plunged, but we had brought plenty of warm clothes. I had learned from my family's moonlight climb four years ago that nights at high elevations in September can be extremely cold. We sat close to our campfire and talked about the summit climb.

I suggested, "We should start early, because it's five miles with a 4,000-foot climb. Then it'll be eleven miles back down to Whitney Portal. That's a long day."

Elsie agreed, "We don't want to be hiking in the dark, there's no moon right now."

Neither of us owned a watch, so we woke often during the night to check the position of the Big Dipper.

Sometime in the night, Elsie said, "Look at the dipper handle. Do you think it's time to start?"

"Oh no, it's too cold," and I fell back asleep.

It was dark when we agreed that it *must* be time to start. But it was still too early, and we lost the trail.

At dawn, we were approaching Consultation Lake when we saw on a note on the top of a boulder. It was held down by several flat rocks. It read, "*Are you lost too?*" We laughed as we found our way back to the trail. I don't know how we stumbled that far in the dark without a trail or flashlight.

After the sun came up, we had a pleasant hike to the top of that dramatic mountain. It was a perfect calm and cloudless day. From the summit of Mount Whitney, I said "goodbye" to the valley and the mountains beyond mountains. I looked across the ridges to the summit of Mt. Williamson where I had stood with Joan and Bill just one year ago. Almost two thousand feet below me, in its granite cirque, Tulainyo Lake sparkled in the sun. I could see the place in the surrounding talus jumble where Joan, Corky, and I had sunbathed on the boulders three years earlier. Below us, the Alabama Hills and the Whoopee Road reminded me of picnics with my cousins. I waved to Winnedumah across the valley—too far away to see, but I knew it was standing tall on the Inyo crest twenty-five miles away.

We stayed on the summit a long time. I said, "Elsie, I have stood on this very rock three times in the last four years. I want to remember this view forever—every peak, every pinnacle, every lake, and every twist of the Owens River.

There were friends and memories in every direction. I said "good-bye" to all, knowing in my heart this place would always be my home.

Afterword

College and After

Joan

Bill offered to drop me off at Pomona College in Claremont on his way to Los Angeles in mid September, 1950. He was returning to the University of Southern California to complete his engineering degree. When the big day arrived, he loaded my boxes and suitcases into his Chevy, and we drove the 250 miles south over Cajon Pass and to the campus.

As we pulled to the curb in front of my dorm, some boys appeared and offered to carry my luggage to my room. It was a tradition that allowed the sophomore boys to look over the freshman girls. Bill confessed to me later that he thought to himself that afternoon, "Well goodbye, Joan."

As I anticipated, there were many challenges at Pomona. Most of the students were from well-to-do families in Los Angeles or other urban areas. And I could tell from their comments and the answers they gave in class, that their education had been more rigorous than mine. But I enjoyed living with the freshmen girls in the dormitory, and I worked hard to keep up academically.

In my sophomore year, I lived with eight other girls in an old house next to the dorms with a warm-hearted housemother. I made lasting friendships, and it was my favorite college year. By my junior year, I had gained academic confidence but was losing interest in the social life and the boys, who all seemed so much younger and less interesting than Bill. We were married the following summer in the beautiful Bridges Hall of Music.

For a semester we lived in married student housing, converted barracks, while I finished a major in education. Bill commuted to work as an engineer for the City at the Los Angeles headquarters. He was soon involved in the design of a spillway for Pleasant Valley Dam in the lower Owens River Gorge. We had our first child and bought a little house, but neither of us liked living in the traffic-congested Los Angeles area. Bill changed jobs, and we eventually settled in the small town of Mill Valley just north of San Francisco. Marin County had hills and beaches and a mountain laced with hiking trails. It had a population that appreciated and worked to protect its natural areas. And it had good schools.

For many years, I was a stay-at-home mom, busy with three sons and a daughter. Then I earned a teaching credential and taught for twenty years in elementary schools. In keeping with my interest in the natural world, I developed outdoor education programs for my students.

While the children were young, Bill and I led summer outings for the Sierra Club Wilderness Threshold program. On each trip, a group of families hiked four to six miles to a mountain location while their food and gear were taken in by pack animals. We stayed for a week, sharing the cooking, before hiking out with memories of watching our children have a grand time. As they grew older, we led family backpack and canoe trips. Our children still refer to those experiences as high points of their childhood.

In our later backpack years, we led Sierra Club trips in Alaska, usually followed by a trip for the two of us hiking down a river or up a mountain route.

Afterword

In 2004, I did a solo hike of the John Muir Trail with children, grandchildren, and Bill helping with the food caches. My pace was slow, averaging five miles a day, but my spirits were high. It was a time of solitude and reflection and memories of many journeys in that unforgettable land.

The World Beyond

Carol

My years at Pomona went by quickly. It was sometimes uncomfortable living among wealthy and cosmopolitan classmates, but I did find kindred spirits and good friends. Claremont was a quiet town with mountains and desert nearby, and it was easy to get out to hike and bike.

The week before we graduated, I married Del Wiens, a classmate who shared my love of the natural world and adventuresome activities. He went on for a Ph.D. and taught biology at the University of Colorado and the University of Utah. His research took our family to many parts of the world. We lived in Ecuador and trekked in Nepal. Our three young daughters traveled with us by Land Rover the length of Africa and the width of Australia, camping most of the time. They taught kids to jump rope across both continents.

We raised our family in Utah, backpacking in the mountains and sandstone canyons, river rafting, and backcountry skiing. As with Del and me, their childhood outdoor experiences have served them well. When the girls were in the middle grades, I went back to school for an M.A. in archeology and worked in that field and later as a wildlife biologist.

Del and I continued our travels after our children were grown. We canoed numerous wild rivers on month-long trips in the Canadian

Arctic. When we retired, we bought a sailboat (Norseman 447) and headed for Australia, 8,000 miles away. We'd had no experience with oceans or sailboats, but we planned carefully, prepared for emergencies, and made good decisions along the way. The self-reliance we gained from our years in the out-of-doors, first as children and continuing to the present, has given us the confidence to undertake new endeavors.

After eight years of sailing, we returned to the sagebrush and mountains and now live in Boise, Idaho.

The Eastern Sierra Water Wars

Joan

The Los Angeles Aqueduct had been operating for twenty-two years when our family moved to Owens Valley. Soon after our arrival, our parents learned about the bitter and futile struggle the Owens Valley people had waged against the all-powerful City of Los Angeles Department of Water and Power (the "City" as we called it then, or the "DWP" as it is called today). According to valley residents, Los Angeles stole their water. But in spite of vigorous and sometimes violent protests by locals, the aqueduct construction was completed in 1913. As Mulholland, Eaton, and Lippincott—the masterminds of the project—had predicted, taking water from the eastern Sierra streams allowed Los Angeles and the San Fernando Valley to grow.

Owens Lake, formerly fed by Sierra streams, had dried to a puddle with a wide soda-ash rim by 1926. Without water, the lake lost its magnificent bird life, and frequent winds blew unhealthy lake dust up and down the valley. The complaints of local citizens were ignored.

When more water was needed in the Los Angeles area, the DWP turned its attention to Mono Lake, 106 miles north of Independence. Sierra streams that fed Mono Lake would be diverted into a system of tunnels and reservoirs to join the existing Los Angeles Aqueduct.

Construction of the Mono Basin Aqueduct was begun in the early 1930s. Men like our father were hired to haul equipment and materials to the site. He was unaware of the environmental impacts resulting from the actions already taken and those to follow. As a young man during the Great Depression, he was in need of a job and delighted to get one in scenic Owens Valley.

The Mono extension was completed in 1940, and Mono Lake began to shrink. From 1941 to 1990 the ecosystem suffered as the lake dropped forty-five vertical feet. In 1978, the Mono Lake Committee was founded to try to save the lake. In 1994, after a decade of litigation, the California State Water Resources Control Board set regulations to restore the lake to a "healthy" level.

Meanwhile, the DWP had begun groundwater pumping in Owens Valley in the 1960s. After a decade, the effect was evident. Meadows and ponds were disappearing and trees and shrubs were dying. As residents saw these changes occurring on the valley floor, they formed a citizens group to bring legal action against DWP activities. Our mother became a leading member of that group.

In the 1970s, after a series of protests and meetings spanning many years, the environmental movement began to gain momentum. Mama was pleased to have local citizens join botanists and other scientists in advocating for what had once seemed like a hopeless cause. She testified at numerous hearings, wrote newspaper and newsletter articles, established a local chapter of the California Native Plant Society, and worked tirelessly to protect the land she so cherished.

For years, hearings were held, petitions were filed, and protests made, all of which the DWP, with more money and power, rejected or resisted. Finally in 1987, the Environmental Protection Agency declared Owens Lake to be the worst dust pollution problem in the United States. The DWP proposed many mitigation measures and experimented with some of them until 1998, when it was legally required to remediate the dust problem or to pay a penalty of $10,000 per day. Since then, mitigation efforts have been implemented and the blowing dust significantly reduced. Under a court order in 2006, the DWP began to release a limited amount of water each spring into the last six miles of the Owens River and into Owens Lake.

To everyone's amazement, shorebirds began to reappear, more birds each year. The Eastern Sierra Audubon Society began an annual count of species and numbers of birds and now calls this area one of the most important avian sanctuaries in California. The birds are protected under the North American Migratory Birds Treaty Act.

Although limits have been set on the amount of water the DWP can take from Mono Lake and Owens Valley streams, the vegetation continues to struggle as the water table continues to drop.

People sometimes wonder what Owens Valley would look like if Los Angeles hadn't taken the water. Would local land companies and ranchers have purchased the water rights of every stream for private farms and ranches? Would fences, gates, and "Keep Out" signs line the roads to the foothills? Could residents and tourists still wander through the sagebrush and up the streams?

Independence Today

Joan

At times, during the 1930s and 1940s, Independence had a population of almost one thousand. Although not as large as Bishop, forty miles to the north, it had job opportunities because it was both the seat of Inyo County and the Owens Valley headquarters of the Los Angeles Department of Water and Power.

The town has seen significant changes since we left and is no longer the vibrant, bustling community of our childhood. The decline may have begun when the City moved some of its offices from Independence to Bishop in the 1980s. Or, perhaps it was when four lanes were completed on highway 395, making it quicker and safer to commute from Bishop or Lone Pine to jobs in Independence. The state also closed the fish hatchery on Oak Creek. Businesses left, and school enrollment dropped. A final straw seemed to be the widening of the highway right through town. Many trees were lost that had served to soften the stark look of the sidewalks and buildings. Although some county facilities have been constructed at the southeastern edge of town—a new jail, juvenile detention center, and Inyo County equipment and maintenance buildings—most employees commute to these jobs from Lone Pine or Bishop. Cars and trucks in ever-increasing numbers pass through town without stopping.

After the school almost closed because of dropping enrollment, a supportive school board agreed to many changes. A highly regarded principal was recruited, and the grounds and buildings were updated. The school now has a reputation for high standards and has begun to attract students from throughout the county, from Bishop to Keeler. Elementary enrollment is up to sixty-four students. The twenty-seven high school students can take advanced placement classes through a program at Cerro Coso Community College in Ridgecrest. The sports program now includes volleyball, cross-country, basketball, and hopes to soon offer tennis.

The historic Winnedumah Hotel periodically opens and closes. The grocery store that we knew first as Bandhauers, then Kraters, and finally as Mairs Market, is closed. A part-time co-op operates at the site. The Kings Pharmacy building now houses the post office. Bishop citizens are campaigning to have a new courthouse built in their town (in the far northern part of Inyo County), while the citizens of southern Inyo want it built in Independence (in the central part of the county).

In spite of these changes, the town endures with loyal supporters. The Eastern California Museum has many visitors; the library still operates. Tourists still turn west on Market Street and head for Grays Meadow or Onion Valley to camp and fish or to hike over Kearsarge Pass. The residents continue to put on the annual Fourth of July celebration. Six miles to the south, Manzanar National Historic Site documents the Japanese internment camp and attracts many visitors.

The town holds on to old-timers and attracts new people whose interests involve the out-of-doors. The magnificent Sierra escarpment still stands above the town, with clear streams rushing down steep canyons to the sagebrush expanse of the valley floor. And from the crest of the Inyo Mountains, Winnedumah still looks down on the town.

Paul and Mary DeDecker

Joan

Paul and Mary never left Independence. After their daughters finished college, they built a new home on the edge of town with many closets and big windows facing the Sierra crest. Paul created another beautiful yard, and he tended a vigorous vegetable garden and Mary's native plant garden. He retired after forty years with the DWP.

Mary worked as the school secretary for over fifteen years and for the Title Insurance and Trust Company for about ten more. When she retired, she was thrilled to devote all of her time to botanical, environmental, and other interests. She published *Flora of the Northern Mojave Desert, California*, was a member of many boards and commissions, and received numerous conservation awards. Paul supported Mary in her botanical and other endeavors, especially with her extensive plant collection.

Focusing their attention on eastern California and Nevada, they traveled countless desert roads to collect plants and to share botanical knowledge with friends and colleagues. They were active members of the Death Valley '49ers, a group that sponsors the annual Death Valley Encampment. Each served a term as president of that organization.

On the night of their arrival in Independence, on November 15, 1935, Mary wrote in her diary, "Expect to stay two or three years and hope to gain much in health, pleasure, and experience." Their life together in Independence and Owens Valley far exceeded their expectations. Mary lived until age 91 and Paul until age 96.

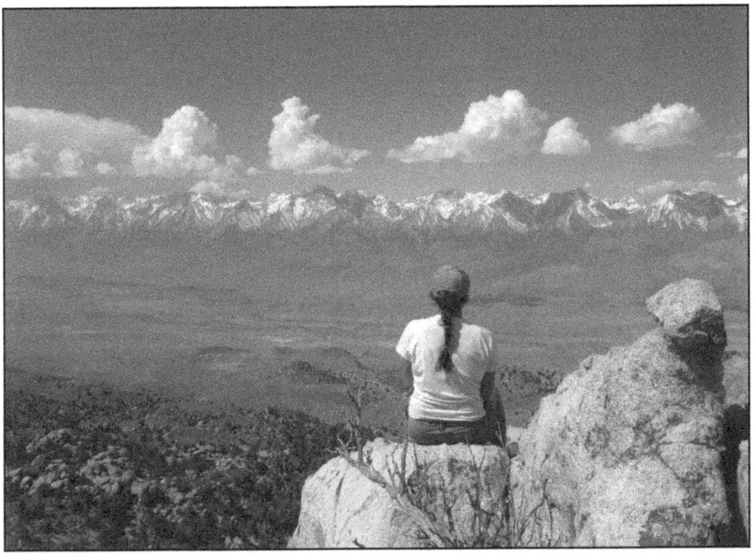

Looking across Owens Valley at the Sierra Nevada from the Inyo crest. Independence is the dark spot to the right of Paula Wiens' head, 2009.

There's a little creek in Inyo, singing by beyond
the town,
Through the pink wild-almond tangle and the
birches slim and brown,
Where all night we'll watch the star-beams in
the shallow, open rills,
And the hot, bright moons of August skulking
low along the hills;
And the Word will wake in Inyo—never printed
in a page—
With the wind that wakes the morning on a
thousand miles of sage.

Mary Austin

Acknowledgments

Many thanks—

To Maggie Wittenberg, who got us started on this project by asking us to speak about our childhood one summer evening on the lawn of the Eastern California Museum in Independence.

To writers and editors who read draft versions and made valuable suggestions: Jean and LeRoy Johnson, Mary Kelly McColl, Elisabeth Sharp McKetta, Jennifer Reese, Amy Richmond, and Wendy Wiens.

To friends and relatives who were generous with their expertise: Genevieve Busby, Roberta Harlan, Jon Klusmire, and Cay Marquart.

To schoolmates and friends who shared their memories: Caroline Goff, Elsie and Bruce Ivey, Bruce Krater, Joy Martin, Arlene Pearce, Tom Poole, Jim Riley, Bill Rowan, Alice Olds Smalley, and our music teacher, Virginia Stephens.

To our husbands, Bill Busby and Del Wiens, who patiently encouraged us as we phoned back and forth between Mill Valley and Boise and spent long hours at our computers. Special thanks to Bill for scanning piles of old photographs.

And to Laurie McAndish King, our copyeditor; Linda Watanabe McFerrin, our developmental editor.

To special people who contributed to our memorable childhood:

Miss Margrave—the Inyo County Librarian who always helped us find the "right" book.

Allie Robinson—the packer who helped our family get started in exploring the Sierra wilderness, and who brought our horse, Lady, into our lives.

Art Reyman—a mountain climber who joined us on Sierra trips and shared with us his love of the wilderness.

Pere McDougall—an elderly neighbor who shared his wisdom and taught us card games.

Anna Kelley—a classmate's mother who drove countless car-loads of school children on field trips, and tow-truck loads of young skiers to Onion Valley.

Vic Taylor—the City snow surveyor who ran the Onion Valley ski lift every possible weekend all winter long.

OK Kelley—the mechanic who helped Vic get the ski lift running each winter, and who organized Sierra trips for the local boys.

Bessie Poole—Mama's dearest friend throughout their long lives in Independence.

Appendix

Names of People Appearing in Photographs

Part One title page. Carol and Joan helping with the chores.

Part One. In our backyard with our cousins.

Joan and Clinton Lathrop on the left side of the teeter totter, Syndey Ann Lathrop and Carol on the right.

Part One. Joan's kindergarten class.

Back row from left: Unknown, Unknown, Marjorie Mercer, Lorna Austin, Barbara Yandell.

Middle row from left: Jackie Baxter, Joan, Jimmy Kelley, Unknown.

Front row from left: Kenny Riley, Norma Harper, Dwight Simmons, Dennis Wilder, Unknown.

Part Two title page. With Silver at Sawmill Lake.

Part Two. The Frank DeDecker family.

From left: Paul DeDecker, Jean Lathrop, Ada DeDecker, Frank DeDecker.

Part Two. Picnic in the Alabama Hills with our cousins.

In back: Carol.

Front row from left: Clinton Lathrop, Sydney Ann Lathrop, Joan.

Part Three title page. Girls in the fishpond.

From left: Geraldine McLaurin, Mary Martha Tatum, Carol, Terry Elliott.

Part Three. With our cousins during construction of Manzanar Japanese Internment Camp.
On left: Joan and Douglas Davis.
On right: Carol and Sharon Davis.

Part Three. A tent sleepover.
From left: Marcia Bateman, Carol, Joan, Patsy Bateman.

Part Three. Dancing in the sprinkler.
From left: Carol, Joan, Patsy Bateman, Marcia Bateman.

Part Three. Campfire Girls on the way to Flower Lake.
From left: Carol Walters (Little Carol), Janice Walters, Patsy Bateman, Unknown, Stella Hunter, Marilyn Kemp, Gladys Mitchell, Marjorie Mercer, Carol, Kay Mercer, Lorna Austin, Patty Lutzow, Barbara Yandell, Joan.

Part Three. With the Goffs at Tyndall Creek.
From left: Caroline Goff, Joe Goff, Paul, Joan, Mary, Carol.

Part Three. Symmes Creek trailhead.
From left: Carol, Caroline Goff, Joe Goff's father, Joe Goff, Paul, Mary, Joan.

Part Four title page. Carol and Billy.

Part Four. Junior high and high school teachers.
From left: Mrs. Wilder, Mr. Weightman, Mr. Storz, Mr. Florrell (Principal), Mrs. Loundagin, Mrs. Newbre.

Part Four. Lunch at Vidette Meadow.
From left: Paul Oakeshott, Joan, Phyllis Oakeshott, Carol, Valerie Mullard, Lady.

Part Four. Riding at Aberdeen.
From left: Billy, Lady, Carol, Sabrina, Janeane, Blaze, Joan.

Part Four. On the John Muir Trail, leaving Muir Pass.
From left: Dad, Mama, Joan, Carol, Art.

Part Four: On Taboose Pass with the Swan family and Art.
Back row from left: Dad and Eddie, Ned, Corky and Ebba Swan.
Front row from left: Carol, Art, Joan.

Part Five title page. A slumber party.
From left: Mary Drew, Carol Walters, Joan, Mary Cole, Dee Persichetti, June Rae.

Part Five. Carol's junior year class. *Owens Valley High School 1950 yearbook.*
Back row from left: Kenny Riley, Arnold Cole, Dan Bostrom, Ernie Harris.
Middle row from left: Bill Aseltine, Suzann Dolley, Mary Drew, Boyd Wilson, Tommy Poole, Bobby Bay, Mrs. Loundagin.
Front row from left: Joanne White, Rita Bottorff, Carol, Jean Nilius, Phyllis Shaffer.
Absent: Bill Hopper and Tom Hunter.

Part Six title page. Sadie Hawkins dance. *Owens Valley High School 1951 yearbook.*
From left: Florence Lockridge, Marilyn Love, Carol Walters, Betty Lou Evans, Unknown, Elsie Lockridge, Mary Drew, Carol, Boyd Wilson, Mrs. Baker (English teacher as Daisy Mae), Mrs. Love, Lora Lee Hare.

Part Six. Summit of Mt. Gould.
From left: Mama, Elsie, Art, Fred, Dad.

Afterword title page. Paul and Mary's grandchildren.
From left: Alison Wiens, Rob Busby, Wendy Wiens, Paula Wiens, Annette Busby, Larry Busby, Bill Busby.